Control

Control

A History of Behavioral Psychology

John A. Mills

BF199.M485 1998

Mills, John A.

Control : a history of
behavioral psychology /
c1998.

NEW YORK UNIVERSITY PRESS

New York and London

NEW YORK UNIVERSITY PRESS
New York and London

Library of Congress Cataloging-in-Publication Data
Mills, John A., 1931–
Control : a history of behavioral psychology / John A. Mills.
p.   cm.
Includes bibliographical references and index.
ISBN 0-8147-5611-5 (hardcover : alk. paper)
1. Behaviorism (Psychology)—History. I. Title.
BF199.M485   1998
150.19'43'09—ddc21   98-19699
                                CIP

New York University Press books are printed on acid-free paper,
and their binding materials are chosen for strength and durability.

Manufactured in the United States of America

10 9 8 7 6 5 4 3 2 1

For Josie, Leila, Julian, and Julie

What is lacking is the bold and exciting behavioristic hypothesis that what one observes and talks about is always the "real" or "physical" world (or at least the "one" world) and that "experience" is a derived construct to be understood only through an analysis of verbal (not, of course, merely vocal) processes.   —B. F. Skinner

    Passions shape the future spontaneously,
              unpredictably, necessarily

                       —Paul-Émile Borduas

The longing for order, a desire to turn the human world into an inorganic one, where everything would function perfectly and work on schedule, [is] superordinated to a supra personal system. The longing for order is at the same time a longing for death, because life is an incessant disruption of order. Or to put it another way around: the desire for order is a virtuous pretext, an excuse for virulent misanthropy.   —Milan Kundera

Contents

Acknowledgments   *xi*

Introduction: Shaping a Profession: Behaviorism in American Psychology   1

1   The Birth of Psychological Behaviorism   23

2   From Apogee to Perigee: Radical Behaviorism Appears but Fails to Take Root   55

3   The Conceptual Basis of Neobehaviorism and Behavioral Science   83

4   The Behaviorist as Research Manager: Clark L. Hull and the Writing of *Principles of Behavior*   103

5   The Behaviorist as Philosopher: B. F. Skinner   123

6   Behaviorists as Social Engineers: Behavior Modification Applied to Abnormal Psychology   152

7   Faithful unto This Last: The Neobehaviorist Hegemony   179

Notes   *195*
Index   *239*
About the Author   *246*

Acknowledgments

I wrote a substantial part of the first draft of this book while I was a visiting research fellow at The University of Melbourne in 1990. I am most grateful to Professor Roger Wales and to the faculty and staff of the psychology department for providing me with a very congenial working environment (and I am especially grateful to Dr. Keith Taylor, who enhanced my knowledge of Australian football). A part of the cost of research and writing was covered by two publication grants and a grant from the President's Social Sciences and Humanities Research Council, all from the University of Saskatchewan. Parts of chapter 4 were originally published as "The Genesis of Hull's *Principles of Behavior*" in the *Journal of the History of the Behavioral Sciences* 24 (1988): 392–401; I must thank John Wiley and Sons, Inc., for permission to quote that material. I would like to thank Yale University Library for permission to quote from Clark Hull's correspondence and Dr. John Popplestone of the Archives of the History of American Psychology for permission to quote from Kenneth Spence's correspondence. I would also like to thank John V. Miller and the staff of the Archival Services of the Bierce Library of the University of Akron, who gave me invaluable assistance.

I could not have written a book as complex as this without a great deal of help from many people. The staff of the New York University Press dealt with business matters promptly, effectively, and courteously. Bruce Grenville chose the illustration on the dust jacket. Franz Samelson most generously sent me photocopies of sections of the correspondence between John B. Watson and Robert M. Yerkes; access to that correspondence was crucial to me. Gail Youngberg exercised her incomparable editorial skills on the introduction and chapter 4; my readers and I are deeply indebted to her. Professor Frederica de Laguna very kindly sent me information about her mother, Grace de Laguna. Fern Winder located much of the reference material I needed for chapter 6 and wrote me a set of working notes; without her help I could not have dealt with a topic that, initially, I found rebarbative. Doug Bates, with inexhaustible energy, collected the research material for Spence and his graduate students in chapter 7. The immediate inspiration for that chapter came from my conversations with Josephine Mills about an exhibition of modernist architecture in Montreal.

Several people read parts of this book or all of it. Andrew Winston and Julian Mills read the introduction and made incisive comments (I was especially encouraged by Julian's response, since he is a stern critic of all prose, including his father's). Franz Samelson and Charles Tolman each set his imprimatur on chapter 2. Hank Stam, Leo Mos, and Kurt Danziger read various versions of the whole manuscript. Their comments and their support were especially important to me. Kurt's comments, especially on chapter 3, were acute and helpful.

Ann Newdigate gave me my title and, above all, the courage and fortitude needed to tackle this very large enterprise. Those who know her work and her writings will recognize her influence on chapter 7. These days, every writer needs a computer guru. I was most fortunate in that mine was Cameron Alexson. During many dark months his interests became mine; I am deeply indebted to him. My debt to Jim Reed is even greater. By using a well-calculated mixture of warm support and downright rudeness he forced me to speak out instead of whispering from behind the comforting ramparts of scholarship. Without him, this book would never have acquired a readable form.

Control

Introduction

Shaping a Profession: Behaviorism in American Psychology

Historians agree that behaviorism was the dominant force in the creation of modern American psychology.[1] Now that psychology has returned to the eclecticism of its earlier years, we can analyze behaviorism's role in American psychology. Yet scholars of behaviorism stand face to face with a paradox. It would appear that we know everything we could possibly want to know about behaviorism, but behaviorism and its role in psychology remain mysterious and enigmatic. We know everything about behaviorism because behaviorists themselves have written numerous accounts of behaviorism in general as well as of various specific aspects of it, because we have a surfeit of secondary accounts of behaviorism and of behaviorist theories, and because we have volumes of critical writing on behaviorism. Even so, behaviorism remains an enigma because its dominance in American psychology blocks our efforts to understand its role and its nature. American psychologists (and many outside the United States or Canada, especially in the English-speaking world) are trained to think behavioristically from their earliest undergraduate years, usually without being made aware, or realizing, that this is the case. A truly committed and highly trained American psychologist who strives to articulate the fundamental elements of his or her research practices will state a set of behaviorist propositions because it is the academic culture of behaviorism that will dictate the seemingly self-evident basis of the psychological enterprise.

Any American psychologist who searches for understanding in a comparison of psychology with other social sciences will have great difficulty in reaching nonbehaviorist territory. Behaviorism was the soil nourishing early American social science. In the late nineteenth

1

and early twentieth centuries there was a symbiotic relationship between social scientists and the intellectual lay public. The writings of the social scientists were read and understood because they took the unformed opinions of their readers and articulated them. Because Americans characteristically view science pragmatically, many of those readers, as well as the social scientists themselves, used what they read as the basis for programs of remedial social action. Those programs, in their turn, provided material for further analysis for the social scientists and, above all, provided the early institutional basis for the growing social sciences. The essence of behaviorism is the equating of theory with application, understanding with prediction, and the workings of the human mind with social technology. Those same equations formed the foundations of the thought of early American social scientists. We now know enough to say with confidence that psychological behaviorism arose not within psychology itself but within American society from about the 1880s onward. It is also clear that the research practices and the theorizing of American behaviorists until the mid-1950s were driven by the intellectual imperative to create theories that could be used to make socially useful predictions.

A critical analysis of the theories of the leading behaviorists, especially John Broadus Watson (1878–1958), Edwin Ray Guthrie (1886–1959), Edward Chace Tolman (1886–1959), Clark Leonard Hull (1884–1952), and Burrhus Frederick Skinner (1904–1990), would in itself be sufficient to reveal the unquestioned—and unquestioning—hegemony that behaviorism established. However, to restrict our analysis to the "giants" of behaviorism would only emphasize their predominance at the expense of historical truth, because their work represented salient expressions of a much broader worldview characteristic of American would-be social scientists. Our best course, then, is to trace the history of behaviorism from its very beginnings not just in American social science but in the intellectual and social context of that social science. Before we begin that examination, however, it is appropriate to pause here and define what we mean by "behaviorism."

Behaviorist and neobehaviorist theories vary widely among themselves, so widely that some scholars would say that no common features can be discerned.[2] The issue is further complicated by the necessity to make two sets of distinctions, philosophical and psychological. Philosophically, we must distinguish between radical behaviorism, methodological behaviorism, and logical behaviorism.[3] A radical behaviorist believes that the mental and the physical are identical and that mental events can be fully explicated in a physicalist language. Skinner is usually said to be a radical behaviorist. When we take unpublished material as well as published texts into account, Hull can also be treated as a radical behaviorist. Most of those American psychologists who were actively engaged in empirical research were, until recently, methodological behaviorists. They believed that all psychological constructs should be defined operationally, that is, in terms of the procedures required to induce concrete manifestations of the behaviors functionally related to the constructs under investigation. They refused to discuss the metaphysical implications of their position. Watson, Tolman, and Guthrie fall into this category. Logical behaviorism is a position taken by some philosophers but is not really represented in psychology (although certain passages in Skinner's writings suggest that he could also be treated as a logical behaviorist). A logical behaviorist asserts that all mental language can be translated, without loss of meaning, into physicalist language (the language in question states what behavior is to be expected when a person claims to be or is thought to be experiencing some mental state). Logical behaviorists resemble methodological behaviorists in that they leave open the question of the substantive reality of mental states and resemble radical behaviorists in that they analyze all mental states with equal thoroughness.

Psychologically, we must distinguish between behaviorism and neobehaviorism. Behaviorism as such flourished most strongly in the 1920s. Early behaviorists shared a common set of concerns, in which negative considerations outweighed positive. All denied any intrinsic life to the mind, none believed that the mind was psychology's primary area of study, and all believed that introspection was a futile and misleading way of gathering psychological data. In a positive sense, all were objectivists (that is, they believed that the only real data were those that could be directly observed). The early behaviorists, with some exceptions, all shared the faith that behaviorist doctrine could be directly applied to human beings and that experimentation with humans provided a direct route to knowledge. Almost all also believed that psychological research would have direct social implications. Above all, no behaviorists produced fully worked out, comprehensive, empirically based theories.

Tolman instituted neobehaviorism in the 1920s. Almost all neobe-haviorists were animal scientists, and unlike behaviorists, they pro-duced highly sophisticated and, in some cases, comprehensive psy-chological theories. The major neobehaviorists, at least, shared the be-haviorist commitment to social application, but believed that such applications should be mediated through empirically tested theories, whose ultimate derivation was the highly controlled environment of the animal laboratory. Such theories, together with those corollaries that provided the theoretical justification for applications, constituted behavioral science, which enjoyed its heyday in the America of the 1950s and 1960s.

Despite the major differences between the various forms of behav-iorism, I believe that all behaviorists shared a set of prior commit-ments. The first of these commitments concerns the relative value given to theory and its applications. The American historian John C. Burnham expressed it cogently. He once said to me that behaviorists wanted their practical work to have a theoretical basis but the partic-ular theory used did not matter to them. That view is expressed in the opening sentence of one of J. B. Watson's articles: "The theoretical goal of psychology is the prediction and control of behavior."[4] Psy-chologist Franz Samelson found that sentence puzzling. Conventional-ly, we think of prediction and control as practical matters separate from (but derived from) theory. He claimed that one could solve the puzzle by assuming that, for Watson, technological imperatives guided the search for theory.[5] Burnham's and Samelson's interpreta-tions are essentially the same. Within that framework of interpreta-tion we can treat Clark L. Hull's ruthlessly instrumental approach to theory building as the fulfillment of Watson's intentions. B. F. Skin-ner's dismissal of the need for theory represents the high point of the behaviorist enterprise.[6] Of all the major behaviorists, only Edward C. Tolman held himself aloof from that enterprise and, in most of his work, showed himself to be a pure theorist. But even Tolman wanted psychological doctrines to have very direct application to everyday life.[7]

A second feature of behaviorism was a suspicion of, or outright hostility to, philosophical speculation. To some extent this is an inte-gral part of psychology's development. In order to establish itself as a profession, psychology had to differentiate itself from its closest aca-demic neighbors. Initially that separation was incomplete because the first American psychologists, such as William James (1842–1910), James Mark Baldwin (1861–1934), and G. Stanley Hall (1844–1924), were all trained as philosophers. The second generation of American psychologists rapidly and forcefully distanced themselves from philosophy. Although that movement was very broadly based, with psychologists as diverse as Robert Mearns Yerkes (1876–1956), Edward Lee Thorndike (1874–1949), and Watson in the forefront, it was the promise held out by behaviorism, a promise that became increasingly alluring from the 1920s to the 1960s, that inspired American psychologists to keep themselves aloof from philosophy. In contrast, European psychologists on the whole remained receptive to philosophical influences.

A third defining feature of behaviorism is the acceptance of pragmatic versions of positivism. Since both pragmatism and positivism are philosophical doctrines, a contradiction lies at the heart of the behaviorist enterprise. Philosophy, by decree, is excluded from the behaviorist club; nevertheless, upholders of some philosophical doctrines are honored members. All behaviorists were positivists, and in behaviorism's early and mature periods (the 1920s to the 1950s), all were pragmatists. Behaviorists were positivists because they believed that one could establish the truth by appealing to facts. For them, a fact was some sort of purely physical occurrence. With respect to the substance of theories, they believed that theories were created out of facts, and that the role of theories was to increase the scope and the precision of prediction. Even for Tolman, theory had a strictly pragmatic role. For all the behaviorists, theory construction was a seesaw process whereby one began with crude outgrowths from observations and slowly created one's theory in such a way that one could make more and more precise observations, building those observations into the theory at each stage. No behaviorist ever considered the possibility of taking existing comprehensive theories of the mind and testing or refining them.[8]

In their pragmatic positivism the behaviorists were archetypally American. While American intellectuals have studied and admired European thought, the leading American thinkers have typically tried to cast their own ideas within a common nationally accepted framework. In particular, Americans have always linked theory closely to application, even at the risk of being simpleminded or crude. As behaviorism developed, the chief outside influences upon it were Gestalt psychology and logical positivism. However, both schools of thought were inspirational to the behaviorists only in a very general way, giving global objectives rather than specific models. In the case of logical positivism, historian of science Laurence Smith showed that Hull, Tolman, and Skinner each created an idiosyncratic version of positivism quite independent of logical positivism.

A fourth defining feature of behaviorism is its materialism. The issues here are clouded because of the behaviorists' dismissal of philosophy and because, in the case of the later behaviorists, they believed that their theoretical approach allowed them to predict and therefore explain behavior without taking any particular philosophical position on the mind/body problem. Nevertheless, a close scrutiny of the writings of the leading behaviorists shows that in various ways they were all materialists. Although Watson started the behaviorist tradition of hedging philosophical bets, he was not willing to state his behaviorist creed openly until he could analyze thought behaviorally. His theory of thinking is clearly materialistic.[9] Guthrie's theory is implicitly materialistic in that he limited his examples to perceptual-motor skills, thereby giving the impression that his analysis could be extended to purely mental events without conceptual change. Hull's belief in biomechanical materialism was the underground force that drove his theorizing.[10] Skinner was notoriously hard to interpret in a clear-cut way. But because he asserted that private events were simply those that occur "within the skin" (that is, mental and physical events were substantively equivalent), and because he claimed that we had to use public criteria to establish the meaning and nature of a mental event, he should, I think, be counted as a materialist.[11]

In writing that psychology's *theoretical* goal was the prediction and control of behavior, Watson succinctly expressed the spirit of his era and behaviorism's fifth defining feature. Even his friend Yerkes, who kept himself aloof from the fervor of behaviorism, was obsessed by social control and social technology. As early American social scientists, both men saw theory as an instrument fitted to achieve beneficial and radical social change. A problem for Watson, as it was for other early behaviorists like Stevenson Smith (1883–1950) and Guthrie, was the large gap between the complex empirical phenomena to be explained and the simple and crude theories. The behaviorists successfully constructed theories capable of supporting their very large ambitions only after the development of inferential statistics in the

1930s and their creation of a form of pseudo-positivism (operationalism). The behaviorists' incorporation of operationalism into their thinking led eventually to the formulation of intervening variables and hypothetical constructs. The motivation behind the development of those constructs was to permit prediction while taking unobservable factors into account (the behaviorists fully accepted the logical positivist symmetry between understanding and prediction). For Hull, the most influential behaviorist theorist, social goals remained paramount, even if they had to be set aside in the interests of creating a believable theoretical structure. More to the point, Hull's approach to theory and the benefits he expected from theory were modeled on the social structures of the American corporate boardroom of his day. Following his excursion into pure research as a young man, Skinner returned to hew the pure Watsonian line. His scorn for theory was matched by an apparent ability to demonstrate that his approach to empirical research yielded limitless practical applications. As so often, Tolman stood on the bank of the behaviorist mainstream. Although he was firmly convinced that behaviorism could eventually yield an applied harvest and although he was a social activist in the private sphere, Tolman was not willing to endanger or dilute the theoretical enterprise by rushing precipitately into the applied field.

The sixth defining feature of behaviorism is very complex and will be discussed again at several points in the book. Although, eventually, behaviorist theories were derived from empirical work in the animal laboratory, the behaviorists' approach to their subjects was distinctively different from that of other animal scientists.[12] First, their data were almost exclusively derived from a very narrow base—the laboratory behavior of two species of rats (*Rattus rattus* and *Rattus norvegicus*) and one species of pigeon (*Columba livia*)—and characterized by a startling absence of comparative observations. Second, the behaviorists, although they eventually gave lip service to the Darwinian theory of evolution, continued to espouse a disguised form of neo-Lamarckism, which underlay many of the theories of learning developed by the major behaviorists in the 1930s and 1940s. Those theories were animated by the belief that, in every important respect, animal behavior was predictable and controllable by factors that could be manipulated in the laboratory. That belief was subtly linked to another, seldom made manifest, that all the crucial aspects of animal behavior were controlled by learning. There is a continuity between that belief and the belief, so characteristic of the early years of American social science, that much evolutionary change originated in the mind. The conviction that the mind was plastically subject to environmental influences and could also control its own destiny was consistent with the belief, forming the driving force behind the thinking of American reformers and social scientists of that era, that human behavior could be shaped to fit social goals by those who understood the nature of those goals and the means of achieving them. It is abundantly clear that some behaviorists (Skinner is the clearest example) were cast in the same mold as their forerunners. Animals were surrogates for human beings, the laboratory and its apparatus were the analogues of social situations, and the experimenter/theorist was the social controller.

The seventh defining feature of behaviorism is a commitment to an extreme form of utilitarianism whereby both values and personal characteristics were seen in strictly functional and instrumental terms. In effect, the person was treated as the physical locus of a set of abstract but operationally definable attributes whose sole function was to promote adaptation to immediate social circumstances. Consistently, values were defined in terms of a particularly stark instrumentalism. The good was that which aided the person or animal to attain certain physicalistically defined objectives (the gaining of food, the securing of shelter, the maintenance of an optimal level of anxiety, and so on).[13] Right was defined in terms of that which yielded immediate personal advantages (like Jeremy Bentham, the behaviorists handled altruism by saying that frequently it was beneficial to defer immediate gratification). "Ought" referred to that which had to be done in order to adapt. Beauty, if dealt with at all, referred to arrangements (of sounds, color patches, objects in space, etc.) that yielded human gratification. Personal relationships were seen solely in instrumental terms and not as ultimate objects of value. Given that the behaviorists' final goal was to demonstrate that their theories applied to all aspects of human life, it is noteworthy that overt treatment of values, morals, and persons was rare in their writings. Even Skinner, who frequently addressed these issues, did not do so in any seriously systematic way.[14]

Although a particular conceptualization of experimentation is, in my view, one of the defining features of behaviorism, a discussion of that topic merits separate treatment, both because of its complexity and because the behaviorist approach came to be shared by all American psychologists until very recently. That approach is characterized by certain attitudes toward quantification and the role and nature of experiments that are surprisingly hard to portray but that rigidly determined the conduct of research. Broadly speaking, mensuration was placed at the center of the scientific enterprise. Only that which could be counted or measured was worthy of consideration as a scientific fact. The lust for quantification reached its apogee in Hull's theories but was centrally important in all versions of behaviorism. Along with the high value placed on quantification we find not only a belief that experimentation is the only sure and safe way to garner facts, but also an approach to experimentation that those outside psychology must find curious.

That approach, which pervaded American psychology, was articulated by Watson as follows: "we may say that the goal of psychological study is the *ascertaining of such data and laws that, given the stimulus, psychology can predict what the response will be; or, on the other hand, given the response, it can specify the nature of the effective stimulus.*"[15] Watson's statement did not merely place prediction rather than understanding at the center of the scientific enterprise. It gave psychologists a crude but very clear blueprint that continues to control the conduct of much psychological research. If one takes Watson seriously, one has to ask what steps we must follow in order to achieve prediction. First, the stimulus itself and all its effects must be made manifest. Second, all the causes of the response and every feature of the response must be open to inspection. Third, each graded increase or decrease in intensity of the stimulus must be reflected in corresponding levels of response intensity. Given the treatment accorded to prediction, the need not just for quantification but for a particular type of quantification became inevitable. This form of quantification in turn controlled both the approach to experimentation and the role assigned to experimentation relative to other forms of fact-gathering.

The exclusive focus not merely on prediction but on making the whole predictive enterprise manifest necessitated a very clear distinction between causes (independent variables) and effects (dependent variables). The obsession with prediction and control yielded a need to separate out the various independent variables. The variation of each in turn and the study of their effects on isolated dependent variables were deemed necessary parts of experimental procedure.

Because contemporary Anglo-American psychologists treat what I have called the behaviorist approach to experimentation as natural and as the sole available approach, it is vital to recognize that it was a construction whose history can be traced in some detail. Andrew Winston has shown that the first formal statement of the approach was in the second edition of Robert Sessions Woodworth's (1869–1962) highly influential text *Experimental Psychology* (the first edition was published in 1938 and the second in 1954).[16] Although Woodworth was not a behaviorist, he elevated experimentation to the highest position in the hierarchy of fact-gathering devices. He published his blueprint for the conduct of experiments at the very time when operationism (the doctrine that concepts should be defined in terms of the processes whereby they are made manifest) had seized the imagination of experimental psychologists. A psychological concept was defined operationally for the first time in the second paragraph of Skinner's Ph.D. thesis, presented in 1931.[17] Skinner's espousal of operational definitions was followed a few years later by two influential articles by Harvard psychologist S. S. Stevens.[18] Thereafter, the concept was rapidly incorporated into American psychology.

Woodworth's proposals concerning experimentation, as expanded by the behaviorists, posed many more conceptual problems for psychologists than they would for a physical scientist. Even in the case of very simple animals, inner, unobservable factors control behavior much of the time. American psychologists, with the behaviorists in the vanguard, eventually dealt with the problem by posing and answering the question, "In principle, what characteristics would unobservable psychological events have to possess if they were to be observable?" It was assumed that the unobserved factors intervened between observed stimulus factors and observed response factors. It was also assumed that the nature of inner events could be fully understood if one could tease them apart into conceptually distinct components and define each of those components in terms of the operations required to make each of them demonstrate its specific effects.

Contemporary psychologists, who have been so thoroughly schooled in this overall approach to experimentation, do not appreciate the crippling limitations it imposes on their ability to generate and explain psychological data. Above all, it defeats the objective that psychology sets for itself, the explanation of behavior. I can illustrate what I mean by discussing one of the classical paradigms in experimental psychology, Pavlovian conditioning. First, the investigator makes the decision to limit her observations to one act (for example, if the experimental animals are dogs, the act might be salivation). Second, and crucially, the observations are quantitative (amount of salivation, latency of the response, response amplitude, probability that the response will occur, etc.). Third, the observations are collected under strictly controlled conditions. The measures of response strength are assigned to what is called the dependent variable, while the conditions under which observations are collected are assigned to the independent variable. In a typical experiment following the Pavlovian model, an investigator might plot the increasing strength of a response as a function of successive trials. In different experiments the animals used might differ (e.g., dogs in one, rabbits in another), the response might differ (e.g., salivation in one, the eye-blink response in another), the operational definition of response strength might differ (e.g., latency in one, amplitude in another), and the range of trials might differ (some responses take longer to acquire than others). But investigators typically find that response strength is an S-shaped function of level of practice.

Even today, if one asked most experimental psychologists to explain the result (that is, to state what causes the response curve to follow a certain time course), they would answer by essentially describing the typical result. They would say that response strength grows as a consequence of reinforced practice. In that account, reinforcement is being granted causal status. But the word "reinforcement," at least in these experiments, merely describes the procedure that the experimenter followed. So the statement "Response strength increases as a function of reinforced practice" should be interpreted as "When an experimenter decides to limit his attention to certain responses and to elicit these in conditions that are totally under his control, then what he has decided to call 'response strength' increases as a function of the experimenter-instantiated conditions." The experiment alone tells us nothing about the causal efficacy of reinforcement (that is, what it is about reinforcement that makes it causally effective). Above all, it tells us nothing about what is going on inside the experimental animals.

I am not saying that psychologists ignore causes, mental states, or brain processes. In the field of animal learning, people have speculated about the processes underlying conditioning from Pavlov's time onward. Those speculations, however, did not emerge solely from experimentation. One can certainly devise experiments to test deductions derived from some theory or to falsify another theory. But experiments do not, in the first instance, produce knowledge.

The approach to experimentation I have outlined borders on the nonscientific. In order to see why, let us consider a piece of research in the field of animal behavior and see how it contrasts with the behaviorist approach. Konrad Lorenz's elucidation of innate releasing mechanisms (IRMs) in lower animals had its origins in his study of egg-rolling in greylag geese.[19] Lorenz's conclusions were based on careful observations, combined with minor experimental manipulations. More to the point, his first step was the development of a model in which he differentiated between the IRM proper and the supporting reflexes, going on to demonstrate that egg-rolling and the supporting reflexes were controlled by quite distinct physiological mechanisms. Having developed his model, he selected a species and a mode of behavior that would allow him to collect the data he needed to verify the reality of the model. Only after he had determined the way greylag geese actually egg-rolled did Lorenz start to experiment. It is vital to note that the role of his experiments was not to discover the nature of egg-rolling (his observations had already done that) but to discover the range of sizes, surface textures, and shapes of objects eliciting the response. The study began where it had ended—with further comparative observations. The function of those was to explain the adaptive role of both egg-rolling and other similar instinctive behaviors. Although thoroughly stereotyped, they are extremely adaptive in natural habitats.

To contrast Lorenz's and the behaviorists' approach, after reading Lorenz you have the feeling that you know what an IRM does and what its adaptive function is. Above all, note that Lorenz discovered that lower animals operate in a machine-like, stereotyped fashion, but by using detailed observations he was also able to demonstrate why, in natural habitats, their behavior seems to be purposive and controlled by human-like factors such as maternal love and solicitude. In a typical behaviorist experiment, the explanation lurks uneasily in the shadows. Besides being vague, behaviorist explanation is circular and deductive. A system of operationalized variables allows one to explain only if one assumes that one is dealing with some sort of mechanism.

In many areas in psychology, it is legitimate to assume that one is dealing with a mechanism (or a system that can be fully understood in machine-like terms). For example, leading researchers in the field of visual perception can explain pattern and form recognition very convincingly by using computer simulation models.[20] A higher-level theory can then, in principle, enable us to incorporate those conclusions into our overall understanding of human beings.

A central point to be grasped is that a great deal of work in contemporary cognitive psychology is devoted to the explanation of how individual minds function. Following psychologist Kurt Danziger's analysis, we can say that cognitive psychologists are trying to create a compromise between the behaviorist and a prebehaviorist psychological paradigm. Danziger maintains that historically, psychology has consisted of a family of paradigms united in a purely nominal sense.[21] Each paradigm had its own way of defining what constituted data, determining what methods should be used to collect data, defining the role and nature of sources of data (that is, idiosyncratic ways of treating minds, persons, or individual dispositional/action systems), dealing with the role and nature of observers, and treating the mind/body problem.

By the 1930s, impelled by impatience with philosophical questions and by their pragmatic weltanschauung, American psychologists had created what Danziger has called the neo-Galtonian model of research. In this approach, the individual was treated merely as the carrier of some variable or variables of interest, and no prior assumptions were made about the mode of action of these variables within the individual. Moreover, the neo-Galtonian model demanded that one should deal with groups, not individuals. The defining feature of the neo-Galtonian model is the use of treatment groups. Experimenters manipulate all individuals in the group in the same way so that the experimenters, rather than the individuals selected for experimentation, become the causal agents. The problem with the neo-Galtonian approach is that it creates sets of purely functional relationships between experimental manipulations and behavioral effects. In a pure neo-Galtonian model, findings consistent with experimental hypotheses would demonstrate only that one's assumptions were logically tenable, not that they were even provisionally true.

Psychologist Tim Rogers has shown us how the behaviorists broke the impasse for their colleagues.[22] The first types of operational definition proposed by psychologists were thoroughly consistent with the neo-Galtonian model. Psychological concepts were defined in terms of the operations required to make the relevant behavior manifest. Independent variables could then be defined in terms of standardized experimental manipulations and dependent variables in terms of selected behavioral observations. Skinner invented a new type of operationalism whereby a construct was defined in terms not of the operations whereby it made itself manifest but in terms of the operations required to produce it, thereby shifting the focus from nature to the laboratory and from naturally occurring behavior to experimentally induced behavior. A good example of such an operational definition is hunger, typically defined in terms of the procedures followed when reducing the body weight of rats or pigeons to 80 percent of their free-feeding level. As early as 1944, Israel and Goldstein pointed out that Skinner had departed significantly from the original purpose and nature of operational definitions.[23] The main purpose of operational definitions was to inhibit people from engaging in fruitless debates about the true essence of the concepts they were using as working scientists. But defining concepts such as atom, electron, or neutron operationally did not absolve physicists from the obligation to understand how those entities functioned in the natural world. A set of causal explanations derived by experiment must ultimately be assessed against happenings in the world of nature.

Skinner's approach, however, "solved" the problem of the relationship between laboratory-induced and real-life behavior by fiat. His form of operationism, which we can call productive operationism, is most effective when applied to intervening variables, such as hunger or thirst. If we define them operationally, we do not need to appeal to inner states as explanations (hunger, for example, becomes what the experimenter induces, not what the animal feels). For many years, the increasing sophistication and success of the behaviorist experimental procedures blinded psychologists to the logical and empirical flaws inherent in productive operationism.

These flaws emerged particularly strongly in the case of drive theory, the most fruitful application of productive operationism. Drive theory assumed that all operational definitions of the same drive were convergent. It fairly soon became apparent that the assumption was not true. Thus, thirst induced in different ways (by depriving animals of water, by giving animals saline solutions, or by feeding them dry food, for example) has differing behavioral effects.[24] So animal biologists have turned to the concept of central motive states.[25] Drive theorists limited themselves to states induced in the laboratory, whereas central motive state theorists deal with states occurring in nature or in very simple experimental situations. The assumptions of the theory were simple and, in principle, empirically verifiable (for example, that any given behavioral disposition temporarily "captures" an animal's entire response system and that each disposition has some definable and observable behavioral manifestation). Central motive state theory is robust enough to allow ethologists to make very precise predictions of the behavior of a wide range of species.[26]

In contrast, drive theory encountered a series of embarrassing failures when experimenters tried to use procedures more complex than those used in the laboratories of the 1940s and 1950s or to extend their work to species other than rats or pigeons. Very frequently, instead of motivating their subjects to perform some experimental task, these investigators induced instinctive drift or adjunctive behavior. Those behaviors were later interpreted as displacement activities induced by stress.[27] Behaviorist theorists of animal learning found themselves in difficulty because of the logical flaw in productive operationism. To take the case of hunger drive, in a simple laboratory experiment with a widely used species it seems to be self-evidently true that reducing free-feeding body weight induces hunger and nothing but hunger. But we accept the validity of the behaviorist claim only on the basis of concealed anthropomorphic premises, not on the basis of some empirical check. The implicit argument on which the behaviorist case rests is "If I reduce the body weight or limit the number of daily meals in a human being then I induce hunger. But I have reduced the food intake of my experimental animals. Therefore, I have induced hunger in my experimental animals." The problem is that unless one has independently verified that the procedure has indeed induced hunger, it does not follow that the conclusion is necessarily true. The procedures could have produced other states in addition to hunger (such as frustration), or repeated exposure to the same operation in particular animals could produce increasing tolerance of hunger. Of course, the required independent checks could have been carried out, but behaviorists did not do so.

Behaviorism has certainly had its successes in the field of animal behavior. But it is essential to realize that in the case of the paradigmatic behaviorist technique (operant conditioning) we have to recognize, on nonbehaviorist grounds, that we are dealing with a system controlled by response feedback. Once that has been established, a wide array of behaviorist techniques is at the disposal of physiological psychologists or psychopharmacologists.[28] In contrast, behaviorism unconstrained by theory has seriously misled animal psychologists.[29]

In the human domain, operational definitions were first applied to the concept of intelligence, but their use rapidly spread to other areas.[30] As in the case of animal work, the overt purpose was to provide psychologists with agreed sets of definitions for their concepts. As in the case of the animal area again, productive operational definitions proliferated. Constructs such as anxiety, nurturance, cognitive dissonance, or need achievement were defined in terms of the operations required to generate instances of them in groups of experimental subjects. Underlying the overt purpose were two major covert aims. The first was a subtle shift whereby the new or "scientific" meanings of the constructs were subordinated to the requirements of the treatment group approach. From the standpoint of common sense, the causal efficacy and experienced qualities of anxiety or cognitive dissonance lie within the individual. When the concepts are redefined in terms of experimental operations, the locus of control is shifted from the individual experiencing the state to the experimenter. At the same time, there is sufficient overlap between the "scientific" and the common-sense meanings to render the findings of psychologists comprehensible to the lay public.

The second concealed purpose was the introduction of what are in effect mechanistic explanations. To take a very simple example, an investigator who defines maternal bonding operationally (in terms of hours spent by mothers with their babies, hours spent vocalizing to their babies, proportion of time spent smiling at their babies, and so on), who defines child/mother love operationally (in terms of numbers of times the child uses a term of endearment, number of occasions per observation session in which the child caresses the mother, and so on), and who finds a functional relationship between the two variables will typically conclude that bonding, as operationally defined, has a causal influence on child/mother love, as operationally defined. Underpinning almost all such work in the fields of personality, abnormal, social, and developmental psychology is adherence to a version of positivism in which the investigative enterprise is supported by a concealed and unarticulated belief in machine-like forces. Bonding, need-achievement, the various forms of depression, or the various forms of anxiety supposedly drive individuals and force them to engage in various behaviors. For example, in the days before codes of ethics proliferated, psychologists had at their disposal an array of techniques for inducing anxiety. It was assumed that those techniques that produced an experimental effect would induce the same behavioral disposition in all the subjects in the treatment group. Mere common sense should have told experimental psychologists that, without some sort of independent check, the conclusion was unwarranted. A given procedure could conceivably have been ineffective for some subjects, induced amusement in others, hostility in yet others, and so on. Many psychologists might reply that intersubject variability would express itself as statistical error, whereas intersubject consistency would express itself in the treatment effect. The problem with that argument is that the treatment effect in this type of work is typically extremely small, so that at best, the induced states account for a very small proportion of the variance.[31] Moreover, one cannot discount the effects of compliance with the perceived aims of the experimenter.

Even if those difficulties are overcome, experimenters in many areas of psychology have to meet the challenge posed by Jan Smedslund, who argues that most psychological research can be interpreted in terms of the psychological language of common sense and that psychologists should relinquish their causal explanations.[32] Smedslund's arguments have considerable force when applied to the "findings" of those working with human beings. To return to my example of maternal bonding, the very use of the term "bonding" automatically implies two or more elements to be bonded. Given that understanding, it follows that bonding must be reciprocal. If a mother has strongly bonded with her child and the child does not love her in return, we ask what it is about the maternal love that has induced the adverse reaction in the child (is the mother dutiful but cold, is the love she proffers smothering rather than nurturing, and so on). Smedslund would argue that in such cases we base our conclusions primarily on a scrutiny of the meaning of the explanatory terms we are using (a part of the meaning of smothering love, for example, is that it induces ambivalence and a need to escape in the child). If we define our terms operationally and then establish that smothering love induces ambivalence and incipient withdrawal, then Smedslund would say that we have done no more than needlessly confirm what had already been established by a semantic analysis of the language of common sense.

Given the logical problems inherent in the use of productive operational definitions, we can ask why their use became not just widespread in psychology but an integral part of the nature of empirical research in the discipline. The answer lies, I believe, in the beginnings of research practices in the United States in the first two decades of the twentieth century. Psychologists were asked to prove their usefulness in the field of mental testing. The primary difficulty was that the nature of the causal factors, intelligence in particular, was completely unknown. The solution to that difficulty was to devise very crude operational definitions.[33] The other difficulty was that close study of individuals in rigorously controlled research settings would not have allowed American psychologists to meet the obligations imposed on them by society in general and industry in particular. The solution to the problem was, once again, conceptual. American psychologists invented the neo-Galtonian research method, an integral part of which was the concept of the treatment group. In the neo-Galtonian approach, the individual became the interactive locus of a number of independent variables, each of which could be manipulated in isolation from the others. Control, as I have already said, was effectively removed from the individual subject and assigned to the investigator. The investigator, in his turn, became a manipulator because, given the equation of science with technology current both within and outside psychology at the time, knowledge was assumed to be derived from action rather than understanding or contemplation, and only those manipulations that had some likelihood of producing socially useful consequences were considered worthwhile. During the rest of the century, psychologists invented more and more precise and more and more sophisticated techniques of manipulation; elegant statistical techniques, especially the various forms of analysis of variance and the various versions of factor analysis, were at their disposal; and they were able to propound their theories and discuss their empirical findings in the language of logical positivism. But I sense an unease, usually expressed in immoderately defensive statements, about this entire enterprise.[34]

The behaviorism described above was the product of the social and institutional context in which American psychology grew and matured. My examination of it begins in chapter 1 with a brief overview of the Progressive movement, concentrating on the symbiotic relationship between Progressivism and early American social science. Both the Progressives and the social scientists believed that science should serve the good of society, where good was defined primarily in terms of material comforts and success. Both groups also believed that it was possible to develop social technologies to shape human beings to serve the ends of society, as defined by an elite with access to objective knowledge of the ultimate purposes of society. Those purposes were defined in terms of a conceptually incoherent but ideologically unified and powerful set of doctrines that are best called "evolutionary naturalism."[35] Initially, American intellectuals were Lamarckian, but Lamarckism was slowly replaced by a particular version of neo-Darwinism in which Darwinian language and concepts were subverted by a continuing and implicit retention of Lamarckian notions. A functional theory of causation and an atomization of the person were also characteristic of American social science from this early period. Ultimately the emerging social sciences in America derived their formative characteristics from Progressivism.

The chapter will continue with an account of the connections between the philosophical doctrine of critical realism and behaviorism. The critical realists, such as Edwin Bissell Holt (1873–1946) and Ralph Barton Perry (1876–1933), developed a distinctive theory of mind that denied that minds had some special status in the universe. They claimed that a moment of consciousness was a physical event whose dominant characteristic was its connection in time with other similar physical events. There were therefore no such creatures as conscious agents. The similarities between critical realism and behaviorism are obvious. Moreover, some of the critical realists and those who developed similar doctrines had direct connections with behaviorists. For example, Perry was one of Tolman's teachers, and Guthrie's doctoral thesis was supervised by Edgar Arthur Singer, Jr. (1873–1954), a philosopher whose views were very similar to those of the New Realists. The bulk of the chapter will consist of an account of what Erwin Esper has called "the great war of words": the speculative behaviorism of the 1920s and its critical response. On the whole, the proponents of this behaviorism were marginalized. The leading behaviorist psychologists of this era (apart from Watson, who deserves his own chapter) were Max Frederick Meyer (1873–1967), Albert Paul Weiss (1879–1931), Jacob Robert Kantor (1888–1984), and Walter Samuel

Hunter (1889–1956). Each devised a unique form of behaviorism; all exerted almost no subsequent influence.

Chapter 2 provides an intensive analysis of Watson's influence, starting with an appraisal of his work as an animal psychologist and a search for the origins of his behaviorism in his popular articles and in his correspondence with his friend Robert Yerkes. I will then analyze the text of his 1913 article in *Psychological Review* and discuss Franz Samuelson's analysis of the repsonses to it. By the 1930s Watson's appeal had faded and behaviorism was in retreat throughout the social sciences. Many psychologists felt that behaviorism had failed to live up to its early promise and was about to become a part of psychology's history.

Chapter 3 will establish the background for a study of the neobehaviorist theories that dominated American psychology in the 1950s and 1960s. The chapter will chart the rise of operationism. By describing the connections between operationism, the behaviorist philosophy of experimental design, and the statistical technique of analysis of variance, I will demonstrate how the newly emerging speciality of learning theory emerged and how it shaped neobehaviorism.

Chapter 4 deals with Clark Hull's theory of behavior. Hull created the only theory in the history of psychology that gave a comprehensive and formal explanation for all behavior, whether animal or human, whether individual or social, and whether normal or abnormal. An analysis of Hull's diaries, his unpublished seminar notes, and his correspondence with Kenneth W. Spence (1907–1967) will demonstrate that beneath the published writings lay an unarticulated biomechanistic theory. That theory, in turn, has to be set in the context of an even less articulate set of views about human nature and the nature of society. Hull's views about the nature of scientific theorizing led him to a particularly stark version of instrumentalism, derived at several removes from his forerunners among American social theorists. His lifework is best interpreted as a prolonged metaphor for his beliefs about the workings of society.

Chapter 5 is devoted to Skinner's theory of mind, his philosophy of science, his utopian social philosophy, and his theory of value. Despite the seeming crudity of his prose, Skinner's position in all those cases was sophisticated and, up to a point, defensible (as demonstrated by the size of the secondary literature his views have generated). In the case of his theory of value, Skinner's novel *Walden Two* is the crucial text. It expresses certain fundamental views about human nature that he imbibed as a young man. Skinner's work is a portrayal, in a seemingly scientific form, of the beliefs about human nature and its place in society held by American intellectuals in the early years of this century.

In chapter 6 I will assess behaviorism's role both as creator and creature of intellectual patterns, societal practices and purposes, and values in America. In order to focus my discussion, I will limit myself to a historical account of the rise and demise of behavior modification, behaviorism's version of psychotherapy. Any full discussion of behavior modification must take account of its scientism, pragmatism, and empiricism. More to the point, I will also deal with the implicit theory of society underlying it. Like their Progressive forebears, the leaders of the behavior modification movement did not merely invent an array of social technologies; they also had a technological view of human nature. Such a view, however, had to compete with others and ultimately fell victim to them.

The chapter will open with an account of the promising developments of the 1920s in the work of such people as Watson, Mary Cover Jones, and William Burnham, moving on to discuss the reasons for the discontinuity between that movement and the emergence of modern behavior modification in the work of Leonard Krasner and others. Their achievements were possible only because the mental health profession had demonstrated that it could deal effectively and cheaply with stress-induced mental illness among service personnel in World War II. During the period of economic growth following the war, the American government funded the creation of a large and complex mental health profession. Given the drive toward large-scale treatments of short duration and proven efficacy, the behavior modifiers eventually became very prominent in the mental health profession. The chapter will close with an account of the impact of the civil rights movement on behavior modification programs in institutions such as mental hospitals. Civil rights lawyers challenged behavior modifiers to demonstrate that their practices were indeed effective, and were often the victors in that contest. They also limited the constraints that the behavior modifiers could apply to their clients. The picture is further complicated by the interaction between the outcomes of the numerous court cases brought by the civil rights movement and the decreasing availability of government funding, starting in the 1970s.

Both resulted in a move to deinstitutionalize the mentally ill, thus robbing the behavior modifiers of much of their clientele. By coincidence, behavior modification's death knell was sounded at the same time as the weight of negative evidence from animal studies brought about the demise of neobehaviorism in academic psychology.

In the 1950s and 1960s, neobehaviorist theorizing and research practices dominated American psychology's subject matter, and that neobehaviorist hegemony forms the subject matter of chapter 7. Neobehaviorists exerted control both intellectually and institutionally. They exercised intellectual control by excluding some parts of psychology (such as perception, thought, and language) from serious consideration and by placing others (especially learning and motivation) in the forefront. The career of Kenneth Spence, Hull's leading acolyte, provides us with the most conspicuous example of institutional control. Besides making formidable contributions to neobehaviorist theory in his own right, he graduated seventy-two doctoral students from Iowa State University. All were carefully schooled in the neobehaviorist habits of thought. Many had exceedingly fruitful careers themselves, and all, with trivial exceptions, remained faithful to the neobehaviorist credo to the end of their careers. Today we still find both behaviorists and neobehaviorists thinly scattered through psychology. However, they lack their former prominence because behaviorism was born in a time of social optimism, rose to its apogee during a period of unprecedented economic prosperity, and collapsed into a group of obscure sects during the current neoconservative era.

1

The Birth of Psychological Behaviorism

Behaviorism derived its unity from social and institutional sources; its intellectual and conceptual cohesion was correspondingly slight. Moreover, forms of behaviorism, usually unacknowledged and unnamed, pervaded American social science from its beginning. I will address four major motivating factors in the history of behaviorism: the search for practical applications, an unacknowledged yearning for philosophical respectability, the need to generate a specifically behaviorist body of theory, and a need to provide an empirical base in animal psychology.

The search for practical applications controlled American social science from its beginning, given that it originated directly from the Progressive reform movement.[1] Both the Progressives and their progeny, the American social scientists of the late nineteenth and early twentieth centuries, believed that science should serve the good of society, where good was defined primarily in terms of material comforts and success. They also believed that practice should shape theory and be the ultimate test of theory. By using, at first, the resources of the American Social Science Association and, from 1876 onward, the resources of new and reformed universities, the Progressives created a cadre of experts imbued with the ideals of American social pragmatism.[2] As mere social scientists, they could not lay claim to the power and prestige conferred by tradition. Instead, they depicted society as an arena exhibiting the interplay of objective social forces. Crucially, they treated persons as mere foci for the reception and projection of those forces. Because those forces bore equally on all, none were automatically privileged. But anybody who had the will and the talent could understand and, above all, manipulate American society. Social leadership then became the prerogative of a meritocracy, not an aristocracy. Those tendencies appeared first in early American sociology, economics, and political science, so that is where my history of behaviorism will begin.

As in the case of the search for practical applications, the need for philosophical respectability first manifested itself outside psychology. A group of American philosophers, the New Realists, together with a like-minded trio (Frederick James Eugene Woodbridge, Edgar Arthur Singer, Jr., and Grace de Laguna), advanced overtly behaviorist doctrines very early in this century. These philosophers published in the *Journal of Philosophy, Psychology, and Scientific Method*. A perusal of the early volumes of the journal shows that several psychologists did likewise, while the New Realist group referred extensively to the psychological literature. Moreover, there are direct lines of descent between the New Realist group and the behaviorist movement. The philosophers Ralph Barton Perry and Singer both inspired and exerted a determinative influence on the thought of two behaviorists (Tolman and Guthrie respectively).

Direct intellectual ancestry, however, does not guarantee a direct influence on the creation and promulgation of inherited doctrines. The New Realists were publishing at the very time when psychology was trying to distance itself from philosophy. The first behaviorist theorists felt the need for philosophical expertise and saw the necessity for dealing with certain philosophical problems (the mind/body problem being the most prominent). But the expertise had to appear to be their own and to be used to solve purely psychological problems. So psychologists had to create a traditional body of knowledge. Because the creation of a tradition requires the passage of several decades, the mature products of two of our forces (the need for philosophical respectability and the need to create a purely psychological body of theory) did not appear until fairly recently in behaviorism's history. Moreover, the two needs also followed relatively independent courses in behaviorism's early years. As a result, an account of New Realist doctrine is a detour from our main story, albeit a necessary one.

A need to generate a discipline-specific body of theory was a vital driving force in all the American social sciences in their early years. That need was historically conditioned. The pragmatism endemic to Progressivism eventually produced a unique form of positivism. By the 1920s American positivism had emerged as behaviorism, which enjoyed a brief hegemony in economics, political science, and sociology and was an influential force in psychology. In the 1930s behaviorism went into retreat, reemerging in psychology in the late 1940s as behavioral science, an empirically and theoretically based endeavor claiming both scientific status and the power to overcome social and personal dysfunctions. In the 1950s behavioral science became a complex hierarchy of theories, research techniques, training programs, and professional organizations. Operationism, the intellectual core of that hierarchy, was the creation of a small group of American psychologists, several of whom were behaviorists. So American behaviorism should be interpreted not as a set of positivist theories of action but as a programmatic attempt to achieve human betterment. Within behaviorism, the very first theories (Adolph Meyer's, Albert P. Weiss's, and J. R. Kantor's) were just that—pure theories. Because they lacked the life-giving link to the practical they were consigned to the margins of psychology's history almost as soon as they were written. They are, nevertheless, very much a part of that history and must be entered into the record.

Similar considerations apply to the need to create a body of empirical work derived from the animal laboratory. In that case, animal psychologists had to develop the practical expertise needed for working with their two chosen animals, the rat and the domestic pigeon. In the absence of a body of laboratory lore, the highly sophisticated work of the midcentury would have been impossible. The generation of a methodology, closely linked to increasingly complex and sophisticated statistical theory, was equally necessary, as was the generation of a theory ("learning theory") specifically designed as an avenue of expression for the laboratory work. The writings of Walter Samuel Hunter (1889–1954), the first behaviorist to base his theory explicitly on animal work, and of Zing-Yang Kuo (1898–1970), who was the first radical behaviorist to engage in animal work, had almost no influence on later behaviorism. Although Hunter was the first to teach a course on learning, his course material looked backward to German objectivism and to Thorndike. His only influence as an animal psychologist was to train some of those who were later to engage in work that resembled or laid the groundwork for the classical behaviorist work of the 1940s, 1950s, and 1960s. Kuo had a very brief career as an American psychologist (1918–23). Thereafter he lived much of his life in China, whose turbulent modern history ensured that he did little research.

Until the last third of the nineteenth century none of the modern social sciences were recognizable as independent disciplines.[3] Disciplinary differentiation began with the emergence of modern universities and colleges in the 1870s and 1880s. The appearance in the 1880s of people with doctoral degrees in their own field constituted a major advance. All these men believed that all science had to be empirically based, deriving that idea in part from the German universities in which they were trained and in part from the successes of evolutionary biology. The American proclivity for social utility manifested itself with varying strength in the various social sciences. The most influential of the new economists placed moral and social values at the center of their enterprise, and the socialists among them pressed for more state intervention. Reform tendencies were weakest in anthropology (since the discipline offered little opportunity for their manifestation), while the political scientists tended to be relatively conservative.

As the modern American university began to emerge, it became increasingly more feasible to take up the role of pure researcher. Men with a strong motive to find social uses for knowledge were attracted to those posts, ensuring that the work of their early graduates would be strongly infused with Progressivism. However, once the universities were established, institutional pressures within them exerted a moderating influence on reform ideals. In the universities, left-wing reformers and traditionalists had to meet and cooperate on a common middle ground. At the same time, university administrators were equally anxious to demonstrate the social utility of their new areas of study and not to give offense to those who were funding the enterprise. The form taken by American positivism ensured that the universities were socially cohesive and promoted their societal influence.

In the universities positivism provided a minimal, agreed set of standards for the conduct of research and teaching. It projected the reassuring image of groups of scholars pursuing objective, disinterested research and then offering their findings to society. It also provided a cloak beneath which value assumptions could operate unseen.

Behaviorism took root early, prevailed for a long time, and was pervasive in American sociology. As early as 1897 the Columbia sociologist Franklin Henry Giddings (1855–1931) devised a scale of sympathy, postulating that sympathy would be closest among those sharing the same genetic makeup.[4] In 1909 he published a more sophisticated version of the scale, which had nine points, varying from native-born of white parents, through various European "races," to orientals, "civilized dark," and finally, "uncivilized dark."[5] The position of a particular person on the scale was to be ascertained by an analysis of objective characteristics (the person's parentage, cultural origin, and skin color). Giddings did not say so, but the new scale could be construed as an expression of prejudice. He attempted to overcome that potential criticism by constructing each scale point out of his objective characteristics. Given that he expressed the values of his day with such fidelity, he did not realize that each of his characteristics was value-laden. He knew that his scale was a scale of ranks, not an equal-interval measure; he solved his problem by deploying implicit behaviorist principles while arguing that all barely detectable differences in degree of fellow-feeling or sympathy had to be equivalent. By "barely detectable" he meant "behaviorally equivalent." Thus, behavior became the only avenue whereby we could judge psychosocial attributes; private mental states, unseen mental causes, and the unconscious were all ruled out. By comparing the 1890 and 1900 censuses, Giddings demonstrated the social utility of his scale. He assigned various population groups to his scale points and proved (to his own satisfaction, at least) that Americans had become culturally more homogeneous during that decade.

All the features of the behaviorist enterprise existed in embryo in Giddings's scales. First, sympathy was defined in terms of measurable behavior. Second, Giddings made no appeal to feelings or other mental constructs; the behavior was directly correlated with supposed biological forces. Third, he made no presumptions about the causal connections between biology and psychology; the establishment of a functional relationship sufficed. Fourth, the desired conclusion was stipulated in advance; had Giddings not supported his hypothesis he would have assumed an error in technique, not an error in reasoning. Fifth, the connection with the dominant social concerns in the United States at that time is obvious.

Versions of behaviorism were to be found at the University of Chicago as well as at Columbia. Chicago graduate Edward Cary Hayes opened the door to behaviorism in 1904 by insisting that sociology limit itself to the study of phenomena (rather than to the states or conditions underlying phenomena) and to the study of functional relationships between antecedent and dependent variables. Such study would be effective only if one could quantify the variables in question.

In Hayes, then, we do not see just behaviorism but a particular behaviorist doctrine—that the pursuit of science is the pursuit of strictly functional relationships between objectively identifiable variables.

Hayes's position was taken further by his colleague Luther Lee Bernard. In 1919 Bernard published an article in which he advanced a position strikingly similar to that of Watson.[6] Behaviorism was to sweep away the mists of superstition that had clouded sociologists' gaze. Superstition comprised not just witchcraft or mysticism but all metaphysics. Bernard postulated a direct connection between activity in neural substrates and mental states or in sociological phenomena, while also insisting that the primary aim of the behavior scientist was to discover statistical regularities in observed behavior. Above all, no science of human behavior could be complete unless it resulted in prescriptions for social action.

Throughout the 1920s the University of Chicago dominated American sociology. The work of the Chicago sociologists demonstrates the formative and continuing role of Progressivism and the convergence of that heritage with a behaviorist positivism. The leading figures of the Chicago school, especially Robert E. Park (1864–1944) and Ernest Burgess (1886–1966), produced eclectically empirical and problem-driven—rather than theory-driven—work. At first sight, it seems Progressivism did not control the development of sociology at Chicago. For example, Martin Bulmer has argued that Park, Burgess, and their followers wished to study sociological phenomena purely objectively. In particular, he refers to the numerous occasions on which Park repudiated the work of the social survey movement, where the intent was to collect data that could then be presented in such a way as to engender ameliorative community action. However, there are substantive continuities between Progressivism and the beginnings of empirical sociology in America. More to the point, there were formal similarities between Progressive thought and the underlying features controlling the research practices of the Chicago school.

To take Park, journalism was his first profession, an early experience that exerted a continuing influence on his work as a sociologist. After abandoning journalism Park worked for Booker T. Washington for several years; during that period he put much time and effort into publicizing the atrocities committed in the Belgian Congo. While teaching at Chicago, Park collaborated with Charles Johnson of the Chicago Commission of Race Relations and was employed by the

Carnegie-funded Americanization study of 1918–19. Another Chicago faculty member, Ellsworth Faris, spent the first seven years of his working life as an African missionary. Finally, the Chicago school's characteristic work had its origins in the work of an early faculty member, Charles Richmond Henderson, who was more of a social worker than a sociologist and had close working contacts with various community agencies. After Henderson's resignation Burgess took over his courses.

With respect to both substance and form there are striking continuities between Progressivism and sociology. From the beginning, empirical work in sociology was supported by foundations such as the Laura Spelman Rockefeller Memorial. Bulmer argues that those controlling the research funds, especially Beardsley Ruml, were scrupulously careful to avoid demanding predetermined findings from their clients. Nevertheless, the foundations inherited from Progressivism a powerful meliorative impulse and, more important, a prior commitment to the solution of social problems via edicts from above rather than communal agreement from below. Such attitudes must have biased the choice of problem areas for grantees. Furthermore, the granting agencies had considerable impact on the very structure of American social science. As British sociologist Harold Laski commented,

> No university today is complete without its research institute; no foundation is worthy of the name unless its directors are anxiously scanning the horizon for suitable universities which can be endowed with such institutes. There are few universities where the movement is not away from discussion of principle to description and tabulation of fact. Everything is being turned into material for quantitative expression, since this best yields to cooperative effort.[7]

That emphasis on cooperative effort was closely linked with the instrumentalism fostered by the Progressives. The Progressives placed practice above theory and limited theory's role to the elucidation of predetermined problems. Within that scheme, science became a communal enterprise managed from above. The managers (thesis supervisors) collaborated with the workers (graduate students) in order to discover the most efficient ways of solving predetermined problems. Faris wrote that as a result of the Chicago school's work, sociology was defined as "*the pursuit of objective scientific knowledge concerning the nature of society and social organization, groups, and institu-*

tions, the nature and effects of processes of social interaction, and the effect of these forms and processes on the behavior of persons."[8] Faris was proposing a purely functional model, in which identifiable social variables controlled behavioral outputs. The same functional model was at work in Burgess's zonal hypothesis of the structure of cities.[9] According to this model, the newer cities of North America showed a characteristic pattern. Each had a downtown core of high-value commercial property. Surrounding the core was a "twilight" zone of low-cost hotels and housing, surrounding that a zone of better-quality blue-collar housing, and surrounding that the commuter suburbs. The Chicago school discovered that the social pathologies characteristic of twilight zones were a consequence of the living conditions forced on new arrivals. As soon as those people became moderately prosperous they moved out and their level of pathology dropped. The continuity with Progressivism is evident. We have a functionalist explanation of the primary data, while the school's conclusions have direct practical consequences.

We can see those same tendencies very clearly in the work of the economist Wesley Clair Mitchell, who was one of the behaviorists among the institutionalist school of American economists.[10] He showed his colleagues how economic theory should be transformed so that it could deal directly with statistical aggregates instead of making deductive inferences from the needs and feelings of fictional individuals. At the same time, the new knowledge was to be socially useful. Mitchell tried to discover the degree of relationship between empirically established variables. He wrote that the same trend was to be seen in psychology:

> Psychologists are moving rapidly toward an objective conception and a quantitative treatment of their problems. Their emphasis upon stimulus and response sequences, upon conditioned reflexes; their eager efforts to develop performance tests, their attempts to build up a technique of experiment, favor the spread of the conception that all of the social sciences have a common aim—the understanding of human behavior; a common method—the quantitative analysis of behavior records, and a common aspiration—to devise ways of experimenting upon behavior.[11]

Mitchell exhorted economists to change their style of work; the lonely scholar with his books was to be replaced by the grant-supported member of a research team analyzing public records. The necessity for empirical manipulation of data meant a change in the conception of the conduct of empirical work. Empiricists in the social sciences could not derive their practices from the delicate physical manipulations employed by physical scientists. Instead, they had to content themselves with relatively coarse manipulations having discernible effects on aggregate behavior. Once again, there are strong analogies between Mitchell's proposed research practices and those of psychological behaviorists. Watson, for example, committed himself from his earliest research to the exploration of relatively crude relationships between globally conceived variables.

From the 1920s onward, behaviorism emerged as a strong force in American political science. "The new science of politics," spearheaded by Charles C. Merriam of Chicago, dominated the discipline.[12] In 1921 Merriam wrote an article very similar to Watson's "behaviorist manifesto" in that he exhorted his colleagues to use new methods but eschewed any mention of theory:

> For our purposes it is not necessary or possible to read the future of social or political science. It is sufficient to say that we may definitely and measurably advance the comprehensiveness and accuracy of our observation of political phenomena, and that the processes of social and political control may be found to be much more susceptible to human adaptation and reorganization than they are now.[13]

Merriam presaged psychology's future ethos. He upheld industry and commerce as models for the conduct of research in political science, claiming that the individual scholar was much less efficient than a team of people using a common method. He also claimed that no real scientific political science was possible until standardized methods of record keeping had been developed. The methods were to be those of science. Merriam compared statistics to the telescope or microscope and claimed that statistics could be used to uncover hitherto concealed facts.[14] He also urged political scientists to pay attention to psychology (predictably, the only psychologist he named was the empiricist Edward Lee Thorndike). According to Merriam, "We seem to stand on the verge of definite measurement of elusive elements in human nature hitherto evading understanding and control by scientific methods."[15]

In the 1920s some psychologists showed a reciprocal interest in political science. For example, Floyd Allport asserted that political science was the study of behavior: "government itself is behavior. Conceived as a structure, or an institution, it is behavior of a different sort from those more obvious and spectacular processes mentioned above: it consists of deeper, more stable, and more generalized attitudes. But it is, none the less, behavior."[16] Exhibiting a Progressive-inspired distrust of participatory democracy, he used the results of intelligence tests to argue that reliance on public opinion was reliance on mediocrity. He proposed no solutions, but claimed that psychologists had presented political scientists with a serious dilemma.[17]

The culmination of the "new science of politics" movement came with the publication of a distinguished and original body of work by people such as Harold D. Lasswell, Harold F. Gosnell, and Quincy Wright from 1927 onward.[18] The distinctive feature of the research was the innovative use of data-gathering and statistical techniques. The new science of politics movement reached its peak in the 1920s and then declined; there is an intriguing similarity to the course of the behaviorist impulse traveling through psychology.

Behaviorist doctrines exerted a powerful influence on American philosophy. Indeed, in that it was a constitutive force among the first group of truly professional American philosophers, the New Realists, one can say that its role in the discipline was foundational. New Realism was a progenitor of psychological behaviorism both because it gave a distinct philosophical expression to certain elements of Progressive thought and because the New Realists advanced ideas that were either behaviorist or allied to behaviorism. It is particularly noteworthy that all the members of the group believed that insofar as it was possible, philosophers and natural scientists should be guided by the same principles.

The New Realists (Edwin Bissell Holt [1873–1946], Ralph Barton Perry [1876–1957], William Pepperell Montague [1873–1953], Walter Taylor Marvin [1872–1944], Walter Boughton Pitkin [1878–1953], and Edward Gleason Spaulding [1873–1940]) were a group of American philosophers who propounded a theory of mind that was objectivist and, in almost every respect, physicalist.[19] The three leading members of the school (Holt, Perry, and Montague) all had doctorates from Harvard and were heavily influenced by William James. Holt and Perry both taught at Harvard (Holt from 1901 to 1918 and Perry for his entire career). Like their mentor, the New Realists were pragmatists. Like James again, they were opposed to the form of philosophical idealism that dominated American philosophy in the late nineteenth and early twentieth centuries; among the New Realists, Perry and Montague led the attack on that doctrine. Holt, the most sophisticated philosopher of the group, converted James's solution to the mind/body problem (neutral monism) into a sophisticated and wide-ranging theory.

The New Realists and their allies played a crucial but seldom acknowledged role in the creation of behaviorism. For one thing, they had a direct influence; because Tolman studied under Perry and Holt at Harvard, he was the only neobehaviorist who believed that the "object of knowledge" must be stated as a proposition. He derived his treatment of purpose, which crucially differentiated his theory from Watson's and Hull's, directly from Perry. But indirect and pervasive influences were, I believe, more important. What we see in the writings of so many early twentieth century American philosophers is a physical treatment of sensations, the abolition of the self as a causal agent with a special status in the natural world, and a treatment of the study of mind as a study of functional relationships between those physical attributes of natural objects of crucial importance to living creatures. All those characteristics played a vital formative role in the creation of behaviorism. The New Realists and those philosophers who shared their views advanced them all on a purely speculative basis in the absence of any empirical research. Since the behaviorists and the New Realists also shared the same goal of applying the exacting standards of the physical sciences to their respective disciplines, both groups had a sympathetic interest in each other's writings.

The members of the school set out their principles in a jointly authored article in the *Journal of Philosophy, Psychology, and Scientific Method*.[20] They believed in the joint solution of agreed sets of problems, they maintained that problems should be approached analytically, they affirmed both existential realism (a belief in the existence of physical objects) and subsistential realism (a belief in the existence of at least some essences and universals), and they were anti-representationist (that is, they were opposed to what we take to be the most distinctive doctrines of Locke, Berkeley, and Kant). We should not study minds or persons, they believed; we should restrict ourselves to the study of the mode of relationships between what are commonly treated as mental "contents" and physical occurrences. Like James and the members of the Chicago school of psychology, they were functionalists. So Perry, for example, saw no differences between psychology and physiology in terms of content; instead, he saw psychologists as dealing with adjustments of whole organisms, whereas physiologists studied the role of organs within living beings.[21] In the same vein, Perry advanced a behavioral theory of cognition, assigning all mental contents, whether overt or covert, to the category *response*.[22]

In a brief account of New Realism, such as this, it is best to concentrate on Holt, since he expressed the group's views most fully.[23] Furthermore, for much of his career Holt worked as a psychologist (he ran the psychological laboratory at Harvard for several years). He defined a consciousness as an entity comprising all the objects of which that consciousness was aware.[24] The term *consciousness*, then, was simply a way of categorizing a collection of objects. Holt treated behavior as the only observable psychological category, and believed that behavior was always organized in order to achieve purposes. Therefore, the study of mind consisted of attempts to discover the functional relationships between behaviors, on the one hand, and the objects toward which behavior was directed, on the other. In his theory, consciousness became the living relationship between living beings and the particular elements in the physical world toward which their actions were directed. Those relationships then became the objects of consciousness. To describe purpose was to describe the objects of which behavior was a constant function.[25] Purpose or volition, however, was not mere behavior but a set of dispositions to behave. Although dispositions were always ultimately directed toward physical objects, they could not be reduced to physical activity. The psychical world infused the physical because all psychical activity was purposive. But talk or thought about the mental always had to find expression via physical objects. Again, we have to remember that the ultimate constituents of physical objects and of the universe as a whole were akin to those of logic, so that Holt's universe had a distinctly mental or conceptual character.

Woodbridge, Singer, and de Laguna held philosophical positions even closer to behaviorism and more extreme than the New Realists'.[26] Frederick James Eugene Woodbridge (1867–1940), who had a Ph.D. from Berlin and who taught at the University of Minnesota from 1894 to 1902 and at Columbia (where he was Montague's department head) from 1902 until his retirement in 1937, was a naturalist and a realist, by which he meant that life, mind, and consciousness were situated in bodies, even though mind, once it had reached a certain stage of development, might come to control certain occurrences, while consciousness was a mere spectator of natural events.[27] Moreover, he shared with the New Realists a tendency to place method above theory. As early as 1904 he was construing consciousness as a mode of maintaining relationships between objects, not some sort of receptacle containing representations.[28] Montague commented that for Woodbridge, sensation was merely a physical event: "It was the first case of acute behaviorism that I had seen, and the first, I believe, that existed. To believe in the outer world was indeed very good, but to purchase that belief at the cost of denying the inner world was too high a price even for realism."[29] Woodbridge refused to treat sensations as the fundamental material of the mind. He claimed that there were acts of sensing, but that from the standpoint of the perceiver there was no fixed, substantive reality associated with each act of sensing. Objects, then, were in consciousness in the same way that objects were in space. When we situated an object in space we merely specified its relationship to other objects.

Edgar Arthur Singer, Jr. (1873–1954) completed his Ph.D. at the University of Pennsylvania in 1894; the title of his thesis was "The Composite Nature of Consciousness." In a series of articles published between 1911 and 1917, he equated consciousness with behavior.[30] We believed in consciousness, he claimed, because one set of behaviors led us to expect others. Singer was advancing a sophisticated form of methodological behaviorism in which he called on his readers to classify and predict actions, not try to uncover the causes for actions within putative agents. He also advanced a form of physicalism in which he located certain functional consistencies in the nervous systems of living creatures; those consistencies tended to lead, statistically, to the preservation of groups. Behavior, then, could not be under the control of creatures who initiated and fulfilled purposive sequences of acts, but resulted from forces operating at a group level. In that scenario, individuals did little more than contribute to the error variance. Correspondingly, the role of the experimenter was not to uncover causal factors within agents but to study relationships between variables.

Although Stevenson Smith and Edwin Guthrie called Singer a founder of psychological behaviorism, he repudiated the role.[31] For one thing, he classified the psychological behaviorists as "mechanists," and wrote that "all the categories of life and mind are to my understanding of them *teleological*."[32] For another, Singer, in common with so many American philosophers of his day, was an essayist rather than a philosopher in the modern sense (that is, someone who states definite doctrines clearly and succinctly and who, above all, carefully considers the implications of those doctrines). As a result, Singer's works are diffuse and a trifle thin. Nevertheless, although he did no experimental work himself, he very clearly enunciated the core of the basic principles that were to underlie the research of the behaviorists and neobehaviorists. Given that he was not an original thinker, his writings show us that those ideas were diffused widely through the American intellectual community long before they were put into practice in experimental psychology.

Grace Mead Andrus de Laguna (1878–1978) (known almost all her life as Grace de Laguna) was strongly influenced by Singer in her early career. She was well acquainted with the work of the psychological behaviorists like Watson and Albert P. Weiss, and they knew her work as well (for example, Tolman cited her). In the mid-1920s, following her publication of a book on language, she abandoned behaviorism.

Her behaviorist affinities emerged strongly in her treatment of perception. She claimed that we had no empirical justification for giving red-, green-, or other "centers" a causal role in color perception. Instead, we had to say that the ability to attend to color patches was dependent on a complex set of sensory and motor connections. Much later, the only person to develop a behaviorist theory of perception, James G. Taylor, built on that foundation.[33]

In a review of the second edition of Margaret Floy Washburn's *Animal Mind*, de Laguna displayed her prescience even more strikingly.[34] She outlined what amounted to an operational approach to research in psychology. She treated the study of sense data as the study of the conditions required to produce prespecified verbal responses (e.g., "red" when people are presented with certain types of paper under certain conditions of illumination). She wrote,

> *The phenomena thus investigated become in effect functions of the factors constituting the standardized conditions of the experiment.* It must not be suggested, however, that this means the identification of psychological research with either physical or biological science. The psychological standardization of the conditions of experiment is almost never equivalent to a

physical or mechanical standardization of them. What may constitute a wide variation in methods mechanically considered, may well fall within the limits of psychological constancy for the particular experiment in hand. Nor is this determined by an unchecked introspection that a given variation does not "look" or "feel" different, but by further experiments which act as mutual checks. In short, one of the most important tasks of the psychologist is the determination of what constitutes the standardization in typical cases.[35]

Implicitly she was asking Washburn to treat psychology as a set of methodological practices, not as a body of substantive doctrines.

De Laguna was also philosophically far ahead of her psychological contemporaries in that she was the first to advance the intersubjectivity argument. She wrote, "it is an essential condition of scientific investigation of any phenomenon that observations made by one individual must be verifiable by others. Otherwise indeed a phenomena [*sic*] is not even identifiable."[36] She did not deny that, when someone looked at a color patch or when someone was in pain, there were private events. The question at issue was, rather, the scientific investigation of those private events. We could not deny experiences, and we knew their nature from verbal descriptions. So, she wrote, "The real scientific observer in the psychological experiment is not the O but the E of the experiment. The series of introspections is a series of responses given by the O under the conditions of the experiment, and observed and interpreted by the E."[37] Long before the enunciation of the principles of the psychological experiment by Woodworth and others in the 1930s, de Laguna was articulating the essential basis of those principles.

De Laguna exhorted behaviorists to abandon speculation in favor of research: "The future of behaviorist psychology will depend on the success with which it treats the specific phenomena of consciousness. To rest its case on the general theoretical advantages, important though they may be, of defining consciousness in terms of behavior, would be to forego the chief claim of any theory to scientific recognition: methodological fruitfulness."[38] Behaviorism, she wrote, had at that point promised much and achieved little. In particular, the central areas of psychology (sensation, perception, and volition) had been left untouched. In part, that was a legacy from behaviorism's origins in comparative psychology and philosophy.

With respect to behaviorism's history, two features of de Laguna's work are noteworthy. First, her positivism was entirely homegrown, a direct offshoot of Singer's (and of the New Realist position in general); in that respect it resembled Tolman's, Hull's, and Skinner's. It was also pervasively rooted in the pragmatism and commitment to social utility so characteristic of American intellectual life in the early twentieth century. Second, de Laguna's methodological principles were elaborated in an empirical vacuum but were very fully elaborated nonetheless. Her work therefore asks us to interpret behaviorism as an enterprise in which laboratory data were constructed in order to lend support to a preestablished philosophical position.

From its beginning American psychology was dominated by an eclectic objectivism and a nascent scientism. Given behaviorism's commitment to objectivism and scientism, when behaviorist positions made their first tentative appearance, American psychologists welcomed them not because they were novel or because they held out the promise of undoing the errors of the past, but because they were familiar. Psychological behaviorism, if it originated anywhere within the discipline, had its beginnings in the inchoate views of the nature of psychology as a discipline that were commonplace in the 1900s.

Fortuitously, the date of the first seemingly behaviorist statement in psychology, by James McKeen Cattell in an address given at the World's Fair at St. Louis in 1904, is the same as the first overt behaviorist statement in American philosophy:

> I can only say that psychology is what the psychologist is interested in qua psychologist. . . . I am not convinced that psychology should be limited to the study of consciousness as such . . . I admire . . . the ever-increasing acuteness of introspective analysis . . . but the positive scientific results are small in quantity when compared with the objective experimental work accomplished in the past fifty years. There is no conflict between introspective analysis and objective experiment—on the contrary, they should and do continually cooperate. But the rather widespread notion that there is no psychology apart from introspection is refuted by the brute argument of accomplished fact. It seems to me that most of the research work that has been done by me or in my laboratory is nearly as independent of introspection as work in physics or in zoology. . . . I see no reason why the application of systematized knowledge to the control of human nature may not in the course of the present century accomplish results commensurate

with the nineteenth century applications of physical science to the material world.[39]

As department head at Columbia, Cattell certainly favored and supported what one might call brashly mechanist forms of objectivism such as Edward Lee Thorndike's. At the same time, he did not make psychology the exclusive preserve of the behaviorist; he reserved some role for the introspectionist.

William McDougall, later to be a vocal opponent of behaviorism, was the first psychologist to use the term *behavior* when defining psychology. In words reminiscent of those Watson was to publish five years later, he wrote that "The insistence upon introspection as the one method of the science [of psychology] tended to prolong the predominance of this narrow and paralyzing view of the scope of the science."[40] McDougall went on to write that "psychologists must cease to be content with the sterile and narrow conception of their science as the science of consciousness, and must boldly assert its claim to be the positive science of the mind in all its aspects and modes of functioning or . . . the positive science of conduct or behavior."[41] Although that passage, taken in isolation, might suggest that McDougall had preempted Watson, we cannot classify McDougall as a behaviorist. His repudiation of introspection was part of his repudiation of hedonism, associationism, utilitarianism, and individualism (so that he was distancing himself from an intellectual tradition that is fully compatible with behaviorism's) and was designed to set the stage for an examination of the forces underlying conduct.

Walter Bowers Pillsbury (1872–1960), although a student of the arch-introspectionist Edward Bradford Titchener, nevertheless defined psychology as the scientific study of behavior.[42] Like Cattell, Pillsbury wished to match his definition of psychology to what he took to be the new science's actual achievements and its potential for enhancing social and psychological efficiency. In the preface of his *Essentials of Psychology* he wrote, "The point of view [in this book] is on the whole functional; more attention is given to what mind does than to what it is. With this goes an emphasis upon the outward manifestations of consciousness and upon the behavior of others to the subordination of the individual consciousness."[43] Like Cattell, Pillsbury believed that consciousness should still be studied. It was a subject of intrinsic interest to us, and he believed that complex actions could be understood only by an appeal to consciousness. Nevertheless he wrote that "At the present stage in the development of psychology, it seems best to subordinate consciousness to behavior. Behavior is to be studied through the consciousness of the individual and by external observation."[44] Thus when Pillsbury wrote that "Psychology may be most satisfactorily defined as the science of human behavior," we should not treat him as a proto-behaviorist even if, for the sake of enhancing psychology's appeal to the practically minded, he was enunciating behaviorist-seeming principles.[45]

The first coherent and wide-ranging behaviorist theory to appear in American psychology was American in form in that its inspiration lay in objectivism. Substantively, however, it did not have an American origin. Its proponent, Max Meyer, earned his doctorate under the German objectivist Carl Stumpf at Berlin.[46] Meyer's chief interests lay in hearing and musical acoustics. His objectivism was born in 1896, when he heard "two Russians" expound the doctrine at the International Congress of Psychology at Munich.[47] In formulating his behaviorism, Meyer drew on his European mentors Stumpf, Hermann Ebbinghaus, and the linguist Lazarus Geiger.[48] According to the historian of psychology Erwin Esper,

> In a letter of June, 1966, Meyer wrote, "In Tonpsychologie Stumpf was a 'behaviorist' without knowing himself this fact, obvious to me now." And in a letter two years earlier Meyer had said that when he arrived in America, "I was then already a behaviorist, although I did not know the English language had such a word. When a subject said, 'That noise must be . . .' I told him not to 'introspect' but to do something, to sing."[49]

In 1900 Meyer was appointed to the University of Missouri and appears to have developed his behaviorist theories partly in an attempt to acculturate himself shortly after he arrived in America. He wrote, "I had to teach psychology to college students. I conceived of psychology as the science of learning; I conceived of learning as conductivity change . . . somewhere in the nervous system."[50] Meyer first formally stated his views in his book *The Fundamental Laws of Human Behavior*, published in 1911, two years before Watson's "behaviorist manifesto."[51] There, he advanced a strict contiguity view of habit formation, claiming that habits had their origin in the nervous system, whose role was simply to make connections between stimuli and responses.

The fullest exposition of Meyer's behaviorism is to be found in his book *The Psychology of the Other One*.[52] Here he abandoned his neurological underpinnings and gave a fairly straightforward exposition of his principles. But they remained the same. The most noteworthy aspect of Meyer's 1921 book was his treatment of language: "The speech functions here described are habits in no essential manner different from other habits. [To assume that they constitute a separate class and to give them] such names as memory, or reasoning power, or thought . . . has little to commend it from the psychologist's point of view."[53] Having treated language as nothing other than a set of habits, Meyer proceeded to claim that the relevant habits had a motor basis. At first language acquisition was a passive process. For example, the child learned that the word "food" was associated with the muscular and glandular changes correlated with hunger and eating. Later, children began to imitate words in conjunction with actions. A vital aspect there was the inevitable self-stimulation (the children received both auditory and muscular feedback from their own vocalizations). The feedback provided a constant link between sets of functionally equivalent but physically diverse events and allowed the child to generalize on the basis of specific behavioral instances. Eventually, actions associated with speech attenuated to undetectable events in nerve and muscle. Those minute events formed the basis for the abstractions we called meanings.

Meyer's major methodological doctrine, according to Esper, was that psychology was to deal only with objective data and only with behavior of social interest. For several reasons, Meyer found almost no audience for his views. In his earliest publications he insisted on deriving all his psychological constructs from hypothetical neural models, a mode of exposition that was foreign to his American readers. In addition, he made no concessions to those readers. Furthermore, especially in his later journal articles, he played the role of the European sophisticate who scorned the intellectual laxity of Americans. When we add that he did not balance his criticisms with any real attempt to enlarge his audience (feeling, one assumes, that his books provided him with the only forum he needed for expressing his views) it is no wonder that he was little read and soon forgotten.

Meyer had one successor, Albert Paul Weiss. Weiss trained, both as a graduate and undergraduate, at the University of Missouri, completing his Ph.D. in 1916. He spent the rest of his career at the University of Ohio. His first publications were in education and in audition. Otherwise, all his efforts were devoted to formulating a comprehensive theory of behaviorism. Weiss died aged 52 after a serious illness.

Weiss's reputation was overshadowed by Watson's and, indeed, his peers seemed to treat him as a spokesman for his better-known colleague.[54] Weiss's treatment of *behavior* was as comprehensive as Watson's; the concept embraced all phenomena from the smallest muscle twitch to all the actions and symbolic processes required to write books, while also extending outwards from the tiniest possible individual acts to the furthest reaches of society. Weiss went beyond Watson, however, in that he treated the difference between physical and mental or between physical and symbolic as a mere scientific convention.

Although, again unlike Watson, Weiss said that behaviorism had to address metaphysical issues, his treatment of philosophy was equally cavalier. He reduced metaphysics to philology and to an analysis of the linguistic habits of those classified as philosophers, dismissing philosophers' concepts as mere fictions. By equating philosophy with metaphysics and by focusing on philosophers' linguistic habits, Weiss preempted the logical positivists in their dismissive characterization of metaphysics as nonsense.

Weiss was asserting that the relevant philosophical issues had been decided and all that had to be done was to arrive at a consensus on terminology. He further asserted that there was no need to use the term "conscious" and that it was up to the mentalists to define it. Indeed, Weiss assigned the problem of consciousness to the margins of psychology: "The success of behavior methods will not depend on how they treat the problem of consciousness; they will succeed or fail according as they do or do not further the general welfare of society."[55]

Consciousness, in order to be known, had to be expressed in action of some sort. He then went on to take a physicalistic approach to the description of action reminiscent of logical positivism. He asked his readers to imagine a situation in which someone introspects and an observer reports the actions of the introspecter. Weiss chose to couch those reports in what amounted to a data language. He focused on the act of writing, claiming that, in recording the events to which both were exposed, the observer and the introspecter would make the same muscular movements. That is, he did not assume that the introspecter was reporting private or inner events (he made the distinction between public and private social, not biological, and he gave a higher epistemological status to physically based than to subjectively based information).

Weiss went beyond Watson in his attempt to demonstrate that behaviorism was monistic in that it could offer a materialist account for all phenomena. To illustrate his behaviorism's epistemological approach he used the continuum from "mere awareness" of an apple to reporting the presence of an actual apple. In awareness, physical stimuli had to be present, but because there were no sense receptors in the brain we could not detect the sources of stimulation. In the latter case we could record the sources of stimulation. Weiss's position allowed him to dispose of any need to consider possible causal relations between the mental and the physical, since the only real domain was the physical.[56] In contemporary terms, Weiss was both an analytic and a radical behaviorist, since he believed that all "mental talk" could be translated, without loss of meaning, into a physical language, while he also claimed that private or implicit aspects of behavior were all derived from a history of physical transactions with the world.

To a contemporary reader, Weiss's refusal to consider the possible role of nonobservable events in the central nervous system in the control of behavior is a strange feature of his physicalism. Weiss believed we could not have a full processing of stimulation in the absence of movement or of the possibility of movement. Using the metaphor of the brain as a telephone exchange allowed Weiss to treat the brain purely as a physico-chemical mechanism so that, when discussing the neurophysiology of behavior, he did not have to introduce a new hierarchy of concepts.

Weiss admitted that behaviorism's seeming description of language solely in terms of the muscular movements required to produce speech or writing made it susceptible to criticism. To overcome that deficiency, he analyzed language as a system of signs designed to communicate meaning and focused on the various acts whereby meaning was communicated, ignoring the precise muscular movements necessary for the production of those acts. No behaviorist other than Skinner was to take that approach.[57] Moreover, both Skinner and Weiss advanced philosophies of language; neither proposed research strategies designed to support their claims.

Weiss's treatment of language was reminiscent of Skinner's not merely in terms of its working stance. In a detailed account of a child's acquisition of the word "orange," Weiss claimed that the word was acquired because of the desirable consequences of using it, so that his explanation resembled Skinner's account of the acquisition of the class of words he calls "mands." There was even a hint that Weiss foreshadowed Skinner's autoclitics in that he claimed that children could learn to insert single words into sentences by imitating their parents' utterances.

Unlike all other behaviorists, including Skinner, Weiss characterized language in terms of its structure. He discussed what Charles F. Hockett called "key properties" of language: for example, any language consists of an infinite, ordered response output; languages make it possible to exchange communications over large spatial and temporal distances; in language, a small energy input into a stimulus can trigger a much larger response output.[58]

When he wrote about thinking, Weiss provided a much more wide-ranging and robust blueprint for behaviorist research and theory than was to be found in the work of his successors. He asked us to define thought in terms of its social consequences: "If thinking is defined according to the biosocial character of the responses that are the solution to the problem stimulus, two thoughts are similar when the solution responses meet similar biosocial requirements."[59] He also wrote, "Thinking is a form of behavior, standardized and conventionalized, and typified by a particular problem stimulus and a solution response. The same forces are operative in thinking as in any other form of behavior."[60] Weiss's strikingly incisive analysis of thinking invites comparison with Wittgenstein's. In that respect, within behaviorism he had no peer. Indeed, it is difficult to think of any contemporary psychologist who had thought about the problem so deeply.

Turning to the social realm, Weiss said that social status was directly established by the overt reaction and, like the stimulus, had a biophysical and an individual-social aspect. Introducing the two aspects allowed him to discuss the issue of the differing significance of actions that are physically identical (his example was signing a check as opposed to signing an I.O.U.). Social status itself was produced by specific and efficiency factors. The former specify one's social role, the latter one's status or power. He then broke down the efficiency factor into variables, claiming that an individual could be defined in terms of his or her relative ranking on all relevant variables. In a footnote he explicated that point:

> Much of the criticism that has been directed against mental testing arises from the failure to see that mental tests are actually social tests; that the mental test score actually gives the individual's social status in the specific activity that is being tested. Mental age, fundamentally, means social age. The criticism that "mental testers do not know what they are testing" merely means that no scientific classification has been developed for normal adult individuals which is based on the overt reactions characteristic of a given group . . . the difficulty with the definition of intelligence means that at present it is impossible to separate the social from the neural factor in the analysis of the overt reaction.[61]

In that passage Weiss showed a remarkably acute understanding of the role mental testing was to play in America from the 1920s to the 1960s. He recognized that the testers were committed to working within the confines of a given set of power and status relationships and that their task was to predict effective working roles for individuals in society.

A Theoretical Basis of Human Behavior was the greatest and most comprehensive achievement of the behaviorism of the 1920s. Weiss explicated behaviorist principles fully, especially in the two key areas of language and thought. He also gave careful consideration to criticisms of behaviorism. Compared to Watson's *Behaviorism*, his is a much more thorough and scholarly book. But he is a sadly neglected figure whose ideas are seldom discussed.

Three reasons can be advanced for that neglect. One is Weiss's early death, which was preceded by several years of incapacitating illness. Furthermore, his death came at a low point in behaviorism's fortunes. The second is his personality. Weiss was a modest, rather retiring man who did little to publicize his ideas. Here, he sharply contrasts with Watson. In particular, Weiss made no attempt to popularize his views. But perhaps the major reason for the neglect of Weiss lay in what was seen as his extreme reductionism. A coyness about reductionism (as in Hull's case) or a successful circuit of what psychologists saw as an epistemological morass (as in Skinner's case) was an essential route to success.

Even though Jacob Robert Kantor continued publishing until 1984 and even though the school he founded (interbehavioral psychology) has many living adherents, I have decided to include an account of his theory in this chapter.[62] Like the other psychological behaviorists who first published in the 1920s, Kantor did not develop a research-oriented theory. Thus he stood apart from the neobehaviorists, despite the similarities between his theory and Skinner's. Besides refusing to create a research-oriented theory, Kantor rejected operationism and did not accept the reality of the concept of *learning*, even if he had intellectual (but not institutional) affiliations with functionalism.

Kantor created his mature theory very early in his career. He resembled his behaviorist confreres because its inspiration was negative rather than positive. He was an anti-mentalist, argued against both mind/body and brain/body dualism, and assigned instincts a fleeting role in the psychological economy. He also resembled the other behaviorists in his acceptance of Watson's aspirations to create an overarching theory of behavior, but he could not accept Watson's means of realizing them. In particular, by taking an antimechanist stance Kantor rapidly distanced himself from Watson.

Kantor was also distinctive in rejecting some of the constitutive tenets of the behaviorist school. For him, physics was not the master or model science; instead, he espoused a scientific pluralism, a pluralism that he applied to psychology as a whole (he claimed that certain concepts and data-gathering techniques were unique to psychology) and within psychology (he claimed that the various areas within psychology had fundamentally distinct features). He did not believe that psychologists could make predictions, and he did not believe that standard models of causation applied in psychology.[63]

There were powerful positive elements in Kantor's thought. Following Watson, he believed that the explanations for adaptive actions lay in a close study of their ontogenesis. In his very first writings Kantor recognized that developing adequate explanations for smoothly and unthinkingly generated human adaptive actions was a crucial problem for any psychological theory.[64] He believed passionately, like all the other behaviorists, that explanations appealing to mind, consciousness, or instinct were not explanations at all. His antimechanism and his distrust of the possibility of prediction led him to develop the concept of the interbehavioral field. The components of any given interbehavioral field were the organism, the stimulus, the media (or medium) of contact, the setting factors, and the reactional biography.[65] Kantor's treatment of the organism did not differ from that of the other behaviorists (he saw the organism as a set of dispositions or response functions).[66] He treated the stimulus, however, very differently. For him, stimuli were simply occasions for reaction and fluently emerged from past actions. For example, presenting a blue flower to human beings elicited an infinite range of reactions, all of which were controlled both by past experience of flowers and by cultural expectations regarding them.[67] Thus, past experience with flowers (some of which was collective, that is, symbolically mediated), constituted the stimulus. Stimuli, then, could not be physical; physical objects and events were mere occasions or settings for actions and could not cause actions.

Kantor used the concept of medium of contact to emphasize the distance between his and all other psychological theories. A medium of contact, he wrote, "is certainly *not* a stimulus in the sense of energy 'mediating' mental qualities by its effect on the brain."[68] Media of contact, such as light or sound, then, were necessary but not sufficient conditions for psychological events. Because he was not a dualist, Kantor did not believe that physical events were registered and interpreted by either the brain or the mind.

Kantor's treatment of media of contact allows us to understand his theory of meaning. Both dualists and materialists would say that events can be meaningful in themselves. For example, a red patch is meaningful merely by being perceived and thereby incorporated into the perceiver's experience. Kantor, however, saw the matter quite differently. First, for him meaning arose from the domain circumambient to an event (as when a child in a dimly lit room sees a teddy bear as a terrifying monster). Second, he believed it was wrong to say that an event could derive its meaning from outside its ontological domain (so that mental states could not be reduced to neurological events).[69]

The complex and varied antecedent and concurrent events in which a specific individual interaction of stimulus and response is embedded were, according to Kantor, setting factors. Other theorists organized them and assigned a causative role to subsets of them under such generic terms as "intervening variable" and "hypothetical construct."[70] Kantor's treatment of setting factors demonstrates how, as in the case of reinforcement, he relegated what was central to neobehaviorism to the periphery of his theory.[71]

Kantor's treatment of responses was very similar to his treatment of stimuli. That is, like Skinner, he did not believe that responses could be characterized solely or even largely by their physical form.[72] Instead, a response was the expression of a complex concatenation of circumstances. It was also the avenue down which psychologists had to travel in order to understand behavior. For example, weeping could have complex origins (anger, sorrow, frustration, etc.). There were also individual differences in the threshold for weeping. Even the various types of weeping showed complex differences (for example, a bout of sorrowful weeping might have various subcomponents such as love, misery, or rage at lost opportunities; some sorrows provoked weeping, others did not).

The reactional biography comprised constituent events distant in both time and space from any given action. Verplanck comments, "The reactional biography can be understood as everything that ever happened to the individual and everything the individual ever did. It delineates the behavior repertoire of the individual."[73] The components of the field reacted with one another in highly complex ways. To explicate the interbehavioral field, I will take the example of the contrasting effects of malnourishment and adequate nourishment in infancy on intellectual development. If malnourishment is sufficiently severe, brain growth is retarded, with a consequent effect on intellectual growth (that is, we apply a linear causal model in deriving our explanation). Kantor would then ask us to consider the effects of normal nourishment. We could not attribute normal intellectual functioning to normal brain growth resulting from adequate levels of nourishment. Instead, according to Kantor, the well-nourished child made contact with its environment on a very broad front. Those contacts were not merely passively recorded. Instead, they formed the basis for further reactions, which themselves constituted a basis for differing reactions.

Even if we take a reaction as simple as sneezing, the sneeze of an infant is quite different from that of a forty-year-old. The infant's sneeze is a simple reflex response and has no further consequences; the adult's might be the portent of an annual spring allergy attack and will result in a visit to the drug store, besides eliciting gloomy thoughts about future red, sore eyes, lassitude, and so forth. Furthermore, the reactional biography included cultural components. A middle-class English sneeze might elicit scornful looks, whereas a German sneeze elicits a good-natured "Gesundheit."

Because Kantor did not believe that his theory could find expression in research or have practical applications, he concerned himself almost exclusively with metatheoretical issues. That is, he tried to establish a secure framework within which to develop a comprehensive behaviorist psychology. Kantor's diffuse writing style constitutes an additional problem for those not already convinced of interbehaviorism's value. To make his difficulties worse, Kantor consistently took on the role of a critic rather than that of an expositor of some distinctive theory; he exacerbated his difficulties in this respect by criticizing behaviorism as freely as he criticized other theories.

Although Kantor did create a school of psychology and did inspire a surprisingly large group of followers, he could not, given his theory's form, inspire a group of research-oriented acolytes. Skinner was far more successful in that respect. Because Skinner's and Kantor's theories were so similar, Kantor, if he lives on at all, lives in Skinner's shadow. Neobehaviorist theories contained explicit research-oriented components, so that adherents were given clear guidelines allowing them to generate findings consistent with their chosen theory.

I can illustrate my point by contrasting Skinner's and Kantor's treatment of reinforcement. For Skinner, reinforcement referred to a class of events designed to control the rate of emission of responses. By specifying the means of measuring and controlling the rates of emission of responses and correlating those rates with the rate of delivery of reinforcement, Skinner could show his followers how to generate an infinite set of research techniques. Kantor almost dismissed reinforcement, treating it as a conceptual device that permitted the neobehaviorists to generate distinctive theories.

Finally, I think we can say that Kantor developed his theory at a time when it would be seen merely as a recondite variant of a psychological doctrine, competing in an ideological war both with its fellows in the behaviorist camp and with enemy theories outside. The key development in behavioral science was the creation of new research technologies in the 1930s. The conjunction of learning theory, operationalism, and research designs based on analysis of variance, combined with an enunciation of the relevant principles in the language of the logical positivists, ensured research productivity for generations of graduate students. Theories deprived of those essential nutrients, Kantor's among them, withered on the vine.[74]

Just as Kantor looked back to the theoretical behaviorisms of the 1920s, so Walter Samuel Hunter looked forward to the research-driven neobehaviorisms of the 1930s and 1940s. Hunter enunciated the behaviorist creed, but did not formulate a distinctive version of it. His one theoretical term, anthroponomy (his name for the science of psychology), was designed to act as a warning sign (banning mentalists), and so did no more than affirm all behaviorists' distrust of the mind and all allied concepts.[75] By the same token, his major innovation was programmatic rather than substantive. Hunter designed the very first course in learning to be given in psychology, thereby setting up the warp for the neobehaviorist tapestry.

Hunter converted to behaviorism in 1922.[76] His contribution to the doctrine was based exclusively on his research on the delayed reaction.[77] In that work, Hunter showed conclusively that raccoons, monkeys, and children could all respond adequately to an internal cue. He inferred that all those species shared the same type of intellectual capacity (all could form symbolic representations of the world). He wrote,

> By applying the term "ideas" to those cues, I mean that they are similar to the memory idea of human experience so far as *function* and *mechanism* are concerned. They are the residual effects of sensory stimuli which are retained and which may be subsequently re-excited. The revival, moreover, is selective and adaptive to the solution of a particular problem, and when aroused they function successfully as a necessary substitute for a definite component of the objective stimulus aspect of the problem.[78]

In order to arrive at a comprehensive theory, Hunter, like his behaviorist peers, assumed that consciousness and language were coterminous—that is, first, whatever we are conscious of is linguistically expressible, at least in principle, and, second, consciousness was nothing other than a mass of verbalizations. By implication, symbolism had a purely functional role: symbols or rules were nothing other than surrogates for full-blown responses. Hunter's position implied that symbolic processes, even though they were entirely derived from experience, were different from all other psychological processes.

In his psychology as a whole Hunter obeyed the behaviorist imperatives. The term "anthroponomy" issued a promissory note to treat the human condition comprehensively. However, he did not redeem those promises himself. Hunter wrote,

> Anthroponomy is the science of behavior of the human organism as a whole. The problems of this science necessarily cover a wide range. Some are shared with the related sciences of sociology, physiology, neurology, physics, chemistry and mathematics, while other problems are studied little if at all outside of anthroponomy. These latter problems concern the characteristics which most specifically define human nature, *viz.,* the learning and use of new forms of response, language behavior, and social behavior, which latter we call the behavior of inter-stimulation and response.[79]

Hunter was the first to define the science of psychology as the study of the acquisition and deployment of habits. Such a definition was implicit in Watson's approach, because he placed the acquisition of habits in center stage, but we do not find formal statements of the role of conditioning or learning in Watson's writings. Hunter was prescient in another respect. It would seem that he derived his formulation of his version of behaviorism from his research, and his work on the delayed reaction provided the paradigm. His behaviorism thus appeared to have an inductive origin, in that respect resembling Skinner's and Tolman's.

Hunter's theory, as expressed in his textbook *Human Behavior*, was rather disappointing.[80] He presented the standard functionalist fare. He treated society as a collection of individuals whose role was to adapt to the situations in which they found themselves. He divided anthroponomy's subject matter into four areas—comparative psychology, the application of psychological tests, abnormal psychology, and social psychology. Despite his opposition to Watson in his most distinctive research, Hunter molded his psychology into a Watsonian form. Psychology was derived from and based its scientific respectability on biology and the physical sciences in general. Its current justification lay in the applied area. Its future lay with proposals to cure society's ills; crucially, those ills resided in failures of individual adjustment. Using ontogenetic techniques derived from comparative psychology and modes of assessment developed by mental testers, psychologists were to act as social technocrats. Hunter's creed is fully expressed in the following passage:

> The sum total of overt and concealed, implicit, behavior which makes up the daily life of the individual constitutes his total personality. These forms of behavior are what they are in virtue of the thousand and one incidents through which the individual has passed since infancy. Undoubtedly if we had a complete and detailed description of the individual's equipment at birth and an equally satisfactory record of the modifications of his responses since that time, we would be in a position to give a satisfactory explanation of his adult personality.[81]

There we have Watson without the bombast. Hunter had firmly grasped the essence of Watson's message. Each of us is the sum total of all the habits we have acquired since our birth. Moreover, all those habits were acquired under conditions that are in principle fully specifiable, and all have consequences that, again in principle, can be completely stated in terms of observable actions.

If asked to name the ultimate behaviorist, most psychologists who know their history would say Watson or Skinner. The palm must, however, be awarded to Zing-Yang Kuo.[82] From 1924 onward, Kuo elaborated an anti-instinct stance into the most extreme version of behaviorism in the history of thought. Astoundingly, heredity was not a psychological problem for him because the existence of heredity could be neither proved nor disproved in the laboratory. He wrote, "Any controversy in psychology must be capable of promoting experimental researches so that the issue can be settled in the laboratory, or it must at least have some particular value for laboratory procedure."[83] Kuo continued,

> I shall define psychology as *the science which deals with the physiology of bodily mechanisms involved in the organismic adjustment to environment with special emphasis on the functional aspect of the adjustment.* (By functional aspect, I mean the effect, or result, or adjustment-value—positive, negative or indifferent—of a response which establishes a new functional relation of the ongoing organism to its environment, social or otherwise.)[84]

Unlike Watson, but like Weiss, Kuo was calling for the creation of a new, physiologically based science of behavior.[85] There could be no compromise with the existing discipline because to compromise was to incorporate psychology's fetid metaphysical past into the growing discipline.

Kuo wished to dismiss purpose from psychology altogether, producing behaviorism's *ne plus ultra*: "The basic principles that have been employed to explain the behavior of a stone should be sufficient to explain human behavior. The behaviorist need not assume an inner motive in the case of human behavior any more than the physicist needs to assume spiritual influence in the case of stone movement."[86] Belief in the directive function of drive, he asserted, implied belief in some spiritual agency. He denied any difference between anticipatory and consummatory reactions, saying that all reactions were to be explained in terms of the operation of current stimulation. Once again he expressed himself in extreme terms: "the organism—animal as well as man—is always a passive machine acting in one direction or another as a result of predominance of chemical or physical forces in the environment."[87]

Even if one says that Kuo caricatured the substance of behaviorism, one has to say that he showed a precise grasp of the nature of experimental method as it was portrayed by both the behaviorists and the functionalists. He wrote,

> the experimenter starts out his experiment with a preconceived end, and when the animal has reached a certain end (*note that this is not the animal's own end*) its ceaseless movements are brought to an end; *e.g.,* when the animal has gone through the correct path and has reached the food box and taken food, the experimenter immediately interrupts its activities and brings it back to the entrance of the maze again. Indeed, if there is any "purpose" in animal experimentation, that purpose belongs to the experimenter.[88]

Kuo believed that the rejection of purpose had to imply the rejection of trial-and-error learning. If one assumed that every movement was passive and enforced by the environment, there was no need to posit trial and error. He reverted to his point that, in any experiment, the animal was totally under the experimenter's control. Further, the abolishment of instinct implied abolishing trial and error because trial and error, traditionally, was opposed to instinct, mirroring the distinction between unlearned and learned reactions. But, with unusual humility, Kuo admitted, "in spite of more than a quarter of a century of animal experimentation we still know very little about the effectiveness of controlling animal behavior."[89]

Just as Kuo typified behaviorism in his portrayal of experimental method, he emulated the behaviorists' cavalier dismissal of any consideration of the central nervous system.[90] Ironically, Lashley, later to be a founding father of the "cognitive revolution" that thrust behaviorism into the shadows, was the only American psychologist to respond favorably to Kuo.[91] Kuo himself took up an academic post in China and ceased to play a role in the behaviorist movement.

2

From Apogee to Perigee

Radical Behaviorism Appears but Fails to Take Root

Typically, the classical neobehaviorisms of the post–World War II period are assigned a continuous history, originating in the empiricism and associationism of Locke and Hume, which culminated in the mature psychological associationism of Alexander Bain and in Herbert Spencer's evolutionary associationism, from which arose, via Darwin's speculations about the evolutionary origins of mind, a widespread and wide-ranging comparative psychology. John B. Watson, who became America's leading comparative psychologist, is the main actor in this dramatic tale. Supposedly the insights derived from his animal work formed the imaginative core of a fully fledged, fully comprehensive behaviorist theory, which eventually (and inevitably) became a group of research-based, theoretically sophisticated neobehaviorisms. Certainly by the early 1920s "behaviorism" had come to mean the doctrines of John B. Watson.[1] By the middle of the decade Watson was advancing a form of behaviorism in which he dismissed mental, spiritual, or, indeed, abstract qualities as unworthy of serious study. He was also propounding a social technology whereby social agents (especially mothers) formed children's personalities, capabilities, and propensities very early in life; more to the point, he exhorted socializing agents to use their powers to produce human beings with predetermined characteristics. However, this socially oriented and crudely speculative behaviorism is a far cry from the highly sophisticated and technical work of the neobehaviorists. I will devote most of this chapter to establishing Watson's true role in behaviorism's history.

Most of the rest of the chapter will be devoted to the behaviorism of Edwin Guthrie. He did not share the limelight with Watson in the

1920s; nevertheless he bridged the gap between early, theoretical behaviorism and neobehaviorism. However, he did almost no research and his theory retained the speculative character of early behaviorism. Hence he was powerless to overcome the temporary decline in behaviorism's fortunes in the late 1920s and early 1930s.

The authors of the first textbooks on the history of psychology claimed that psychological behaviorism had its origins in the American comparative psychology of the first two decades of this century.[2] It is certainly true that Watson was America's preeminent early comparative psychologist and that he eventually became a behaviorist. It is also true that America's first comparative psychologist, Edward Lee Thorndike, invented instrumental learning, one of the two constitutive paradigms of behaviorist learning theory. However, there is no clear line of descent from Watson's animal work to his behaviorism, while Thorndike, although he briefly flirted with behaviorism, soon renounced it. Finally, neobehaviorist learning theory was almost exclusively animal science; in its first manifestation, behaviorism was a human science.

Others have dealt fully with Watson's contributions to comparative psychology.[3] Robert Boakes concludes that Watson, to a very large extent, allowed others to set his agenda for him.[4] He does, however, pinpoint some themes distinguishing Watson's work from that of his contemporaries. First, Watson gave some priority to psychological development, starting with his doctoral research, published in 1903. One of his students, J. Allen, carried out a further developmental study a year later. During his fieldwork on the Dry Tortugas Watson studied the behavioral development of young terns. Watson's work on the psychological development of animals came to an end in a study with Karl Spencer Lashley.[5] Boakes suggests that Watson pursued this research theme in his work with human infants and that it is only there that we see a continuity between Watson's animal and human work. Second, Watson did some work on the relationship between instinct and learning in terns. Third, Watson knew that if one was to make effective comparisons between the psychological abilities of higher animals and those of people, one had to develop complex learning tasks, such as delayed reaction and multiple-choice. However, he did no sustained work there. Oddly enough, during his period of animal research Watson showed little interest in the processes of habit acquisition.[6]

As an animal researcher, Watson was a classical functionalist (that is, he believed that mind played an adaptive role in animal life). Although he never mentioned the evolutionary psychologist James Mark Baldwin, it is certainly clear that he shared Baldwin's views on the role of evolutionary forces in animal life.[7] The most significant modification Watson eventually made to Baldwin's (and his functionalist heirs') position was to extirpate the concepts of mind and consciousness. But given the functionalist equation of mind with consciousness, and given the limited role assigned to the latter, the patient scarcely needed an anesthetic. That removal aside, Watson's (or, rather, his student Harvey Carr's) theory of habit formation was remarkably similar to Baldwin's. Watson and Carr assumed that animals acquired many of their adaptive habits during their lifetime.[8] As did Baldwin, they further assumed that young animals had at their disposal a vast array of random movements and that habits emerged from that pool via a process of selection. Watson and Carr, again like Baldwin, stressed that what was new about a habit was the organization of a set of components, not the components themselves.

There were three key elements in Watson's approach to animal learning: first, a mistrust of Darwinian theory; second, a belief that he had discovered a principle allowing him to explain the rapid acquisition of a large number of habits early in the life of the individual; third, a commitment to experimental work in the laboratory over fieldwork. If one accepts these as the defining parameters of Watson's research practice, then the derivation of his ideas from predecessors such as Baldwin is very clear. It is also clear that he needed to make very few conceptual modifications when he transferred his attention from animal work to research on infants. It also becomes inevitable that those following in his footsteps should do the same.

To assume that Watson's behaviorism never comprised a coherent set of doctrines makes the discovery of its origins a well-nigh impossible task. We can merely read the historical evidence and see what help it offers us. In an often quoted statement, Watson claimed a very early origin for his behaviorism.[9] There are many problems with that statement. First, Watson switched to the use of human subjects with the utmost alacrity from 1916 onward, and as we will see later, his behaviorist principles were applied to human rather than to animal subjects. Furthermore, Watson's published animal work shows no trace of a behaviorist position. Second, what Watson meant by "keeping close to biology" needs careful explication. For instance, in a 1909 letter to Yerkes he wrote, "Damn Darwin. The Neo-Darwinians and Neo-Lamarckians, etc. are in a worse hole than the psychologists."[10]

In 1905 Watson reviewed Jennings's *Reactions to Heat and Cold in the Ciliate Infusoria*.[11] Although he showed consistency with his mature views by criticizing Jennings for equating "pleasure" with "interest" and for maintaining that even unicellular animals inevitably acted in their own best interest, Watson denied that such animals showed genuine trial-and-error behavior because they had no means of judging what constitutes "error" and what "success." In 1905, it seems, Watson attributed at least elementary mental processes to higher animals.

In a later discussion of Jennings's work, Watson made level of adjustment the criterion of consciousness—the more complex the level, the greater the probability that we were dealing with a conscious being.[12] In order to arrive at a judgment of complexity, Watson claimed, we relied on an examination of the facts of behavior. However, he was prepared to go beyond the facts by saying that, were we to appeal to introspection, the more complex the act of adjusting to some environmental event, the greater the amount of conscious content. So, as in 1905, Watson was denying consciousness to lower animals. But he was also assigning a role to the conscious mind (the capacity to make relatively sophisticated adjustments to the environment).

In the same issue of the *Psychological Bulletin* Watson reviewed Loeb's *Dynamics of Living Matter*; he wrote, "A paper in the *Journal of Experimental Zoology* . . . shows that [Loeb] still fails to grasp the fundamental principle of psychology—viz., that a physico-chemical statement of behavior can never *interfere with* nor be *substituted for* a psychological statement." He added the footnote, "I.e., so long as we assume psychophysical parallelism as the working hypothesis of experimental psychology."[13]

According to John Burnham, the first sign of Watson's behaviorism was his use, from October 1907 onward, of the phrase "afferent control" as a replacement for consciousness.[14] For example, replying to Robert Yerkes's comment on one of his articles, Watson wrote,

> I should not quarrel with you about the elimination of "sensation." I am willing probably to go further than you in denying a high degree of con-

scious development in these animals. My work should probably have been phrased differently here. To my mind it is not up to the behavior man to say anything about consciousness. I tried all through the paper to phrase the work in terms of "afferent control"—this at least was what I meant to do.[15]

I see no need to say that Watson was advancing an incipient behaviorism in that passage. His "afferent control" was an objectivist—not necessarily a behaviorist—term. Psychologists of the day, such as Yerkes, Washburn, James Angell, and Mary Calkins, saw no contradiction in combining introspectionism with objectivism.

In 1908 we see signs of the emergence of a systematic and comprehensively articulated psychology in Watson's thought. In that year he expressed the essence of his current thinking in a departmental seminar at Johns Hopkins, in a lecture to the department of psychology at Yale, and in a paper to the Southern Society of Philosophy and Psychology.[16] However, it seems that those theoretical aspirations were not engendered by a concern about the state of psychology but were stimulated by a contract to write a textbook about comparative psychology.[17] Watson first mentions the book in a letter to Yerkes:

Shall we try to combine a popular book with textbook—shall we make it a wholly text book, or wholly popular? I want the book to be [a] *psychological* i.e. *not merely a behavior treatise*. I want it to be used as a companion to Angell, Judd or Titchener in a one year course in *introductory psychology*. Shall I write a chapter on care of animals one on apparatus and methods etc. and give at [the] end of each chapter [a review of important terms] such as "trial and error", "Retention" "Imitation"—practical tests or shall I leave them to Bentley? I don't believe he has enough experience to do the thing I want done in the introductory experimental line.[18]

Watson was not contemplating applying objectivism to the human situation; he went no further than proposing an expositional strategy. We also see him positing a disjunction between the study of behavior and the study of psychology. To Yerkes, he expressed the fear that such a commitment to the study of behavior would place him among physiologists rather than psychologists:

one chapter will have Behavior a biological problem—the scientific determination of modes of behavior and the *modus operandi* of behavior—a part of the problem of natural selection—the second the psychological implications in modes of behavior. My interests are all in the first where an objective standard of determination is possible and where interpretation takes the line of the *importance* of the *observed facts*—for the theory of selection—facts—and interpretation possible without mentioning consciousness or deviating from a (wide) biological point of view. What is then left? Am I *a physiologist?* or am I just a mongrel? I don't know how to get on.[19]

In a later letter to Yerkes we do see the emergence of a tentative behaviorist theory, though still not one in which consciousness would be banished: consciousness would be retained as a provisional observational and interpretative category. Watson wrote,

I am a physiologist and I go so far as to say that I would remodel psychology as we now have it (human) and reconstruct our attitude with reference to the whole matter of consciousness. I don't believe the psychologist is studying consciousness any more than we are and I am willing to say that consciousness is merely a tool, a fundamental assumption with which the chemist works, the physiologist and every one else who observes. All of our sensory work, memory work, attention, etc. are part of definite modes of behavior. I have thought of writing . . . just what I think of the work being done in human experimental psychology. It lacks an all-embracing scheme in which all the smaller pieces may find their place. It has no big problems. Every little piece of work which comes out is an unrelated unit. This would all be changed if we would take a simpler, behavior view of life and make adjustment the key note. But I fear to do it now because my place here is not ready for it.[20]

The phrase that requires analysis is "a simpler, behavior view of life." Throughout the letters he wrote to Yerkes from 1905 to 1914, Watson uses the term "behavior" as a synonym for "comparative psychology" and the term "behavior men" as a synonym for "comparative psychologists" (Margaret Floy Washburn was treated as an honorary man).[21] In the letter of September 18, 1908, from which I quoted above, "behavior treatise" means "text book of comparative psychology."

Watson's conception of comparative psychology's role in psychology was fully developed by 1912. He wrote to Yerkes,

[Thorndike] has been after me once or twice since then to come go [*sic*] over into experimental pedagogy. He too seems to think that I belong there so I am more than interested to find you more or less of the same mind. In my point of view I am already doing the scientific side to experimental pedagogy. Ulrich has just completed a problem on the distribution of learning in rats which is really a remarkable piece of work. We are planing [*sic*] to carry out a similar line of tests upon human beings. If this type of work is not scientific experimental education I guess I don't know what the latter is.[22]

Earlier that year Watson had described himself to Yerkes as an "experimental educationalist" and wrote that "I am pretty sure that any careful investigator in experimental education will have to be an animal psychologist."[23] In the same letter he had a long discussion of a proposed study of the spectral sensitivity of the birds (presumably, the noddy and sooty terns) of the Dry Tortugas. So by 1912 Watson seemed to be treating experimental pedagogy as comprising human and animal research. Apparently he did not see animal research as a branch of what we would now call behaviorism. Instead, the comparative psychologist was to bring to bear all his expertise, irrespective of his theoretical background or predilections, to the problems of human developmental psychology.

As early as 1910, however, there are indications, in some popular articles he wrote for *Harper's*, that Watson was starting to widen his conception of the nature of mind. In selecting *Harper's* as an avenue of publication Watson displayed what Franz Samelson sees as his customary caution. The academic who writes popular articles can always be taken at his word by his immediate audience (and have the added satisfaction of knowing that the words he has chosen will not be subjected to critical scrutiny and thereby will preserve their ambiguous meaning) while he can safely disavow his apparent (but possibly deeply felt) meaning to his academic colleagues. Watson duly played that game in a letter to Yerkes:

> Thank you for your letter about my Harper [*sic*] article. I think you took it a little too seriously. I was rather more interested in vocational training than in the other subject. Yet I do feel that the two hang together completely. I tried not to say anything in the article so far as the experimental side is concerned which was exaggerated or untrue to the facts. The rest of it was a matter of opinion. That opinion is likely to change with my mood. I think such an article must be taken in somewhat of a humorous way. I think it ought to be realized by scientific men that such things are "pot boilers" and are written for the money that is in them. If I did not need it I should never write them. The only thing I try to do well in them is not to falsely state the experimental position. I was much amused by your saying that I must have done this between experiments. It was the hardest article to put into shape that I have ever written. I pegged the way on it [*sic*] off and on for about three months.[24]

Besides playing a role in Watson's current psychic economy, the article was a harbinger of the future, because he was to find his true voice and have his deepest influence in the popular realm. It was the "lay public," not his colleagues, who were the first to receive what could be construed as a statement of classical behaviorism. Watson wrote,

> A little reflection . . . will show that we are forever debarred from studying the mind of our human neighbor [by direct inspection of its contents]; yet surely no one in this day would be hardy enough to deny that we can and do get a very definite and scientific notion of the way our neighbor's mind works. We study our human subject in two ways—by watching what he does under given and controllable conditions and by attending to what he says under those conditions. Still further reflection will show that speech is only a refined and highly organized way of acting and behaving. Instead of reacting with the arm or leg our human subject when speaking reacts with the muscles of his throat. If it is admitted that speech is only a refined mode of behavior (and of this there is no doubt), we are forced to the conclusion that all of our knowledge of the minds of others comes from our observation of what they do. If we control the conditions under which a human subject reacts, and record such reactions, as is done in the psychological laboratory, we get that body of knowledge which is called "human experimental psychology."[25]

Although Watson equated the expression of thoughts with the movement of the speech muscles, he did not equate thought itself with those movements, as he would in 1913. But after a discussion of work on sense discrimination he wrote, "When all such evidence is in, we shall have an invaluable body of facts which will all but revolutionize the present popular way of looking upon mind as the proud possessor of the human race."[26] There, perhaps, Watson adumbrated what was to come.

In 1913 Watson published "Psychology as a Behaviorist Views It." Nowadays the article is known as "the behaviorist manifesto" and treated as the first statement of behaviorist principles in psychology.[27] More to the point, there is little disagreement that the appearance of Watson's article marked a sea change in psychology. As Roger Brown put it so robustly, "In 1913 John Watson mercifully closed the bloodshot inner eye of American psychology. With great relief the profession trained its exteroceptors on the laboratory animal."[28] Would that history were as clear-cut as that. By 1913 behaviorist principles and behaviorist ways of thinking were already widespread in American social science, even if they were not labeled behaviorist. Remove that context and Watson, retrospectively, appears unique. Replace it and his ideas are difficult to distinguish from those of his peers.

Watson delivered what we now know as the manifesto as the first of a series of eight lectures at Columbia University in the winter of 1912–13 (he was appointed a nonresident lecturer for that purpose). He first mentions the course of lectures in a letter to Yerkes:

> My *second* lecture takes up the actual problems of animal behavior. If you are in need of a general article during the year, I shall submit this. If you find it any good at all, you might keep it on hand in case of scarcity of material. . . . All eight of the lectures will go in bodily as a part of the book.[29]

Later he wrote, "I have been generally upset by having to give the lectures at Columbia" and "My first lecture will appear in the March number of the Review."[30] On the lectures in general he commented to Yerkes,

> I am on the home stretch in my Columbia lectures now. I have been surprised at the way in which the crowd has held up. I have had on the average of one hundred and fifty to two hundred people, and since I had not planned to make the lectures popular, I wonder sometimes how they find so much to interest them. I am sending you a reprint of my first lecture. If you don't like it, I hope that you will cuss me out.[31]

It seems that Yerkes did not cuss Watson out, because the latter wrote,

> I am greatly obliged to you for your comments on the paper. I think our main difference lies in this: you are willing to let psychology go its own gait, whereas I have probably an earlier and a deeper interest in psychology than you have; consequently I am not willing to turn psychology over to Titchener and his school. The wise way would probably be to do as you suggest,—call behavior physiology or biology, and leave psychology to the introspectionists. But I have too sincere an attachment to psychology to do this way [*sic*]. I believe that it can be made a desirable field for work. I think it is probable that my *second paper*, which is now ready, will clear up some of the difficulties in the way and show you why I am not willing to turn psychology over to Titchener.[32]

Watson's primary aim in delivering the Columbia lectures, then, was not to propose a radically new form of psychology but to proclaim the merits of his version of comparative psychology. Moreover, the core of his case was not in the first lecture (what we now know as the "manifesto") but in the second.[33] Furthermore, Samelson points out that the second lecture expressed views more revolutionary than those in the *Psychological Review* article.[34] But it is very seldom cited.

Watson himself did not accord his article revolutionary significance, even retrospectively. Franz Samelson notes that he did not list it in the bibliography appended to his autobiography.[35] Watson certainly never aggrandized it with the title "Behaviorist Manifesto." That name first tentatively appeared in print in R. S. Woodworth's *Contemporary Schools of Psychology* in 1931: "Watson's behaviorist manifesto, as we may call it . . ."[36]

An analysis of the text of "Psychology as the Behaviorist Views It" is a crucial first step in any attempt to understand its significance. We have three such analyses already, but given the foundational status of the article in psychology's history, I feel no qualms about undertaking my own.[37] In the first sentence Watson merely characterized psychology as objective (Wundt or Titchener would have agreed heartily). The second sentence is deeply mysterious and requires a lot of unpacking.[38] In the third sentence Watson marginalized introspection but did not banish it altogether. Nor was consciousness dismissed as an object worthy of serious study, even if it was no longer to be accorded a preeminent position. Later in the article Watson suggested that his colleagues should "practically ignore consciousness in the sense that is used by psychologists today," which was, again, a mysterious statement. Did "practically" mean "for all practical purposes" or "pretty well ignore except in certain experimental situations"? Also, what did "in the sense . . . used . . . today" mean? Did it mean that consciousness could still be an object of scientific study, provided that psychologists talked about it in the right way? In the fourth and fifth sentences Watson suggested that psychology should be unified, but without really saying how.

For the next few pages Watson attacked the psychology of his day. His attack culminated in the assertion that attempts to establish criteria of consciousness had led to no resolutions and had no bearing on the conduct of animal research, which in any case yielded factual outcomes. He made an analogy with the Darwinian theory of evolution. The original driving force of the theory was the search for human origins. Contemporary biologists had no interest in the matter. In the same way, the desire to know more about the mind was the original impetus of the science of psychology; now, he said, we could turn our attention to other matters. But note once again that Watson was not saying consciousness did not exist, merely that psychology could do without it, at least for the time being. Besides dismissing structuralism, Watson criticized functionalism. There his argument was practical—behaviorism would allow one to avoid becoming embroiled in either parallelism or interactionism. Psychology could finally come of age by banning all philosophical discussion; in that respect it would then resemble physics.

It was only on the ninth page of his twenty-page article that Watson presented some positive arguments for his position. He asserted, first, that animals adjust via habit and instinct and, second, that particular stimuli elicited particular responses. He then continued by maintaining that the same methods applied to the study of noddy or sooty terns, to Australian aborigines, or even to educated Europeans. At this point, Watson said he wanted a psychology usable for "the educator, the physician, the jurist and the businessman." "One of the earliest conditions which made me dissatisfied with psychology was the feeling that there was no realm of application for the principles which were being worked out in content terms."[39] Immediately after that sentence he praised applied psychology for its vigorous growth, calling it "truly scientific." Significantly, he also said there was no need to invoke consciousness in precisely such fields. Watson then returned to a survey of experimental psychology. Before proceeding with his very rapid and sketchy survey he added this highly significant observation: "I am more interested at the present moment in trying to show the necessity for maintaining uniformity in experimental procedure and in the method of stating results in both human and animal work, than in developing any ideas I may have upon the changes which are certain to come in the scope of human psychology."[40]

We should read Watson's words in the context of the passages I quoted from his letters to Yerkes. If we also take into consideration the state of Watson's research, we can interpret the passage as the core of his thesis. He was, quite explicitly, not calling for the creation of a new version of experimental psychology. Instead, he was asking his colleagues to apply the rigorous methods of experimental animal psychology to their work.

Watson then proceeded to claim that sensory psychology could gather data by objective means alone, citing his and Yerkes's work on sensory discrimination in animals. Samelson stresses that Watson dealt with imagination, judgment, and reasoning in a footnote. His observation is extremely important because John Burnham and Albert E. Goss, in their analyses of the birth of behaviorism, say that Watson's thinking progressively evolved but that he had to come up with a behaviorist explanation for the higher mental processes before he publicized his beliefs.[41] Samelson goes even further, suggesting that the footnote was written in two stages. He believes that the first part of the footnote was written after Watson, who was editor of the *Psychological Review*, had read a manuscript entitled "Inner Speech during Silent Reading" by Rudolf Pintner, which was published in the *Review* in 1913. Although Pintner discounted the motor theory of speech, he cited a 1899–1900 study by H. S. Curtis on movements of the larynx during thinking. When Watson edited the *Review* article for insertion into his 1914 book he incorporated the footnote into the text and added a reference to an article by Anna Wyczoikowska on a method for tracing tongue movements during silent speech (published in the *Review* in November 1913).[42]

In summarizing his views Watson wrote, "Certainly the position I advocate is weak enough at present and can be attacked from many standpoints."[43] That is hardly the sort of statement one would expect to find in what has retrospectively been treated as a ringing declaration of faith.

In his second Columbia lecture Watson discussed two concepts that were to give behaviorism great difficulty, images and affection (emotion).[44] Images (centrally aroused sensations) provided the more difficult problem because they confronted behaviorists with what was later to be called the no-particular-behavior argument (private cognitive events are occurring but, from behavioral evidence alone, we cannot specify the nature of those events). Watson's solution was, for that period in his career, uncharacteristically radical—he proposed abolishing the concept of images. He suggested replacing images with implicit behavior, equating thinking and imaging with tiny laryngeal movements. Significantly, he said such movements would be potentially, not actually, observable. Above all, he made no attempt to suggest how the physical analysis of laryngeal movements would correlate with detailed reports of thought and imagery.

With respect to his analysis of emotion Watson was far more modest. He defined emotion (affection) as an organic sensory response in which pleasure and pain impulses were directly assessed. Following Freud, he assigned the origin of pleasure impulses to the tumescence of sexually sensitive tissue and of pain or unpleasure to the shrinking of such tissue.

He concluded his article by stating what certainly sounds like the essence of a behaviorist credo:

> Having thus summarily dismissed the image and the affective elements, I crave permission to restate the essential contention of the behaviorist. It is this: the world of the physicist, the biologist, and the psychologist is the same, a world consisting of objects—their interests center around different objects, to be sure, but the method of observation of these objects is not essentially different in the three branches of science. Given increased accuracy and scope of technique, and the behaviorist will be able to give a complete account of a subject's behavior both as regards *immediate response* to stimulation, which is effected through the larger muscles; *delayed response*, which is effected through the same muscles (so-called action after deliberation)—these two forms comprising what I have called *explicit behavior*; and the more elusive types, such as the movements of the larynx, which go on in cases where action upon stimulation is delayed (so-called thought processes). This latter form of behavior, which manifests itself chiefly in movements of the larynx, but which may go on in (to the eye) imperceptible form, in the fingers, hands, and body as a whole, I should call *implicit* behavior. For years to come, possibly always, we shall have to content ourselves with experimental observation and control of explicit behavior. I have a very decided conviction, though, that not many years will pass before implicit behavior will likewise yield to experimental treatment.[45]

Read in isolation, that paragraph does sound like a manifesto. But if it were, why would Watson have published it in a philosophical journal, even in one that many psychologists read and in which they published? In any event, Watson was doing no more than to tentatively suggest enlarging the scope of an objectively based experimental psychology. He certainly gave no examples of how such an enlargement might be achieved.

If either "Psychology as the Behaviorist Views It" or "Image and Affection in Behavior" were a manifesto, we would expect that there would have been a response from academic psychologists, especially from the structuralists and functionalists. John Burnham says that there was a furor.[46] Samelson looked for signs of the furor and could find none.[47] Titchener, as one might expect, belittled the originality of Watson's ideas and reasserted the claims of his own structuralism.[48] His tone was, however, remarkably conciliatory. Fred L. Wells, one of

Watson's former graduate students, commented of the manifesto, "It is an unusually concrete statement of a central idea that has always claimed certain adherents among us, at least as an idea. Therefore the way in which so many have received it seems to be due not so much to either its source or content as to a changed attitude in those who read its words."[49] Samelson's comment on his search of the contemporary literature is that he would often find "a tantalizing reference to the popularity of behaviorism among a certain group of persons, [but when] we ask just who was involved and how it was expressed, [we find] the concrete evidence to be very elusive."[50] That elusiveness is illustrated by a comment in Christian Ruckmich's 1916 review of the previous decade's work. Ruckmich concluded that "introspection has contributed more generously to normal, human, adult psychology . . . than has any other method."[51] Essentially the same point had been made by Pillsbury in a paper given at the 1914 APA conference.[52] Pillsbury did not believe that Watson had introduced a revolutionary doctrine but, as Samelson summarizes him, merely a change in terminology. Nor was Pillsbury especially sympathetic to Watson's demand that psychology be relevant to practical concerns.

One of Samelson's most telling points is that responses by supporters and opponents of Watson were remarkably similar. For example, Mary Calkins published a short article in 1913.[53] Samelson finds three themes in it: first, the usefulness and indispensability of introspection; second, the practical relevance of psychology; and, third, what Samelson calls a "cooptation" theme (in Calkins's case it took the form of arguing for a functionalist self psychology). By 1922 Walter Hunter (who described himself as a semi-behaviorist) could find only two behaviorists in psychology—Watson and Albert Weiss. Watson and Weiss, as we have seen, had very different intellectual pedigrees.

Nine years after Watson's purported call to the barricades, the number of acknowledged behaviorists was pitifully small; it is possible, however, that the term *behaviorism* had gained acceptance. But even here the evidence is negative. In 1918 the APA published a report on terminology. The report was based on a questionnaire sent out by Knight Dunlap to more than a hundred members in 1915. Of the fifty-eight respondents, only two rejected the term *consciousness* and replied in a behaviorist manner (Watson and the philosopher W. T. Marvin). It did not contain the term *behaviorism*. By chance, Samelson discovered a preprint of the published report. The published report contains twenty-eight terms. The twenty-ninth term on the preprint is *behaviorism,* but it has been crossed out in ink. Like so much archival evidence, that is infuriatingly inconclusive.

Now we come to the question of who were to be the workers and who were to interpret and use the data. In "Psychology as the Behaviorist Views It," Watson had hinted that his proposals would find their most ready acceptance among applied psychologists. In the 1912 *Harper's* article he made that point very clearly. He started by saying that there was a great public interest in techniques of child instruction and in mental development in general.[54] Thus there was a concomitant interest in instinctive behavior in both children and animals. He also claimed that there was widespread dissatisfaction with the Darwinian concept of instinct, which demanded that all instinctive action automatically serve the fitness of the species and promote the interests of individuals. He continued by claiming that experimenters had been successful in experimentally controlling the course of evolution. (Here Watson was suggesting that the laboratory control of behavior gave us genuine insights into its causes, whereas field study enabled us only to identify cases requiring more rigorous study.)

Watson continued by asking how habits could replace and improve on instincts. He recommended the isolation method for the study of "uncontaminated" instincts. The method would at least allow us to differentiate perfect from imperfect instincts and both from instinctively based random behavior. He cited Yerkes and Bloomfield's work on mice killing in cats and his own work on predator avoidance in terns as examples of perfect instincts and Conradi's work on the learning of canary song by sparrows as an example of an imperfect instinct.

He then went on to discuss random behavior at length, saying that "From the casual observer's standpoint there is no difference between a perfect habit and a perfect instinct. We can separate the two only by the 'genetic' method I have already described."[55] The practical benefits of his techniques would manifest themselves through early and thorough training, Watson claimed, thus bringing about an optimal balance among the inborn tendencies of an individual: those tendencies that were potentially harmful could be suppressed and the potentially beneficial enhanced. Watson gave the following examples; "exaggerated opinions of one's own capabilities and powers, tendencies towards seclusion; tendencies toward the acquisition of property and ideas belonging to others, leading on the one hand possibly toward paranoia, melancholia, and other fundamental nervous diseases, and on the other hand toward criminality."[56] Watson concluded his article by attacking the current system of education because it produced conformism and gave no training in "the real problems of life." He suggested replacing teachers with what one might call "researcher/ controllers," each of whom would work with groups of twenty children, following them from primary through high school, using the genetic method to track changes in their charges and to socialize them. Watson was saying that those who had received the optimal training in method in the human sciences could impartially recognize what social skills were required by society and would impartially instil them into others.

The article gives clear premonitions of the future direction of Watson's thinking, whereas "Psychology as the Behaviorist Views It" and "Image and Affection in Behavior" do not. Furthermore, the *Harpers* article was directed at the lay public, the same audience to whom, eventually, he would direct his behaviorist doctrine. Watson appeared to have been hedging his bets—preaching an enlarged version of comparative psychology to academics and a form of social technology to the public at large.

Up to this point I have been arguing that Watson, at least until 1913, equated behaviorism with comparative psychology. I have also argued that behaviorism as a doctrine or theory was the exclusive possession neither of Watson nor of psychology, since versions of behaviorism pervasively underpinned American social science from the end of the 1890s to the 1920s. At the same time, Watson did eventually become a behaviorist in the usual sense of the term. However, it is exceedingly difficult to discover when and in what form he enunciated his doctrine for the first time. Indeed, it seems that classical, overarching behaviorism crept upon him like a thief in the night.[57]

Watson, I suggest, first stated his classically behaviorist principles in an article entitled "Behavior and the Concept of Mental Disease," published in 1916.[58] The article is diffuse and tentative. Fortunately, we know quite a lot about the circumstances in which it came to be written, allowing us to understand what Watson meant by "behaviorism" in 1916 and his conception of its role in psychology. The article emerged from Watson's association with Adolf Meyer (1866–1950), the Swiss-born psychiatrist who played a prominent role in establishing American psychiatry.[59] Meyer became head of the department of psychiatry at Johns Hopkins and director of the Henry Phipps Psychiatric Clinic in 1908. He was influenced by functionalism and eager to make use of comparative psychology. Consistently, he also believed that psychology should be allied with the biological sciences. He was extremely eager to collaborate with Watson.

Meyer helped kindle Watson's interest in human psychology, and the latter began to read psychoanalysis under Meyer's tutelage. Historian Ruth Leys claims that Meyer influenced Watson's thinking in direct and concrete ways:

> It is worth noting that Meyer's was a psychology that, in advance of Watson's behaviorism, stressed the behavior and conduct of the individual. He also shared Watson's ambition to make psychology an empirical science, arguing that only by subjecting the study of man to the norms of the empirical sciences could psychiatry hope to justify its inclusion in the academic curriculum.[60]

The first fruit of Watson's collaboration with Meyer was a paper he presented on a proposed psychology curriculum for medical students.[61] There was perhaps more concentration on topics like the acquisition of skills, work, and fatigue than there would be in other psychological courses, but otherwise the curriculum was an abbreviated version of the typical psychological course of the time.

In 1916 Watson started working in the Phipps Clinic. He sent Meyer the manuscript of "Behavior and the Concept of Mental Disease." Meyer objected strenuously to Watson's text, claiming (in his words) that it did not express "a sensible objective psychobiology" and that it opened the way to a dualism between a physiological or biological approach to the study of actions and a nonscientific, introspective approach. He also urged Watson, as editor of both the *Psychological Review* and the *Psychological Bulletin*, not to publish a dogmatic statement of an unsupported position in either journal. Watson complied with Meyer's wish and published his article in the *Journal of Philosophy, Psychology, and Scientific Method*.

Watson used Freud's theories as his starting point, asserting that he was convinced of their truth but wished to ground them in biology.[62] He wrote,

> The central truth that I think Freud has given us is that *youthful, outgrown and partially discarded habit and instinctive systems of reaction can and possibly always do influence the functioning of our adult systems of reac-*

tion, and influence to a certain extent even the possibility of our forming the new habit systems which we must reasonably be expected to form.[63]

In amplifying that passage Watson appealed to William James's interpretation of the wish, whereby socialization thwarted most of the courses of action entertained by young people. The tendency to enact the suppressed sequences remained, however, even if people could not verbally express the suppressed possibilities. Watson explained unconscious behavior as the inability to express action sequences verbally.

Watson's position was a foretaste of what was to come in the behaviorist movement. Throughout its history, behaviorism has treated psychoanalysis as both enemy and source of inspiration. Behaviorists have used the concept of habit as a surrogate for the psychoanalytic unconscious. Habit structures acquired early in life purportedly exerted control over adult behavioral patterns, thereby playing the same role as the complexes of psychoanalysis. Watson's thinking looked backward toward his own genetic method and forward to the conquest of psychoanalysis and its assimilation into a behaviorist doctrine.

His first published statement of theoretical behaviorism was "I believe that the description of 'mental cases' can be completed as well as begun in behavior terms."[64] Watson illustrated his meaning with the hypothetical example of a neurasthenic dog. He imagined a dog whose handler had instilled in it a whole battery of maladaptive habits and then took it to a veterinarian for examination. Since the veterinarian had no knowledge of the dog's psychological history, his explanations for the dog's symptoms would be absurd. Once again, Watson was accurately predicting behaviorism's future. The behavior modifiers of the 1950s and 1960s would claim, following Skinner, that the psychological makeup of an animal or person is nothing other than the history of sequences of past reinforcements and would mock the pretensions of depth psychologies. Watson was predicting the future in another sense. Anybody acquainted with dogs knows that nobody could instil some of Watson's maladaptive habits. Watson's hubris led him, like his neobehaviorist successors, to make outrageous and unrealistic claims for his behaviorist technology. Neobehaviorism could emerge only when animal psychologists ceased to make objective and dispassionate studies of animal life. Like his successors, Watson could become a behaviorist only when he had abandoned animal science.

Watson dealt with the highest reaches of cognition by conceiving language as an array of conditioned responses. He defined speech as a set of signals correlated with underlying habits. Maladaptive responses, both verbal and nonverbal, because they had come into being in specific ways, could be abolished and replaced by adaptive counterparts.[65]

The received view asserts not just that Watson produced a comprehensive blueprint for behaviorism but that his later work provided the required research paradigms. After all, he had a superb record as an animal experimenter, and behaviorism's appeal to the profession of psychology as a whole was, purportedly, its ability to generate cast-iron laws of behavior in the animal laboratory. The historical evidence does not support the belief.

Watson's first foray into human psychology was an attempt to photograph and record laryngeal movements.[66] Unsurprisingly, he rapidly abandoned the attempt. Next Watson moved into conditioning. There he did very little work himself, leaving most of it to his associate, Karl Spencer Lashley. We can get some impression of how much Watson knew about work in conditioning from his 1915 presidential address to the American Psychological Association.[67] He understood, but did not elaborate on, the distinction between Ivan P. Pavlov's and Vladimir M. Bekhterev's approaches, calling the former the study of conditioned secretion reflexes and the latter the study of conditioned motor reflexes. He concentrated on Bekhterev solely, it seems, because his techniques offered fewer technical difficulties than Pavlov's. Watson's aim was to convince his colleagues that conditioning offered a way of collecting data quickly in many fields. His chief example was the rapidity with which one could measure perceptual thresholds in animals. At the beginning of his article he suggested that conditioning could replace introspection as the favored method in psychology. Thus, psychology would be unified in terms of method rather than in terms of content.

Substantively, Watson's major contribution was in the area of the experimental induction of conditioned emotional reactions. His first attempt, intended to offer an environmental or associationistic explanation for the fear of lightning, used a strong light as the conditioned stimulus and a loud sound as the unconditioned stimulus and seems to have been inconclusive. His next attempt was with the famous Little Albert, an eleven-month-old infant whose mother was a wet nurse at the Harriet Lane Home for Invalid Children in Baltimore.[68] In 1919–20 Watson made psychology's first film; the closing sequences show Little Albert's behavior before and after he was conditioned (but not the conditioning itself).[69] Watson used a white rat as the conditioned stimulus and the striking of a steel bar with a claw hammer as the unconditioned stimulus. There were seven pairings of conditioned and unconditioned stimuli in two sessions one week apart. On the film one sees Albert's responses to the generalization tests. We see discomfort and distress, but not necessarily fear; we cannot assign causes to his feelings. If conditioning did indeed occur, we cannot decide whether it was Pavlovian or Bekhterevian.[70] Mary Cover Jones reported in 1974 that Watson tried to replicate the Little Albert study on her daughter, but failed. In addition, there were three other attempted replications in the 1920s and 1930s.[71] In the first (1940) edition of *Conditioning and Learning* Ernest Hilgard and Donald Marquis reported that there was no evidence for fear conditioning in infants.[72]

By 1917 Watson was beginning to treat psychology in terms of a unifying set of principles. In that year he published a draft of the first chapter of his second book (and only general textbook), *Psychology from the Standpoint of a Behaviorist*, which he had at that time entitled *Human Psychology*.[73] The article resembled the chapter in tone and scope, but there were big differences in content. One major similarity was that by 1917 Watson had formulated a rule stating the essential aim of psychology (prediction and control): "the goal of psychological study is the *ascertaining of such data and laws that, given the stimulus, psychology can predict what the response will be; or, on the other hand, given the response, it can predict the nature of the effective stimulus.*"[74] His edict was derived from his work with conditioning.

During the five years following Watson's forced resignation from Johns Hopkins, the academic community continued to hold him in high esteem.[75] Between 1921 and 1925, 30 percent of the articles in the *Psychological Review* cited him. From 1926 onward his academic reputation declined; in the period 1926 to 1930 only 12 percent of the articles in the *Psychological Review* cited him.[76] Thereafter he played an ambivalent role in psychology's history. In a purely ritualistic sense he is venerated (by those psychologists who remember him) as one of the founders of modern scientific psychology, but only a handful of scholars know anything about his work.[77] Indeed, a sophisticated contemporary psychologist would be repelled by the crudity and lack of polish in Watson's thought and writing. One can appeal to psychoanalysis (the doctrine that behaviorists tried to discount) to explain the treatment that Watson's successors accorded him. In his popular writings Watson had tried to solve American psychology's enduring problem. The discipline simultaneously tries to reach a mass audience and maintain scientific credibility. To do so it must work with a few paradigms, since a lay audience could not deal with numerous paradigms. To have broad appeal, those paradigms must be simple. At the same time, they must potentially be capable of technical elaboration. American psychology's fundamental failure resides in its attempt to replace sophistication in terms of comprehensiveness, power, and subtlety by a commitment to a contentless technological sophistication. Psychologists' inability to resolve that very deep dilemma, I believe, generates acute discomfort. Watson's work is a mirror that reflects the profession's unacceptable face. Psychologists resolve their ambiguity by making a classically Freudian move. They conceal their fears about Watson from themselves by according him an empty respect; to explore the basis of that respect would be to expose the deficiencies of the discipline.

Even if Watson's doctrines had no immediate impact on psychology after 1930, he exerted a powerful (though indirect) influence on neobehaviorism. In his only systematic book, *Behaviorism*, Watson did eventually make Carr's theory of habit formation his own, and it constituted his most enduring legacy to behaviorism.[78] His theory grew out of his use of the genetic method and his attempts to overcome circularity in the reasoning of his contemporaries. Whenever we encounter a habit, he said, we should not assume that an animal was striving to achieve some purpose. Instead, we had to discover how the act became a permanent part of the animal's response repertoire and why it was elicited by a limited range of stimuli. Watson believed the answer lay in the observed fact that the goal-gaining act was inevitably associated more frequently with reward than was any other. "Nonadaptive" acts therefore fell away by attrition.

Watson's formulation of his law of habit was masterly. It was schematic and yet permitted investigators to carry out definite investigations with definite outcomes. It was ruthlessly objective, appealing only to observable events as sources of explanation. In that respect it was even more objective than Thorndike's Law of Effect (which appealed to the unobservable processes of stamping and stamping out). Its defect lay in its failure to allow animal scientists to conceptualize or control inner processes (what were later to be called drives and motives). The operationalism of the 1930s took care of that problem, and it was then possible to create the complex and sophisticated neobehaviorist theories of the 1940s and 1950s.

Admittedly, the pursuit of Watson's program ultimately led animal psychologists to the fiasco of the 1960s and early 1970s. But that should do nothing to dim the institutional achievement. Skinner, Hull, Tolman, and Spence realized Watson's goal—the creation of a behavioral science from the ground up. To realize that goal they and their colleagues had to generate theory and data rapidly. Even if Watson's contemporaries received his message coolly, his successors learned a lot from him.

Those successors, however, refuse Watson a place at the forefront of their pantheon, instead treating him as a remote and rather reluctantly admired ancestor. They treat Edwin Guthrie with far more respect.[79] Like Kantor or Weiss, Guthrie was a typical early behaviorist in that his speculations about the nature of mind and behavior were almost entirely supported not by his own research, but by arguments and examples, typically drawn from everyday life.[80] Guthrie also resembled Weiss, Meyer, and Kantor in that he did not acquire his behaviorism from Watson. Instead, he said that he became a behaviorist after hearing Edgar A. Singer give the lecture "Mind as an Observable Object" at a meeting of the American Philosophical Association in 1910.[81]

Unlike his peers of the 1920s, however, he established some of the guidelines for the neobehaviorist revival of the late 1930s while maintaining a strong attachment to the associationist tradition. He was also part of an older tradition in his robustly instrumentalist approach to theory. In contrast to Tolman, Hull, and even Skinner, he viewed theory as a mere device or framework for presenting facts. Thus he opposed the use of even low-level theoretical terms such as *latency* or *trials to criterion* on the basis that researchers' attention would be directed toward the recording of mere outcomes and away from noting the details of behavior. For him, the use of outcome measures was theoretically self-defeating in that no constraints were placed on the search for explanations that attempted to account for those outcomes directly. Thus animals and people were treated as devices that could impose purposes on behavior, whereas he believed purposes arose from the flow of behavior.[82] Guthrie therefore resembled the Progressivist forebears of American social scientists in his insistence that clear statements of the facts of the case constitute explanation.

Guthrie straddled the old and the new traditions in his placement of learning and habit formation at the center of psychology. Since the time of James, American psychologists tended more and more to push the study of sensation and perception to the periphery of the discipline and, at the same time, to interpret cognitions in strictly functional terms. Guthrie treated mind in terms of functions and processes, rather than contents or attributes, and he defined mind in terms of habit-forming capacities: "Mind must be for us a mode of behavior, namely, that behavior which changes with use or practice, behavior, in other words, which exhibits learning."[83]

Guthrie was definitely consistent with the emerging trends in neobehaviorism in his treatment of Pavlov. English translations of Pavlov's work were available to him and to his fellow neobehaviorists, giving them a great advantage over Watson. Like all other American behaviorists, once more, Guthrie treated Pavlov's book as a repository of techniques rather than an account of a phenomenon that demanded explanation both in terms of its role in the functional and adaptive repertoire of various animals and in terms of its origin in brain processes. Although Guthrie and his colleagues were perfectly justified in rejecting Pavlov's fanciful account of brain processes, they failed to see the broader biological significance of conditioning.

Guthrie also set the stage for developments in neobehaviorism with his conception of the relationship between theory and application. Unlike Watson, he steadfastly refused to ensure that practice would follow directly from theory (and certainly did not want practice to drive theory).[84] At the same time, by interleaving his exposition of his theory with everyday examples, he left his readers with the distinct impression that the relationship between theory and practice was, if not immediate, at least very close. There are also indications that Guthrie was typically American in his relative evaluations of practice versus theory and the life of action versus the life of contemplation. For example, in one of his autobiographical comments he wrote, "A too brief acquaintance with the economist Carleton Parker who . . . persuaded me to undertake in 1917 a mission to interview loggers in the state's camps for the Secretary of War, and a very brief career in both an infantry and artillery OTS in 1918 served to turn attention from books to men."[85]

The most striking feature of Guthrie's theory is his treatment of the intellectual framework within which the neobehaviorists were to develop specific theories of learning and habit formation. Although one cannot call his treatment an innovation, since he did no more than formalize certain tendencies in behaviorist thought, he certainly grasped the essential issues very firmly and provided neobehaviorism with parameters that were part of its essence. He started by applying the objectivist or positivist imperative to the fundamental problem of learning. We all agree that learning must be defined as a permanent change in behavior. Furthermore, the various forms of learning are dispositions; that is, habits remain dormant until the relevant eliciting situations appear. At first sight, then, learning requires explanation in terms of factors that are not open to empirical investigation. For the psychological positivists, however, all terms or concepts had to be, at least ultimately, expressible in an empirical language. The way out of the difficulty was to define learning in terms of observable and manipulatable antecedent or controlling conditions (stimuli) and physically manifested outcomes (responses). Learning theorists were then faced with two broad alternatives. They could either say that learning was the study of relationships between stimulating conditions and response outcomes or say that learning was what intervened between stimuli and responses. If they chose the latter, as Hull and Tolman did, they had to assign a content to learning; if they chose the former, like Guthrie and Skinner, they escaped that demand.

Guthrie was also at one with his brother behaviorists in that he conceived of learning very broadly and in a value-neutral way. That is, he refused to restrict the study of learning to the intellectual domain and insisted, equally strongly, that the study of learning was not the study of the acquisition of improvements or benefits; the acquisition of French should be treated on the same footing as the acquisition of tics or phobias.[86]

Toward the end of his life Guthrie wrote a comprehensive account of his version of scientific theory that allows one to see how he reconciled the conflicting claims of purpose, science, and common sense.[87] In effect, he advanced a form of operationism in which meanings were nothing other than verbal conventions. The essence of science, he asserted, was prediction. Prediction consisted in saying that, within a certain margin of error, given an event of category A, an event of category B was likely to follow. Therefore, a necessary preliminary step was the categorization of phenomena. Along the way, much of the complexity of experience would be lost, but in the interests of formulating meaningful predictions, such a simplification of experience was essential.

Finally, Guthrie was totally opposed to intervening variables. As a result, he was the most starkly empiricist of all the neobehaviorists. He claimed that to explain meant to point to the physical stimulus that, in any given situation, provoked a physical response. When we said that an animal was not attending, we meant that the animal was not emitting any identifiable responses. Guthrie wrote, "Whatever the mechanism of learning, it must establish a causal chain of connections between stimuli and movement patterns."[88]

Guthrie's theory of learning was a particularly striking instance of the projection into psychology of Progressivist thinking. It was not just the case that learning was interpreted in terms of control of situations by experimenters.[89] From the very close observation of the facts of the case it followed that one could exclude fictitious entities such as reinforcement from one's explanatory armamentarium. Explanation became prediction and prediction became the discovery of highly specific relationships between discrete events.

Throughout his writings Guthrie insisted that meanings were nothing other than verbal conventions. Extending that analysis to theories, he said that theories were merely devices that rendered sets of facts orderly and meaningful to particular audiences.[90] Guthrie's desire to be a good empiricist was limitless (after all, the basic fact about discourse is that it occurs between individuals and that any given piece of discourse is tailored to the needs, knowledge, and emotional characteristics of individuals). But, equally characteristically, empiricists want to draw reasonably widely generalizable inductive conclusions that will stand the test of time. That was clearly the stronger tendency in Guthrie's approach, and he never showed how he could reconcile his social relativism with his absolutist tendencies.

The most serious criticism of Guthrie's theory, however, revolves around the issue of its supposed simplicity. For Guthrie, his theory's simplicity was its greatest merit. It allowed him to offer seemingly art-less explanations for a wide range of phenomena. Mueller and Schoenfeld's examination of his theory leads them to conclude that it is simple in appearance only.[91] One source of the difficulty lay in Guthrie's failure to define the key terms "stimulus" and "response" independently of each other. Thus a stimulus was not any sensory pattern but a pattern that called forth a response. In the same way, a response was that which was called forth by a stimulus. Those circular definitions meant that, in logical terms, Guthrie could offer no proof for his fundamental assertion that learning consisted of bare associations between specific stimuli and specific responses. In order to do so, we have to point to instances where a radical change of adaptive behavior has followed such connections, and nothing other than such connections. A further requirement is that the antecedent events (stimuli) and consequent events (responses) should be defined in terms of independent criteria. If the requirement is not satisfied, then a critic can argue that, in any given instance of Guthrian learning, only those characteristics of stimuli and responses satisfying some unstated prior criteria are noted in experimental protocols or in cases of naturalistic behavior.

Another source of the concealed complexity of Guthrie's theory lay in his failure to deal with the problem of breaking the flow of behavior into significant components. His associationism led him to presume that any observable response had to be made up of a group of subresponses, each, in principle, separately conditionable. He tried to capture the distinction between a gross, overall response and a specific component by postulating his distinction between acts and movements, claiming that it was only the latter that were conditioned. But when faced with actual situations, he found it impossible to make the distinction. A movement, then, that seems at first blush to be an example of a brute, irreducible fact turns out to be a construct.[92]

Finally, Guthrie was curiously coy about the status of his principle of conditioning. For example, he wrote both that association was "assumed to be the basic event in learning" and that "the principle amounts to a convention that we shall use associated stimuli for the prediction of responses. It has no provision for measuring the relative effectiveness of different signals or the extent of similarity required in the practice and in the test situation."[93] Guthrie's coyness was explicable when one considers that his own theory was a mere restatement of common sense. Given the differences in what passes for common sense between cultures or across time in the same culture, it is no wonder that Guthrie, if he is read at all, is read only by historians of psychology.

In 1938 A. A. Roback published his *Behaviorism at Twenty-five.*[94] He wrote that one title he considered was *The Passing of Behaviorism*. He had originally intended publishing an article dealing with behaviorism's first quarter century in *Harper's*. But his proposal was rebuffed by one of *Harper's* editors, who wrote,

> While we published a series of articles on behaviorism some years ago when there was a widespread interest in the subject, we did not sponsor Dr. Watson's ideas nor do we now.
>
> Our reason for returning this manuscript is that, in our judgment, it comes too late in the day, and that the behavioristic philosophy has already been pretty well discounted.[95]

In the same year that Roback's book appeared, the University of Illinois psychologist Willard Harrell and his colleague from Johns Hopkins, Ross Harrison, produced a scholarly obsequy.[96] They wrote,

> Behaviorism must be viewed now as essentially an historical development of the recent past. Watson has withdrawn from psychology, Lashley has become quiescent on controversial matters, and both Peterson and Weiss are dead. Tolman has been drawn under the mantle of Gestalt and purposive psychologies and the resulting eclecticism is behaviorism in name only. Hunter and Kuo have forsaken the Watsonian orthodoxy but their deviations have attracted few followers, while the younger converts to behaviorism have become strangely silent. Of recent years the volume of literature on behaviorism has dwindled into a barely perceptible stream, and psychologists have grown weary of the very words. A portion of the theory has been assimilated into the main body of psychology with consequent loss of identity as "behavioristic." Radical behavioristic psychology in brief has been safely confined to that limbo of abandoned theories whence there is escape only through a process of theoretical reincarnation or resynthesis.[97]

In regard to the behaviorist theories I have reviewed in this chapter and the preceding one, Harrell and Harrison wrote, "Even such a cursory summary [as their article] brings into striking relief the paucity of original ideas in the systematic formulations of radical behaviorists."[98] I found it particularly striking that this early radical behaviorism was dismissed on the basis of ill-formulated and weak criticisms, a further demonstration of the weakness of the theories. Crucially, the behaviorists of the 1920s totally failed to explain the actions of conscious, rational agents. So people like Wilson D. Wallis thought they had disproved behaviorism simply by stating that, for example, behaviorists could not differentiate between mere actions and goal-directed acts.[99] Wallis had in mind examples such as this. Movement of the limbs (like the restless, meaningless movements one might see in certain schizophrenics) and the act of walking toward some location are radically different. In the latter case, running, leaping, hopping, and so forth would all be equivalent means of reaching the same goal. In the former, different types of act are not necessarily equivalent (differences between them would constitute the basis for reaching various diagnoses). Wallis was assuming that behaviorism was coterminous with Watson's doctrine and that Watson failed to differentiate mere movement from goal-directed acts. Neobehaviorists such as Hull, Tolman, and Skinner devoted much of their energies to developing a behaviorism incorporating both a fully fledged philosophy of science and versions of agency and purpose.

3

The Conceptual Basis of Neobehaviorism and Behavioral Science

The new behaviorisms of the 1940s and 1950s, consisting of precisely formulated and conceptually rigorous theories, were radically different from their predecessors. Empirically, neobehaviorism derived its support from extensive work in animal laboratories, so that there was a complete contrast with the speculative behaviorisms of the 1920s. A new movement demanded a new set of paradigms, a new core speciality from which the rest of psychology could be invaded, and a new epistemological basis. The paradigms were provided by the now familiar tasks that had to be solved by rats in mazes, shock boxes, and Skinner boxes and by pigeons in Skinner boxes. The new speciality was learning theory. The new epistemological basis was the doctrine of operationism; the rise of operationism was closely tied to the emergence of learning theory.

When behavioral science reigned supreme in psychology, learning theory and neobehaviorism were coeval. The concept of learning as deployed in psychology is so curious that some prior discussion is necessary. The dictionary meaning of learning implies that learning is a process whereby knowledge is acquired in a consistent and formalized fashion. In contemporary psychology, however, the term is broader in terms of content or application and conceptually much more restricted than it is in ordinary discourse. Psychologists, for example, talk of rats learning to run down a straight alley for a food reward or of young children learning the personality pattern of self-abasement as a consequence of prolonged abuse within a family. Those two cases would not be treated as examples of learning outside psychology. We would say that the rats had been trained, implying that they were malleable. Although we would also say that young children learning arithmetic are malleable, we would not say that they had learned arithmetic unless they could self-consciously apply their new skills in a wide variety of situations (and we would not believe that to be true of the rats). We would say that personality patterns are acquired by a complex, largely passive, and unconscious set of processes very different from those underlying formal or academic knowledge.

The concept of learning could be given broad application only if its meaning was greatly restricted. Two steps were necessary. First, following Thorndike's and Watson's lead, American psychologists treated all forms of learning as skills. Maze running in rats, the learning of arithmetic by schoolchildren, and the growth of a personality pattern could then be treated as the incremental growth of some sort of underlying habit structures. Second, those habit structures were said to be under the control of input (or independent) variables and to express themselves in output (or dependent) variables.

For behaviorists in particular and for pragmatically, instrumentally oriented American psychologists in general, habit, which operated out of sight, was a serious problem. As I have already said in chapter 1, we can see how the problem was solved by analyzing Woodworth's treatment of experimentation, which was closely linked to his treatment of learning.[1] Both conceptually and historically the first step was to claim that experimentation was the sole route to the discovery of causes, a claim sustainable only if one treated causation as nothing other than the discovery of close functional relationships between input and output variables.

The next step was to make habits the paradigm for unseen factors. Woodworth made that move in the second edition of his *Experimental Psychology*.[2] He and Schlosberg analyzed the phenomenon of reminiscence in perceptual-motor learning at length.[3] The paradigm task was the pursuit rotor, in which subjects had to maintain contact between an electrically activated stylus and an electrically activated disc mounted on a gramophone turntable. In conditions of massed practice (where the subjects have very brief rests between brief periods of practice), performance initially increases and then starts to decline. If the subjects are allowed to rest then, on their initial reexposure to the task their performance shows a dramatic improvement. Moreover, even if the rest period is as long as a month, performance remains at a maximal level (forgetting sets in after a month, but reminiscence still occurs with rest periods of up to two years).

Those working in perceptual-motor learning had to account for two phenomena: (a) the ultimate decline in performance characteristic of massed practice; and (b) reminiscence following rest. The solution was to link (a) and (b). It was said that performance was a function of two counteracting factors, practice and some inhibitory factor. Prior experiments had demonstrated that the inhibitory factor could not be physical fatigue. The negative factor was then named "inhibition." Inhibition was defined as a state that counteracted the effects of practice, that was an inevitable concomitant of practice, and that progressively declined with rest. It followed that inhibition should progressively decline as the length of the rest interval increased up to some relatively short interval (beyond that interval the beneficent effects of reminiscence would be counteracted by forgetting).

We then have to deal with the issue of reminiscence's epistemological status. It had already been decided that it was not a physical state. To define it as a mental state would mean that we would have to explain all behaviors on a case-by-case basis and that all such explanations would be speculative. For example, we could argue that for some people the performance decrement was due to boredom. Or there might be people who knew what to do but could not be bothered (I know from personal experience that the pursuit rotor task is simultaneously trivial and frustrating). We could explain reminiscence as a renewal of interest in the task.

In order to avoid mentalist explanations, behaviorists argued that the factors governing the acquisition of habits were intervening or organismic variables mediating between independent and dependent variables.[4] Epistemologically, intervening variables were given an abstract, nonmentalist status. Mental states, if they were discussed at all, were denied a causal role. Instead they were treated as fleeting events that did no more than contribute to error in sets of observations. The only way to give meaning to intervening variables, it was said, was to treat them as entities causally producing concomitant behaviors in carefully specified situations. Reminiscence, then, was defined as the increase in performance occurring after a period of rest at the end of massed practice with particular laboratory tasks. That is, it was defined in terms of the operations required to produce it.

The abstract and operational definition of intervening variables allowed the new generation of behaviorists to circumvent the epistemological problems that had haunted their predecessors. Psychologists could set unsettling epistemological issues to one side and proceed with their research largely because questions concerning the nature of knowledge had been converted into questions concerning the way knowledge was used. Functionalism had finally triumphed over structuralism. Making habit formation central meant that all knowledge was reduced to knowing *how*, not to knowing *what*. The achievement of mastering the intricacies of a scientific theory or gaining insight into one's place in the world as a moral being was placed on exactly the same footing as learning how to walk or how to type. Psychologists, then, did not have to ask questions about the nature of mental objects or the relationship of knowers to the world. Because the factors supposedly determining the growth of habits were totally abstract, they could be assigned indifferently to people or to animals. As a result, the psychology of the 1950s was radically different from pre–World War II psychology. Most researchers were studying the habits, skills, and dispositions controlling adaptation to social and physical settings in both animals and humans. It became possible, in principle, to generate new intervening variables and to test hypotheses regarding the behaviors supposedly controlled by such variables in the animal laboratory. Given that learning theorists worked with relatively global notions such as *drive, incentive, frustration,* or *fear*, research could be produced at a higher rate with animal than with human subjects.

Learning theory alone, however, did not suffice to create behavioral science. One can convert content into process and still maintain that the processes are cognitively controlled. In order to excise mentalism altogether from psychology, behaviorists had to define mentalist concepts in some objective way. The solution was to define them operationally. An operationist believes that to understand is to give causal accounts that leave no room for the action of forces lying outside the physical realm. We can give causal accounts only if we can control the situations in which identifiable phenomena occur. In psychology the problem is that actions and beliefs are controlled by factors beyond the reach of observation. The solution was to treat those factors as causal variables with specifiable and distinctive behavioral outcomes. Causal accounts could then be produced as follows. One limited one's observations to dependent variables, which can be defined as physicalistically defined outcomes (behaviors produced in carefully specified conditions). One stringently controlled the situations producing those outcomes by devising procedures for eliminating or randomizing the effects of various background variables. One also controlled the conditions instantiating "hidden" factors such as motives, expectations, values, attitudes, and the like. Then one studied the effect of manipulations of the strength of variables triggering action under prespecified conditions (that is, one instantiated independent variables). One then said that one had provided a causal account when the obtained outcomes matched the predicted outcomes.

The rise of operationism was closely linked to the rise of learning theory. When we have learned, said behavioral scientists, we have acquired a disposition to behave in particular ways given the occurrence of a situation that appropriately triggers the disposition. That is, a habit or disposition remains out of sight until its manifestation is called for. The behaviorists of the 1920s claimed they could give physicalist accounts of hidden factors, but none of their claims were convincing. It was only when certain behaviorists, of whom Tolman and Skinner were the most prominent, demonstrated that such hidden factors could be defined operationally that the behaviorist enterprise could find an accepted place in the social sciences. The use of operational definitions then spread to the rest of the discipline.

The received account of the introduction of operational definitions into psychology is that in the 1930s an alliance was forged between logical positivism and psychology. As a result, it is said, a group of psychologists at Harvard (the leading figures being Edwin G. Boring, S. S. Stevens, and B. F. Skinner) became acquainted with Percy Bridgman's proposal to define all theoretical terms in physics in terms of the procedures whereby they are measured or observed.[5] Like the logical positivists, Bridgman wanted to induce a consensus on the meaning of all scientific terms and concepts. In all sciences, the consequence of such a program would be that work performed in any given laboratory would be comprehensible to all working in that particular discipline. The ultimate aim of the logical positivist program was to purge scientific discourse of all surplus meanings and all uncertainties and doubts. From American psychologists' vantage point, however, the logical positivist program was a secondary consequence of their own. Ultimately, the laboratory was a place from which socially useful findings had to emerge. However, findings could be socially useful only if they were publicly verifiable and commanded universal assent. That meant, in turn, that the findings from one laboratory could be replicated in another. The first step was to find a common data language, that is, to express all findings in terms of behavior. The next was to gain control over the hidden, the implicit, or the unobservable. As I have already said, behaviorists gained such control by defining each hidden factor in terms of its behavioral consequences and then devising procedures for producing those consequences in the laboratory. The laboratory thus became a training ground for social technocrats who could induce socially desired outcomes in natural settings.

Elsewhere I have shown that American psychological operationism had its origins in the way two German experimental psychologists, Gustav Theodor Fechner (1801–1887) and Hermann Ebbinghaus (1850–1909), conceived of experiments and, more especially, data.[6] For both of them, to perform an experiment was to do nothing other than establish numerically expressed functional relationships between strictly defined antecedent variables and strictly defined outcome variables. Besides conceiving of experiments in that narrow sense, both Fechner and Ebbinghaus put their data into a numerical form at the very outset. Thus, Fechner allowed subjects to make only the responses Yes/No or Right/Wrong (that is, responses were coded either 0 or 1), while Ebbinghaus's outcome variables were also fully quantified (number of trials to a predetermined criterion, for example). For both men, objects of study were not persons or situations but sets of abstract variables.

For American psychologists, Ebbinghaus was more important than Fechner. The fundamental unit of measurement for Ebbinghaus was not a single datum (such as a nonsense syllable) but a trial (that is, the presentation to the subject of a predetermined ordered sequence of events).[7] Psychology's role then became the creation of particular tasks that forced experimental subjects (or clients, such as schoolchildren) to perform in precisely defined ways at precisely defined rates of output in obedience to sets of external requirements. The abstract portion of psychology, then, was linked in definite and measurable ways to the social order.

American psychologists, especially the personnel psychologist Walter Dill Scott (1869–1955) and the educational psychologist and mental tester Edward Lee Thorndike (1874–1949), applied these concepts to the study of individual differences. Both Scott and Thorndike conceived of the person as a set of discrete variables, each of which produced overt and measurable effects on his or her actions. Such an account of human life is, of course, tautologous. If we ask, "How do we know these variables exist?" the answer is that any given action self-evidently demonstrates the reality of a particular variable. If we ask, "How is any given variable's nature expressed in behavior?" the answer would be that action of any sort must have a cause analogous to its nature. That is, Scott or Thorndike assumed, without further reflection, that any given cause was expressed directly as behavior.

Edwin G. Boring showed psychologists a way out of that difficulty. Of the nature of intelligence, he wrote, "no harm need result if we but remember that measurable intelligence is simply what the tests test, until further scientific observation allows us to extend the definition."[8] Boring was making an Ebbinghausian move. Provided that an experiment or a test produced definite and predictable outcomes, psychologists did not need to ask awkward questions about the nature of inner events. Indeed, in that the manipulation of posited variables (such as intelligence) yielded gradational outcomes along numerical scales, and in that there was a consensus respecting the means of setting up such scales, one could say that posited variables could be defined in terms of the operations required to instantiate them. Boring, then, had proposed psychology's first operational definition.

During the 1920s a major source of dissension among American psychologists was the division between "pure" (experimental) psychologists and applied psychologists. At the same time, both parties to the dispute had to find ways of making psychology commercially viable. The Depression of the 1930s greatly exacerbated the discipline's problems, but by the end of the decade a solution had emerged. The problem had different manifestations for pure and applied psychologists. The latter, as we have seen, could achieve results, but these had no conceptual or causal basis. We have also seen Boring suggesting that testers cut the Gordian knot and simply assert that the mere application of a test was a guarantee for the meaning of its results (an approach that psychologist Tim Rogers calls "pragmatic operationism").[9] The experimentalists, in contrast, faced an institutional problem: their numbers were so small that they were an endangered species. Moreover, they had no niche at the institutional, the broader educational, or the societal level. The solution to their difficulties had to be twofold. They had to achieve intellectual respectability and demonstrate that experimental psychology could be socially useful.

Once again, Boring (this time with considerable help from others at Harvard) found a solution to the issue of intellectual respectability and indirectly showed American experimental psychologists how they could achieve social utility. Rogers, whose terminology I use once more, calls this approach "representational operationism." However, although the published record tells us that Boring was both pure and applied psychology's savior, his role in the latter case was deeply enigmatic. During the 1920s Boring was an *éminence grise* who overinflated the experimentalists' role in the American Psychological Association and kept applied psychologists out. Furthermore, he had a prolonged dispute with Truman Kelley about the meaning of psychological data.[10] The dispute centered around psychology's use of statistics. For Boring, statistics was no more than a convenient, concise way of presenting data. The experimenter used his judgment to determine the meaning of the data. For Kelley (and for the psychological testers in general) statistics was a source of meaning. For example, Kelley believed that the psychological significance of a set of data was an inverse function of the amount of the probable error. The size of the critical ratio (the ratio of the mean difference between two samples to the mean of the probable error of the two means) would then directly tell us whether we had a meaningful and interpretable result. Against Kelley, Boring argued forcefully that an experimenter, on the basis of his background knowledge and his acquaintance with a specific experimental situation, had a perfect right to ignore or discount a large critical ratio or accept a small one as meaningful.[11]

Boring carried his dispute against applied psychologists further by writing a dismissive review of Carl C. Brigham's *Study of American Intelligence*.[12] Brigham argued that data from intelligence tests showed that individuals of non–Anglo-Saxon descent had less intellectual potential than Anglo-Saxons. Mathematical data expressing a tendency within a group could be extrapolated to all the individuals in the group. Boring argued that the mathematical data referred only to the group means and that mathematically based statements could refer only to them. Generalizations to individuals had to be made on some nonmathematical basis.[13] Boring carried his argument further in his criticism of an article by Murchison and Gilbert.[14] Among their other findings, Murchison and Gilbert reported that in a sample of prisoners, unmarried blacks had lower scores on an intelligence test than married blacks, whereas the reverse was true for their white counterparts. Boring argued that one could draw no conclusions from the data without knowing something about the social and familial factors operating on the individuals in the groups. An inference from Boring's argument was that drawing a random sample cannot in itself guarantee that the psychological characteristics of any individual will necessarily resemble group characteristics. Indeed, characteristics emerging when one sums across individuals could be the least important feature of all the individuals in the group. The argument will fail if one has prior grounds for assuming that the characteristics in question are genetically or even innately determined. In the case of intelligence, however, this is the very point that has to be proved.

With respect to the nature of the inferences legitimately following from scientific data, then, the Boring of the 1920s had nothing in common with the operationists of the 1930s. There was also an epistemological difference. The 1920s Boring was a realist, not a positivist. In his address as retiring vice president of Section I, Psychology, of the American Association for the Advancement of Science at New Orleans in December 1931, he argued that psychology had to have access to both consciousness and brain events. He stated that we introspected brain events, expressed as the feelings of intensity, extensity, duration, and a rather diffuse fourth dimension that he called quality.[15] In a later article he equated the term "empirical" with "experiential" and gave no role within scientific psychology for empirically minded philosophers like Brentano.

Throughout the 1920s, however, one can detect a slow change in Boring's views. In 1926 he and Peak published a study in which they tried to isolate at least one of the factors controlling intellectual potential.[16] They claimed that there were two fundamental types of item in intelligence tests, those testing power and those testing speed of mental functioning. They relegated power tests to a secondary status, claiming that they tested achievement rather than potential. They claimed that speed could have either an interstitial or an inherent role. If one divided an intelligent act into components, they argued, then speed would play an interstitial role if intelligent and unintelligent people could complete each component at equivalent speeds. The differences in overall score would be a consequence of distractions at points of transition from component to component. However, speed would play an inherent role if the unintelligent completed each component at a slower rate than the intelligent. Their data supported the second hypothesis because they got high correlations between overall intelligence test score, speed of completion of individual items, and overall reaction time.[17] Peak and Boring concluded that intelligence was the expression of some neurologically based power.

However, Boring had advanced beyond his 1923 position (assuming the conclusions were his). He had suggested a way of identifying the causes of intelligent behavior. As a philosophical realist he believed that the cause was neurological. Boring's interpretation of his findings also had profound implications for American psychology's future. He treated the cause of intelligent behavior as an unseen factor identifiable in terms of the specific effects it exerted on actions carried out in specific situations. In the case of intelligence, one tested for the strength of the supposed underlying factor by administering specially designed tests. The most appropriate tests would be those best predicting the outcome. One would avoid circularity by carefully specifying in advance the precise nature of the expected outcome. Even slight divergences from expectations would demand a reformulation for the basis of future predictions. The basis for making predictions was strictly empirical; it was not necessary to make any reference to the "real nature" of the causal factor. The philosophical basis for experimental psychology had become positivist rather than realist.

Within psychology, positivism expressed itself as behaviorism. We can characterize contemporary operationists as overt positivists who are closet philosophical realists. Boring, as we have seen, was an overt realist. In his correspondence, however, we find evidence of at least sympathy for the behaviorists. Given American psychologists' renowned philosophical ambiguity, we can say that those who wished to amplify and apply the Harvard operationism could readily fit it into a positivist framework.

As early as 1923, in a letter to Mary Calkins, Boring acknowledged behaviorism's preeminence in the psychology of the day.[18] Boring also displayed his tolerance toward behaviorism in a letter to Leonard Carmichael, who had asked him whether the *American Journal of Psychology* would publish articles on comparative psychology. Boring replied that the journal was by no means averse to receiving such manuscripts: "[The journal] has emphasized introspective or phenomenological work largely because people at other extremes have tended to publish in other places, so that it has been involuntarily more of an organ for consciousness than for movement."[19]

Apparently, during the 1920s at least, Boring saw behaviorism as deployable in a restricted field, since, like the young Watson, he appeared to equate behaviorism with comparative or with physiological psychology. At the same time, various passages in his correspondence imply that he considered a behaviorist psychologist (in that narrow sense) to be essential to the complement of an effective department of psychology. Thus he made several attempts to recruit Leonard Carmichael to Harvard between 1928 and 1934.[20]

A letter he wrote to Clark L. Hull seems to show that Boring had developed what amounted to a homegrown version of logical positivism by 1938. Throughout the letter he stressed that the role of operationism was to maintain agreement respecting the meaning of terms. At the same time, because he appeared to treat some operations as more fundamental than others and because he was not prepared to espouse Bridgman's position regarding a necessary lack of convergence of apparently similar operations (of measures of length, for example), he left a residual role for realism. At the same time, he recognized that any attempt to universalize operationism involved an infinite regress, because all terms, including *operationism* itself, would be operationally defined.[21]

Although Boring had grasped the principle of representational operationism, his graduate student, S. S. Stevens, was the first to state it.[22] Claiming Carnap and Bridgman as the source, Stevens wrote, "Such a procedure is the one which tests the meaning of concepts by appealing to the concrete operations by which the concept is determined." He defined an operation as "the performance which we execute in order to make known a concept."[23] Representational operationism was conceptually more subtle than pragmatic operationism because Stevens and others attempted to establish what types of operations could serve as a definitional basis for psychological concepts. Meaning, then, was assigned to concepts prior to their use instead of emerging as a consequence of use, as in pragmatic operationism. However, the pragmatic operationists took over the language of their representational counterparts, thereby blurring the distinction between the two families of concepts.

Stevens explicitly expunged hypothetical concepts from psychology and claimed that a concept was real only if we could point to instances of it. To be able to point reliably we must discriminate. We knew what a concept meant, Stevens claimed, when we could discover all the types of situation in which instances of the concept could be recognized. A further essential aspect of the determination of a concept's meaning resided in the capacity to discriminate between subtypes of a concept (for example, we would know the meaning of *pleasantness* only when we knew how many types of pleasantness human beings could reliably discriminate).

Stevens's supposed progenitors Carnap and Bridgman had a definite epistemological basis for their operationism. Like a good psychologist, Stevens was epistemologically ambiguous. Some passages suggest he was a methodological behaviorist (so that, philosophically, he should have been a positivist). For example, he wrote, "Operationism requires that we deal only with the reportable aspects of experience. Not only must the experience be reportable; it must be actually reported, verbally or otherwise."[24] He also wrote, "The *experience*, then, upon which physical science is founded would seem to be nothing more than a term which, implicitly at least, denotes the sum total of the discriminatory reactions performed by human beings, for to *experience* is, for the purpose of science, *to react discriminatively*."[25] However, he withdrew his seeming behaviorism in a footnote in which he argued that to report was not necessarily to refer to a state of immediate awareness. He also left a role for more complex mental states. In that passage Stevens was a realist in the tradition of objectivists like Warren or Angell.

At the same time Stevens was formulating his version of behaviorism, Boring was working on the same topic with another of his graduate students, Douglas McGregor. Boring sent McGregor's completed manuscript to Langfeld, the editor of the *Psychological Review*, claiming that it was the best article so far written on the subject.[26]

Boring and Stevens had reconceptualized psychology only in a general and schematic sense. Other psychologists had to show how their scheme could be applied to particular concepts. Edward Chace Tolman, arguably the greatest neobehaviorist, played a leading role in this enterprise. Tolman was admirably fitted for the role because of his connections, via Holt and Perry, with New Realism. His operationism, in which his treatment of purpose was a key element, was immanent in his theory from the beginning. He knew, from work originating in Lloyd Morgan's and Thorndike's animal experiments, that, in animal behavior at any rate, purposes did not precede or guide habits until they had been thoroughly learned because, typically, habits were acquired by trial and error; purposes emerged as a function of training. Although we could observe raw action, we could never observe raw purpose. At the same time, the distinction between purposive action (purposes revealed in or embedded in action) and random action was intuitively clear to us.

For an objectivist like Tolman, however, intuitive clarity could not provide the basis for a viable scientific theory. Furthermore, he had to expunge all traces of mentalistic language from his discourse. He eventually realized that he could achieve his aims not just by adopting the language and approach of operationalism but by equating operationalism with behaviorism.[27] Tolman showed his fellow behaviorists how they could eat their positivist, scientifically respectable cake and keep in their cupboard a metaphysical realism that they could sell to neophyte psychologists and the public at large. His operationalism was derived directly from Holt's and Perry's realism and pragmatism.

In the late 1930s Tolman published a series of articles in which he formally operationalized the concepts in his theory.[28] His operationalism represented the culmination of his metaphysical realism. He conceived of his concepts as real entities. In no sense of the word, then, was Tolman a positivist. But even if he was not a positivist, he wanted to promulgate a science of behavior that was as pure and adamantine as the logical positivist version. In pursuing his vision, he had to steer a careful course between the trackless jungles of mentalism and the arid plains of a molecular, physiological behaviorism. I surmise that the latter danger weighed more heavily on Tolman's mind than the former. To molecularize, mechanize, or physiologize behavior was to commit the fallacy of discussing what was self-evidently purposive or fluidly adaptive in terms of inappropriate mechanical analogies.

To resolve his problems Tolman fell back on what he had learned from Holt and Perry. Like Holt, he conceived of the mind as nothing other than a piece of the world seen from a particular perspective. For Tolman, the mind was a device that selected certain features of the environment and organized them in ways that yielded patterns capable of exerting control over adaptive behavior. As a matter of expository convenience we could talk of minds as though they were independent substances. We could portray the concept of such minds as interlocking sets of cognitive maps linked to environmental and bodily input variables (stimuli arising from the physical world outside the body and motivational factors arising from within the body) and to action systems. Such portrayals (the numerous diagrams occurring in Tolman's writings) were, however, no more than formal devices. Reality was, ultimately, an array of psychophysical moments.

I would, however, be doing Tolman a serious injustice if I portrayed him as nothing other than a New Realist. Although he used his philosophical training to solve his problems, he derived his problems from behaviorism, and behaviorism played a powerful role in his thinking. He inserted New Realist solutions of the mind/body problem into a behaviorist framework. His approach to theory was remorselessly behaviorist. He wrote, "the ultimate interest of psychology is solely the prediction and control of behavior."[29] To generate a predictive system he took over Guthrie's treatment of habit or learning. Habits were to become dispositions or implicit patterns situated between independent and dependent variables. Independent variables were instantiated by experimenters. Experimenters also exerted control over internal or implicit states ("demands," in Tolman's terminology). The demands were the intervening variables. Independent and intervening variables exerted conjoint control over dependent variables (response outputs or actions systems). Behaviorism's and New Realism's requirements were met when intervening variables were defined in terms of the physical operations required to instantiate them.

Tolman divided independent variables into five categories: "(1) *environmental stimuli*, (2) *physiological drive*, (3) *heredity*, (4) *previous training*, and (5) *maturity*."[30] The categories could be placed in two classes. He called environmental stimuli and physiological drive (that is, drive as induced externally by depriving animals of biological necessities) "releasing variables," saying that they initiated behavior. The remaining three were governing or guiding variables; they provided the channels into which behavior was directed. Behavior was, then, a functional consequence of the states of the independent variables. These states occurred at two levels, categorized as f1 and f2. Tolman assigned his predictor variables to two levels because, in order to make predictions, one needed first- and second-order functions—environmental manipulation alone did not permit prediction. These second order functions were intervening variables, defined as "objective entities, defined in terms of the f2 functions which connect them to the S's, P's, H's, T's, and A's, on the one hand, and to the final common B, on the other."[31] The f2 functions included what Tolman called "demands" (the instantiation of putative internal states such as drives or motives), discriminanda, manipulanda, means-end fields, traits, and capacities.[32]

Tolman's intervening variables constituted much more of a mixed bag than those of any other behaviorist. All the other neobehaviorists had some version of demands (Hull's drives and drive-stimuli and Skinner's drives, for example). Discriminanda and manipulanda were, however, representations of objects or events to be discriminated or of objects that assisted animals to reach goals (the closest equivalents would be Hull's stimulus traces). A means-end field was a cognitive map (an internal representation of a problem situation). A trait was an acquired or genetically induced psychological attribute. A capacity was so vague that it defied the sort of precise definition supposedly offered by operationism. Tolman himself placed his intervening variables into two categories—those that could be characterized as mental events and those that could be characterized as mental traits or capacities.[33]

Finally, one had to establish the procedures for defining intervening variables. Tolman said that the requisite definitions could be obtained following experiments in which one held constant all but one (or some well-defined group of) independent variable and recorded the functional relationships between the selected variable and particular dependent variables. His only examples concerned demands, so that it is only here that we can gain any full interpretation of Tolman's treatment of intervening variables. He said that we required parametric experiments because intervening variables were the expression of relatively complex inner processes, and that these processes were ultimately physiological, expressed themselves directly in behavior, and could be defined as functional relationships between independent and dependent variables.[34]

Tolman gave only one fully worked out example of a parametric experiment, that of C. J. Warden's obstruction box.[35] Hungry rats were obliged to cross an electrically charged grid to get to food. Number of crossings per twenty-minute period was an inverted U-function of the number of hours of food deprivation.[36] Tolman's choice of an illustrative experiment suggests that there was a tension between his metatheoretical imperatives and the need to have a theory that would meet positivist criteria. His definition of drive would have satisfied a Skinnerian, since it was couched entirely in terms of the operations required to instantiate it. The following passage suggests that there was, indeed, a "Skinnerian" element in Tolman's thinking in the late 1930s: "it appears to me that it is primarily the job of us psychologists, or at any rate of the 'purer' among us, to gather the psychological facts and laws and leave it to our less pure, physiologically minded brethren to gather the neurological, glandular, and biochemical data which underlie such psychological facts and laws."[37] There Tolman opposed a strictly empirical psychology (whose laws were to be expressed as strictly functional relationships between reliable empirical findings) to physiology. Curiously, then, he appeared to leave no room for what is usually considered to be his own version of psychology.

However, toward the end of his career he made some efforts to find a compromise between his realism and the prevailing positivism. For example, in his last published work he differentiated between "values" and "valences."[38] The former were the objective settings of independent variables and were defined operationally as the amount of effort an animal was prepared to expend to reach a goal or overcome an obstacle. The latter were the internal assessments of values. Tolman made no attempt to define valences operationally. Nevertheless, he felt that the concept of valence fulfilled a major purpose of operationism because it ruled out explanations of a mechanist or a mentalist type. Tolman wanted rich accounts of the idiosyncratic details of individuals' lives. But he did not want to phrase those descriptions in terms of personal, private events ("raw feels"). So, as Stephen Pepper pointed out, Tolman couched his descriptions in terms of relationships such as "getting to," "getting from," "means object," or "shortest path to the goal." A valence, then, was an individually constructed relationship that expressed the relative amount of effort worth expending in the search for a particular goal. In Tolman's eyes it was operationally defined because it had to have a reference to objective states of affairs.

In 1949, following MacCorquodale and Meehl's distinction, he said that his intervening variables were hypothetical constructs.[39] He also said that hypothetical constructs had to form part of a model and that one had to use the model as a whole to make predictions.[40] Tolman's switch of terminology was closely tied to his realism. We can see how his realism functioned in this instance by considering his position on the role of drive-reduction in learning. Tolman's views on drive-reduction will also yield some understanding of his version of operationism. One instituted drives, according to the prevailing view, in order to set up internal states crucial to learning. Each attainment of reward reduced the intensity of the state. Those reductions were inevitably associated with goal-gaining responses so that the probability of their occurrence would increase with each successive exposure to the learning situation. In Tolman's approach, drive states were only indirectly linked to learning per se. Moreover, drive-reduction was operative only when deprivation levels were high. Learning itself, according to Tolman, was controlled by specific positive wants peculiar to particular learning situations. Tolman believed that once the appropriately physiological techniques became available, we would know the physical nature of those states. Their physical description would, he said, constitute an operational definition.[41]

We can get some idea of what he meant by considering his treatment of cathexes, Tolman's new name for what had previously been means-end-readinesses. A cathexis was a representation of a particular reinforcer operating in a particular situation.[42] He wrote that cathexes and instrumental beliefs were "to be conceived of as hypothetical channelings between successive value compartments in the personality structure. . . . A cathexis is a channel between a drive-subsidence compartment and a goal-object compartment. Our immediate task is how to arrive at an operational definition and measurement of such a channel."[43]

Another late concept that could be classified as a hypothetical construct was "perceptual discrimination space," defined as "a discriminable perceptual dimension conceived as radiating in a circular arc in front of the perceiving end of the organism."[44] At the same time, Tolman introduced another new concept, perceptual satiation, which referred to a supposed tendency to switch attention from a stimulus following a period of fixation on it. By combining the two principles he gave a physiological explanation for vicarious trial and error (VTE-ing).[45] For example, when faced with a black/white discrimination a rat would initially search the environment for an intermediate shade matching its current adaptation level. Eventually, perceptual satiation guaranteed that the rat would start to attend to the black and white discriminanda alternately (VTEing would begin). If two discriminanda lay close together along a perceptual dimension then the satiation from one would generalize to the other, so that VTEing would be less in that situation. With a black/white discrimination, however, there would be no satiation and hence much more VTEing. Even though common sense would predict a progressive increase in VTEing as the similarity between the discriminanda increased, Tolman found that the results supported his hypothesis. However, if rats were trained on an easy discrimination and then transferred to progressively more difficult discriminations the amount of VTEing increased with the difficulty of the discrimination. In this case, Tolman claimed that the VTEing was under the control of an action system, not a perceptual system, and that the VTEs represented error tendencies.

By 1940 operationism had provided American experimental psychologists with a language with which they could describe complex and implicit psychological concepts. They also had at their command a set of techniques allowing them to produce controlled outcomes. The next step was to produce experimental simulations of the complex situations of real life and to demonstrate that the hidden factors could be introduced and could be forced to control detectable outcomes. The required procedure was Sir Ronald A. Fisher's analysis of variance.[46] Fisher devised analysis of variance for experimental agriculture. For example, suppose one wished to detect the differential effect of a particular fertilizer on the yield of three varieties of potato. The yield of any given plant will be determined by its variety, the amount of fertilizer it has received, the fertility of the patch of soil in which it has been planted, the amount of moisture it receives, and so on. By controlling the first two factors (fertilization and variety) and by randomizing the effect of all other factors across varieties and administration of fertilizer, one can make estimates of the real effect of fertilization and variety on mean yield per plot.

Fisher and his collaborators were interested solely in outcomes, not causal analyses. By combining analysis of variance with operationism, one could give causal accounts of behavior. Early in his research career Tolman saw that if one treated hidden causes (habits, drives, motives, dispositions, values, attitudes, and the like) as factors of varying intensity, one could detect their effects on behavior. For example, in an experiment on the role of reward in learning, he and Honzik ran four groups of rats in a maze. The rats were either slightly hungry before entering the maze or extremely hungry. The hungry and nonhungry rats were subdivided into two further groups, who were either fed on reaching the goal box or fed two hours after the end of the day's trials.[47] In contemporary terms, Tolman and Honzik had designed a factorial study with two variables (hunger and reward) with two levels of each variable. In modern terms, again, they got an interaction between their variables (reward had a much greater effect on the performance of the hungry than it did on the nonhungry rats). However, they made no statistical tests of the differences between performance during or at the end of the experiment, solely relying on a visual inspection of the learning curves.

Tolman showed his grasp of the principles underlying analysis of variance elsewhere in his major book, *Purposive Behavior in Animals and Men*. For example, his discussion of Spearman's theory of intelligence shows that he had in mind the type of experiment that would support Spearman's supposition that intelligence manifested itself as g and as s.[48] From Tolman's treatment of Spearman's theory one can infer that he believed one could test it by selecting two groups of items, one saturated with a particular s and one g-saturated. One would then select four groups of subjects—those who were high in g but low in the chosen s, those who were high in both g and s, those who were low in g but high in the chosen s, and those who were low in both. On the s-saturated items those who were high in s would perform well irrespective of their level of g, whereas the converse would be true for the g-saturated items. In terms of experimental design, then, we have the analogue of the potato-yield study. Conceptually, however, we have a causal study because we have treated g and s as hidden factors definable operationally in terms of their expression in test scores on stipulated types of item.

It is not surprising, therefore, that Tolman coauthored (with Crutchfield) one of the first articles on the application of analysis of variance to psychology.[49] Oddly, however, Crutchfield and Tolman failed to address theoretical issues, concentrating instead on the superior efficiency of analysis of variance designs as compared with single-variable designs.[50] It was left to Hull to show how analysis of variance could, in principle, detect concealed interactions between two factors.[51]

Skinner took the final step required for the causal treatment of concealed variables by treating operationally defined constructs as the means for producing desired forms of behavior. Once operationism had reached its full development in psychology a two-tiered differentiation of researchers was possible. On the one hand, there was a role for the Tolmans, whose primary interest was theoretical (but who were always aware of the possible practical applications of their work). On the other, we had those (especially Skinner and his followers) whose primary interest was in developing behaviorist-based social technologies. A commitment to social control linked the two tiers of behavioral science. Analysis of variance and allied techniques of inferential statistics were derived from neo-Galtonian premises. Individuals were treated as mere conduits for the production of data caused by forces operating equally in and on all.

4

The Behaviorist as Research Manager

Clark L. Hull and the Writing of Principles of Behavior

Hull's major work, *Principles of Behavior*, which he and his friends always referred to as his magnum opus, was the first attempt to write an all-embracing psychological theory using the principles of behaviorism.[1] Hull intended the *Principles* to be the first part of a trilogy, since it did no more than state a set of general principles. It was followed by the second part, *Essentials of Behavior*, in which he demonstrated (to his satisfaction, at least) that his principles yielded precise quantitative behavioral predictions.[2] The third (unwritten) part would have dealt with applications of behaviorism to social and ethical questions.

Although Hull was the first behaviorist to produce a comprehensive theory, his work was by no means without precedent. Tolman, Guthrie, and Skinner all had a considerable start on him. To some extent, Hull played a role that his three possible rivals refused. Skinner's ambitions to produce an overall theory of behavior seem to have been deferred until the publication in the early 1950s of *Science and Human Behavior*.[3] Guthrie published comparatively little. Tolman, who had an early start, was not a proselytizer or system builder, in part because it would seem that his assessment of the difficulties involved was more realistic than Hull's. Hull always knew that Tolman was his only peer but realized early on that Tolman would never be his rival.[4]

Hull's method of work has left a unique archive. As both a diarist and a correspondent he recorded his mental life prolifically. From 1935 onward, Hull maintained an exceptionally rich correspondence with his leading disciple, Kenneth W. Spence.[5] The two discussed each phase of the writing of the book in great detail. It is therefore possible to chart the development of Hull's thinking very closely. Hull's *Research Memoranda*, the record of the topics discussed at the seminars Hull chaired at Yale's Institute of Human Relations, also give a detailed picture of the course of Hull's thinking from 1936 to 1944.[6] From 1929 to 1943 Hull published twelve theoretical articles in the *Psychological Review*, hoping in this way to develop his ideas, get feedback from his colleagues, and, above all, stake out a claim as the sole creator of a comprehensive behaviorist theory.[7] The most significant article in the series appeared in 1937, when Hull laid out the so-called mini-system (the precursor of the fully worked out theory).[8] Unfortunately, by the time Hull started to work in earnest on *Principles of Behavior* he was fifty-five, and two years after its publication he developed a serious cardiac condition. As a result, the projected third part of the trilogy (on applications of behaviorism to social issues and ethics) was not written.

In this chapter I analyze the development of Hull's magnum opus from a number of perspectives—his stance as a theorist, his early work on the theory of the gradient of reinforcement, and the influence of several external and internal influences on the final form of the theory of behavior as it appeared in the *Principles*. Throughout, I have attempted as much as possible to follow the historical development of his theory, allowing for a certain amount of deviation from strict chronology to follow individual themes.

The work on the *Principles* can be divided into two phases. The first was a long preparatory period starting with a seminar course on behaviorism that Hull gave at Wisconsin in 1925–26 and ending in 1938. During the preparatory period Hull seems to have been envisaging a work of much broader scope than the *Principles*. In it he would have made detailed references to many aspects of human behavior. Toward the end of the preparatory period Hull started work on his mathematico-deductive theory of rote verbal learning and, during most of 1939, suspended work on the *Principles* altogether. Given Hull's views on the nature of theory, we can include time spent on the rote-learning monograph as a prelude to work on the *Principles*.[9] From letters to Spence we know that the work on the manuscript itself began some time in the first week of October 1939 and ended at 5:20 P.M. on December 28, 1942, when Hull mailed the corrected galley proofs to the publishers.

From the beginning (that is, even before Hull started to work on the book itself), it seems that he wanted to develop a mechanistic version of behaviorism that would allow him to make quantitative predictions.[10] It would also seem that, initially, he was going to concentrate on the higher mental processes. Hull's views on theory were the same as those of the logical positivists, although, as Larry Smith has shown, Hull developed his own version of positivism.[11] Just like the logical positivists, he believed in the unity of science and that physics was the master science. That meant that only knowledge generated and validated in a manner analogous to the way physicists generated and validated it would be regarded as "true" knowledge. Once psychologists were pursuing a truly scientific enterprise, Hull believed, disputes between the adherents of competing theories would cease.[12] Hull also resembled the logical positivists in that he wished to put an end to fruitless and unresolvable controversy. Furthermore, both Hull and the logical positivists believed that the source of much controversy outside physical science lay in arguments about metaphysical issues.[13] Like the logical positivists again, Hull believed that there was a "symmetry" between explanation and prediction. Hull's understanding of this symmetry was that the conflicting claims of theories purporting to operate in the same domains could be resolved if it could be demonstrated that one theory made more and more precise predictions than any of its competitors.

However, Hull's idiosyncratic version of positivism distanced him from logical positivism. He tried to derive his postulates directly from experimental data by curve fitting. The logical positivists, who were using already well established theories in the physical sciences as their models, would have found that approach very odd. Hull's approach to causation was also oversimplified. He believed that the laws of molar behavior would be discovered to be uniform and exact; he was not prepared to grant that they might be probabilistic. The logical positivists believed that all metaphysical discourse was nonsense; although Hull fulminated against metaphysics, it is clear that his quarrel was not with metaphysics as such but with what he construed as "bad" metaphysics—the idealism of Jeans and Eddington and the vitalism of Whitehead and Driesch.[14] Smith believes that Hull shared Karl Popper's belief that the ultimate epistemological distinction was between science and nonscience.

Hull's obsession with mechanism and with quantification also divided him sharply from the logical positivists. Smith shows at length how Hull's fascination with mechanical devices was a part of his thinking before he was a behaviorist and exerted a powerful control over his theory. The types of mechanism that interested Hull were those in which a hierarchical control system determines the operation of all the parts of the device. The shift in Hull's interest from particular mechanisms that controlled specific aspects of behavior to abstract devices that could control the complete behavior of living animals was not paralleled by a willingness to consider more complex types of control. Hull's obsession with quantification has been extensively discussed.[15]

Hull's conception of the role of a theorist was unique. He referred to theorists as "sponsors," strongly suggesting that he saw a theorist primarily as the spokesman or publicist for views that he had not necessarily generated himself.[16] Further indication of Hull's calculating attitude toward the presentation of theory is to be found in a passage from his diary: "people apparently are impressed by the mere external appearance of rigor. This is a factor of considerable importance in the matter of propaganda. I shall certainly heed the evident moral when I write up the system as a whole."[17] That passage suggests that, in some respects at least, Hull distanced himself from his own theory, treating it merely as a means of advancing his own status in the psychological community.

When he started work in earnest on his theory, Hull's view of the theorist as a sponsor enabled him to act very much like the president of a corporation, who sets the overall goals of the enterprise but delegates much of the decision making to his subordinates. In Hull's group the atmosphere was, up to a point, extremely open and democratic. Hull welcomed criticism of specific theoretical formulations and, while working on the *Principles*, frequently modified various portions to meet those criticisms. But the overall goals of the enterprise (which was, implicitly, viewed as a social mechanism) remained strictly in Hull's hands. Hull's managerial style of theory construction had the full support of Mark May, the director of Yale's Institute of Human Relations.[18]

During the 1930s Hull collaborated in some empirical work; the available archival evidence on Hull's early work on the gradient of reinforcement allows us to follow the growth of one of Hull's most fruitful concepts. He began with a rather crude, undifferentiated notion that became more subtle and precise by a fairly slow process of accretion, incorporating the work of both supporters and critics. Hull's gradient of reinforcement (for which his earlier name was the goal gradient hypothesis and which he later renamed the delay-of-reinforcement gradient) was the foundation that supported much of his theorizing. Neobehaviorist Gregory Kimble describes the concept as "one of the most important applications of conditioning principles to more complex behavior situations."[19] The hypothesis was paradigmatic because, in principle, it permitted Hullians to analyze a complex act into its components, apply conditioning principles directly to each of those components, connect the components with one another, and thus synthesize the theoretical analogue of the complex act itself.

Hull believed that the hypothesis had the potential for research applications well beyond the limits of his own discipline. In the early 1940s he claimed that the gradient of reinforcement would engender a behaviorist theory of value, whereby sequences of acts would be good (pleasurable) if positively reinforced and bad (unpleasant) if negatively reinforced. Moreover, he believed that his concept could replace Freud's *cathexis*.[20] He derived the hypothesis from the work of Margaret Floy Washburn and of Edward Lee Thorndike. In 1926, in a discussion of an experiment involving the speed of movement of white mice in a maze, Washburn noted that only the speed of running resulting from hunger was associated with the elimination of errors. She wrote, "The hardest thing to explain about the drive . . . is its backward direction, the fact that food at the end of the maze makes an animal readier to perform a turning at the beginning of a maze."[21] She offered a mechanistic solution to the problem, saying that as a result of past learning, hunger would be associated with running, and that, furthermore, because drive was a continuous stimulus, it would be persistently associated with running. Moreover, the degree of reinforcement of any act would be negatively related to the distance between the goal and the point at which the act was performed.

As work on the goal gradient proceeded, Hull and his associates began to differentiate between stimulus-response and response-reinforcer gradients. In the former, one is concerned with the operations of incentives that "drive" an animal toward a particular goal. In the latter, one is concerned with the effect that reinforcers have in enforcing the process of learning. Washburn was, fairly clearly, concentrating on the incentive aspect. It would seem, then, that Hull initially conflated a stimulus-response (incentive) interpretation, derived from Washburn, with a response-reinforcer (associationistic) interpretation, drawn from Thorndike.[22] The Thorndikian concept that most resembled the goal gradient was the spread of effect, which Thorndike first reported in 1933.[23] Thorndike concentrated on response-reinforcer relationships, asserting that if a stimulus-response connection was rewarded or punished, the effect would spread automatically to temporally adjacent connections. Hull's conceptual confusion arose in part from his own uncertainty regarding the role of reinforcement in learning. He was inclined to concentrate on the incentive interpretation during the 1930s because he was thinking hard about such notions as "the pure stimulus act" and goal-gaining anticipatory responses. He set that aspect of his theory aside late in the fall of 1939, once he started to work on the *Principles* in earnest.[24]

When Hull wrote his first paper on the goal gradient hypothesis, published in 1932, he did not subject the rather tentative notions put forward by Washburn to conceptual analysis.[25] Instead, characteristically more interested in quantification, he asked what sort of mathematical function would emerge if one plotted some measure of the strength of a learned reaction against distance from a goal. He chose a negatively accelerated curve derived from a logarithmic function, basing that function on Weber's law, and using the results of an experiment by Yoshioka as support. In 1929 Yoshioka had shown that it was the ratio between the lengths of long and short paths that determined ease of discrimination between such paths in maze learning.[26] In their experiments Hull and his coworkers tried to verify predictions based on the goal gradient hypothesis in three areas (the speed of locomotion gradient in the straight alley, the choice of short, as opposed to long, paths in the maze, and error patterns associated with the elimination of blind alleys in the maze). Their important 1934 study on the speed of locomotion gradient in rats is typical of their work.[27] They showed that once the rats were habituated to the maze, they would accelerate their speed of running from start box to goal box. Furthermore, as trials proceeded, the point in the runway at which animals reached top speed moved progressively toward the start box. But it was also true that the rats would slow down a little just before the goal box. Hull noted that the gradient tended to flatten with increasing practice, but he did not discuss the point.

The 1934 study yielded successful predictions, but a close reading yields some puzzling points. It seemed that, as demanded by the hypothesis, reward exerted a progressively greater effect on performance as training proceeded. In order to interpret his results Hull replotted one of the learning curves he had obtained as a linear function and compared it with a plot of the electrical stimulation required to stimulate nerve-muscle preparations as a function of the amount of prior stimulation. Because the behavioral and the physiological functions had the same shape, Hull concluded that his animals were being "driven" by some physiological force or incentive.[28] But in some conditions, the rats were run to extinction and then reward was reinstated. The reinstated gradients were markedly U-shaped. One explanation of the flattening of the U-shaped early gradients is that the rats showed anticipatory fear of the goal box, which was regained on the first post-extinction trials and subsequently dissipated, flattening the gradients. Hull mentioned that explanation as a possibility, but made little of it.

Numerous studies of the goal gradient were published in the 1930s, two of which, published by Buel and by Drew, endangered Hull's position.[29] Buel analyzed work on the elimination of blinds in mazes. With regard to linear mazes, he concluded that both excitation and expectancy operated evenly throughout the maze (i.e., there was no expectancy gradient).[30] With regard to complex spatial mazes, Buel concluded that the hypothesis, as formulated by Hull at that time, was in some difficulties. He claimed that at least ninety factors controlled the elimination of errors in complex mazes and that all would have to be incorporated into Hull's theory. So, he asked, "How useful would a learning theory be which contained some ninety special conditions for one type of problem?" All could, in principle, be incorporated into formulae, but the formulae would be hopelessly cumbersome. Moreover, he showed that the error pattern on the first trial was very highly correlated with the error pattern on succeeding trials, leaving very little scope for the operation of the goal gradient.

The 1939 study by Drew was particularly damaging to Hull's hypothesis. He studied the goal gradient under a number of experimental conditions. Some of his findings supported Hull's position, but I am interested only in those findings that created difficulties for Hull. First, Drew showed fairly conclusively that the slowing-up in the pre-goal sections of a runway was caused by anticipatory fear. Second, in two of his types of apparatus he baited several sections with equal amounts of food and still got a gradient, suggesting in both cases that the gradient could be explained by cognitive rather than by motivational factors. Third, he showed that the gradient appeared only if the trials were massed (five per day) rather than distributed (one per day). Furthermore, Drew's work strongly suggested that the gradient of speed of running was an artifact. In the massed condition, with each successive trial on any given day, the rats ran successively more slowly in the early sections of the alley. In contrast, in the distributed condition not only was the gradient flat but the running times per section showed a progressive decrease from one day to the next. (In contemporary terms, we would say that a performance factor masked the learning that was taking place.) As Drew commented, "the position is one in which a theory purporting to explain learning is only applicable when inefficient learning procedures are used."[31]

Drew concluded his article with a devastating argument. He had shown that when each section of a runway was baited equally and a massed condition was used, a gradient spanning the whole runway nevertheless appeared. Since on Hull's terms, the sole evidence for the gradient of reinforcement was amount of time that elapsed between the start of a reaction and the attainment of the reward, gradients such as those obtained by Hull himself in his 1934 study were inexplicable by his own theory.

Hull took Buel's and Drew's work very seriously indeed, and responded with a characteristic mixture of defensiveness and serious attention. He wrote at length to Spence in 1938 about the work of both men, revealing in great detail both his personal and his intellectual reactions.[32] The remainder of the letter seems to indicate that Hull was preparing for a shift in his thinking. In order to give himself time, it would seem, he gained a recantation from Buel.[33] He also published an article in which he restated his existing position.[34] Then he and his associates temporarily abandoned work on the incentive aspect of the goal gradient and concentrated on the response-reinforcer aspect.[35] After that, Hull returned to the incentive aspect of the problem and, toward the end of the 1940s, was able to generate a mathematical formula that explained the U-function he had obtained in his 1934 straight-alley experiments.[36] As with every aspect of his theory, Hull's solution to his problems has since been subjected to detailed and damaging criticism.[37]

From 1929 onward, Hull never ceased to be preoccupied with his magnum opus. Until 1939, however, his other commitments prevented him from working on the project full-time. By 1934 his favored title was *The Conditioned Reflex in Man*, which suggests that the project had become broader in the sense that the higher mental processes were not to be the exclusive topic of the work. The new title shows that Hull had become acquainted with Pavlov's work. As the end of the decade approached, the drive to get his views before the public in an appealing form became Hull's major concern, a concern that overrode the necessity for validation, and even his desire for a comprehensive system. On October 2, 1938, he wrote, "At last I have decided to write my long-projected work on psychological theory. It cannot be longer delayed with advantage, even though hardly a single postulate of the system is fully substantiated."[38] Hull's early intention to direct his book to the general public rather than to a specialized audience is implicit in the following passage: "Possibly a compromise may be reached by weaving the concepts, definitions, and so on into an interesting story—make the facts interesting in themselves by throwing light on our everyday activities."[39] By the end of the first period we seem to have a plan for a book stressing human psychology aimed at the general public. Then came a one-year gap during which he completed his work on the rote learning monograph. When he restarted, his plan for the form of the book had changed.

Hull's work on the *Principles* during the second phase was influenced by four major factors: Hull felt compelled to distance and differentiate himself from the Gestalt school; he had an unalterable bias in favor of quantitative predictions; he believed strongly in the ultimate possibility for theoretical unification; and he was driven to incorporate a mechanistic form of biological speculation into the theory. There was a close relationship between these influences. The drive to quantify was an expression of Hull's belief that the essential requirements of a scientific system were objectivity and certainty.[40] If the facts of the case in any particular instance could be established, Hull believed, then dispute would automatically cease. In that respect, he thought that he was contrasting himself with the Gestalt psychologists and their (as he saw it) futile attempts to persuade by means of argument.[41] Hull wanted to end the warfare between the adherents of opposing psychological theories and so saw a need for theoretical unification. Once again, it was the Gestaltists that he was most anxious to win over, since Gestalt theory provided American psychologists with a very attractive alternative to behaviorism. Finally, in his mechanico-biological speculations, Hull set himself against the emergentism and antimechanical beliefs of the Gestalt psychologists. I will deal with each influence at length.

Gestalt theory appears to have influenced Hull in two ways. First, it provided him with a definite articulated position against which he could react. Up to a point, then, his theory was conceived in opposition to Gestalt theory. As Hull himself admitted, he was better at conveying negative criticism than formulating positive doctrine.[42] In saying that Hull relied on Gestalt theory, I do not wish to belittle his originality. Apart from his desire to outdo the Gestaltists, he firmly believed in the explanatory powers of a behavioristic, mechanistic, materialist philosophy. Even so, it was his encounters with Koffka in 1926–27 that stimulated him to make definite efforts to explore the implications of that philosophy.[43]

The other influence of the Gestaltists was their success in disseminating their ideas. This influence was less direct but perhaps even more powerful than the reactive influence of Gestalt theory; the competition for general acceptance fueled the fires of Hull's already powerful ambitions. His response is vividly and affectingly expressed in the following passages from Hull's letters to Spence:

> these Gestalt people are so terrifyingly articulate. Practically every one of them writes several books. The result is that whereas they constitute a rather small proportion of the psychological population of this country, they have written ten times as much in the field of theory as Americans have.

> Meanwhile the responsibility of getting this material [i.e., systematic behavioristic theory] before the public in a systematic manner seems temporarily at least to rest upon my own shoulders.[44]

Hull faced serious problems in persuading psychologists and the intellectual public to accept the value of his approach. For both him and Spence, one gained scientific precision by dehumanizing and depersonalizing behavior.[45] Any theory that had a place for humane values and the expression of individual, subjective interests and strivings but that was also objective and scientific was a strong threat to their enterprise. Kurt Lewin, the younger colleague of Köhler and Koffka, had produced such a theory.[46] The Hull/Spence correspondence is peppered with uneasy references to him. That unease was fully justified because of the broad scope of Lewin's work, because of its capacity to incorporate his empirical findings into a consistent theory, and, perhaps above all, because he provided American experimental psychologists with a theoretical alternative to Hull's version of behaviorism and to the rather dry operationism of people like McGeoch.[47] The power of Lewin's theory is beautifully illustrated by his comments on one of Hull's papers.[48] In it he cogently criticized the Hull/Spence mechanistic approach and showed that his theory could yield the same predictions as Hull's. For example, he demonstrated how expectancy could be inserted into a postulate system and that there were a number of experimental studies showing that expectancy could be manipulated as an independent variable.

Another Gestalt psychologist who posed a powerful threat to Hull and Spence was Ralph K. White. In the same year in which *Principles of Behavior* was published, one of his articles came out in the *Psychological Review*.[49] It was expressly designed to illustrate the superiority of the Tolman/Lewin approach over Hull's neobehaviorism. White claimed that scientific theories could be judged in terms of four criteria (operational meaning, rigor, economy, and experimental basis). He went on to claim (very persuasively, in my view) that the Tolman/Lewin approach satisfied all four and that it was superior to neobehaviorism on the third and fourth.

Hull's fears of the proselytizing powers of the Gestaltists, and of the strength of their intellectual position, were well founded. Given the power and comprehensiveness of Gestalt theory, and given the number of adherents it had secured among American psychologists, it seems that Hullian theory triumphed not for intellectual but for social reasons. Kenneth Spence played a pivotal role. Both personally and through the work of his many graduate students he ensured that Hullian-style research would dominate American animal science and American human experimental psychology for many years.[50]

Hull's approach to mathematical psychology was quite different from that of anyone else working in the field and, partly for that reason, he had very few followers. Unlike others, he did not try to discover what functions might directly underlie his input and output variables, nor did he treat his intervening variables as abstract entities that necessarily interposed themselves between input and output. Instead, he tried to develop direct mathematical expressions of those variables. In that way, he hoped to convince other psychologists that, when making statements about his intervening variables, he was making statements about existing states.[51] Hull considered his quantitative work to be his greatest intellectual achievement.[52]

Hull's drive to make quantitative predictions found its strongest expression in his discussions with Spence regarding the form of the function for habit strength (that is, the fundamental shape of the acquisition curve in learning).[53] Hull had discussed the shape of the acquisition curve at least twice before returning to the problem while writing the *Principles*. In his article in Murchison's *Handbook*, published in 1934, he concluded that it was very likely that if one started with a state of no prior learning and followed the learning process right through to its conclusion, an S-shaped curve would result. He explicitly contrasted such S-shaped curves with "conventional curves of learning," in which a period of positive acceleration early in learning was absent. Failure to obtain an early period of positive acceleration, he suggested, was due to a failure to study the learning process from its very beginning. Later, in the monograph on rote learning, published in 1940, Hull and his colleagues showed that the probability of successful recall was an S-shaped function of increasing numbers of presentation.[54]

Hull and Spence always discussed the issue of magnitude of reinforcement and the issue of the shape of the function together.[55] Hull first raised the question in a letter to Spence of October 2, 1940, saying that he had set up an equation for habit strength as a function of the number of reinforcements and also that he had produced a negatively accelerated function, but giving no details. In reply Spence raised the issue following some questions about the relationship between habit strength and the magnitude of reward. He asked Hull why he had selected a negatively accelerated function when there was considerable evidence to show that most curves were sigmoidal (that is, had an initial section showing positive acceleration). After discussing the issue of magnitude of reward and making some proposals of his own in which he suggested that magnitude of reward had an indirect rather than a direct effect on habit strength, Spence pointed out that in conditioning, most acquisition curves were S-shaped.[56]

Hull replied to Spence on February 8, 1941. Taking up the issue of magnitude of reward first, he said that his belief that there was a direct relationship between magnitude of reward and habit strength was based on two studies, one by Grindley and one by Gantt.[57] Regarding the form of the curve of acquisition, Hull suggested that mathematically, sigmoid functions could be converted to an exponential form. However, the text of *Principles of Behavior* shows no sign that Hull attempted such a conversion, so we have to assume either that his attempt at reconciliation failed or that he made no such attempt. Also we have to bear in mind that the evidence for a negatively accelerated function in the case of magnitude of reward was almost nonexistent. We must also add that Hull had written to Spence that, although he believed that magnitude of reward had an effect on the rate of habit formation, "I do not believe that this is proven conclusively by Grindley's experiment in part because of the far too few animals and in part because the matter of incentive was not sufficiently controlled to be fully convincing."[58] By this time the required evidence, on Hull's own admission, had almost completely disappeared.

I think we can explain why Hull derived a negatively accelerated function for habit strength with a scale of magnitude along the abscissa as follows: He wanted to make precise quantitative predictions. To achieve these, he was obliged to assume that if a need is going to be reduced, then the greater the amount of reduction the greater will be the habit strength, and, furthermore, that the relationship between need and habit strength would be strictly proportional. Most of the experiments available to Hull concerned numbers of reinforcements, and these also provided him with his most reliable data. But for someone interested in the *principle* of making precise quantitative predictions, such data are unsatisfactory because they do not produce infinitely divisible values (except if one makes a rather implausible assumption). A scale based on magnitude, however, does have the required form; hence Hull found it irresistibly attractive.

In regard to the form of the function, I suggest that we can recapitulate Hull's reasoning in the following way. At the commencement of learning, when need is strongest, the diminution in need associated with a "correct" response is also at its highest point. Thereafter, each successive correct response is associated with progressively less diminution in need. Such reasoning is valid only if we assume that satisfaction and needs have no inherent qualities, that they derive all their motivational power from their association with the physical constraints that determine the physical survival of animals. It is clear from Spence's comments that even by the 1930s there were data that would have allowed Hull to test the reality of his derived curve of habit strength. He chose to ignore the evidence.

The third influence (the drive toward theoretical unification) operated strongly on Hull well before he started work on the *Principles*. In the early pages of his 1934 paper "The Conflicting Psychologies of Learning: A Way Out," Hull discussed at length the conflicts that prevented psychologists from following the route leading to a genuinely scientific psychology. His general solution was "Let the psychological theorist begin with neurological postulates, or functional postulates, or organismic postulates, or Gestalt postulates, or hormonic postulates, or mechanistic postulates, or dynamic postulates of dialectical materialism, and no questions should be asked about his beginning save those of consistency and the principle of parsimony."[59] That passage shows that Hull had no concern whatever for the rational or theoretical integrity of scientific concepts. For him, the role of a postulate was to permit the deduction of theorems. The role of theorems was to provide the basis for experiments. The experiments, in turn, provided the sole basis for passing judgment on the truth of the theorems. Provided that the theorems had been correctly deduced from the postulates, they had to be true. The intellectual provenance of the postulates was irrelevant.[60]

The operation of Hull's laissez-faire policy with regard to theory is best illustrated by his strangely prolonged flirtation with Guthrie's theory. The flirtation demands explanation because of the considerable differences between Guthrie's approach and what is usually taken to be Hull's. Hilgard has concluded that Guthrie relegated drive to the periphery of his theory, that he treated repetition idiosyncratically, and that he gave an indirect role to reinforcers. All approaches differentiated him very sharply from the published version of Hull's theory.[61] Yet Hull expressed a strong interest in incorporating Guthrie's theory into his own for over a year, largely because a Guthrian theory would require relatively few postulates.[62]

On May 11, 1940, Hull suggested that Spence write a critique of Guthrie. A similar delegation of responsibility occurred earlier. In 1937 Hull asked Carl Hovland to comment on two of Spence's papers on stimulus generalization (see letters from Hull to Spence on February 2 and 16, 1937). Delegation of responsibility regarding theoretical formulations to others in the group was linked to the need for theoretical unification and derived from Hull's attitude to theory. Hull, it seems, looked on any theoretical task, no matter how complex, simply as a task, and as any good manager knows, any task can be delegated. So he was perfectly willing to use Guthrie's solution of at least some theoretical problems (and so, in effect, to delegate that responsibility to Guthrie in advance). Here we have two of the many examples of Hull's astonishing willingness to delegate work to others. I can think of no other theorist who would hand over the work of formulating centrally important *theoretical* doctrines to someone else.

Despite his delegation of work, Hull either had not formulated or was not satisfied with his diminution-in-drive hypothesis by December 1940.[63] In the meantime, he had obtained some help with his proposed critique of Guthrie's work from a source close to Guthrie himself. On January 13, 1941, Fred D. Sheffield, one of Guthrie's graduate students, sent Spence, at Hull's request, a five-page single-spaced letter outlining Guthrie's system in order to help Spence in writing his critique of Guthrie. But by then Hull had arrived at a mathematical formulation of the diminution-in-drive hypothesis, and the flirtation with Guthrie was over. What that flirtation tells us, I think, is that Hull's views on the constitution of scientific theories were highly idiosyncratic. Hull was trying to find consistent patterns for the presentation of data rather than consistent patterns in his data. Moreover, so long as the data fit a given pattern Hull was not concerned about their origin (again, he was not concerned with theoretical consistency in the conventional sense). Theory, as usually understood, played a secondary role in Hull's thinking. Any behaviorist theory could be made to serve his purposes provided that it yielded some sort of framework for the presentation of his chosen data.

With respect to Hull's biologism, there is no doubt that under Darwin's influence, Hull was clearly impelled to explain adaptive purpose. Psychologists Edmund J. Fantino and Cheryl A. Logan claim that in his explanation of adaptive behavior, Hull extended Darwin's explanation of phylogenetic change to the realm of ontogeny by proposing that reinforcement operated as a selective mechanism on the random responses produced by initial reaction potential.[64] In a 1945 article Hull made a formal attempt to incorporate innate and species-specific differences into his model, which up to that time had concentrated on the behavior of individuals.[65]

Hull's biologism remained speculative and, above all, closely linked to his urge to engage in mechanistic speculations, which was a powerful but subterranean force in his thinking. Larry Smith, in his excellent discussion of Hull's mechanico-biological ruminations, shows clearly that Hull's biologism, his mechanism, and his approach to theory were closely linked.[66] Until at least 1935 Hull hoped to produce a machine that displayed not just adaptive behavior but the power to arrive at novel solutions to problems. If successfully designed, such a machine would have been a physical rebuttal to the emergentists, Bergsonians, and others who believed it necessary to appeal to *élan vital*, life-force, and so on. For various reasons, Hull suppressed the direct expression of his search for adaptive mechanisms and gave that role to his theory. Like the gears and cogs of a machine, the postulates and theorems were designed to produce predictable physical outcomes. Since these outcomes would refer to the learned, adaptive responses of animals, we would have, Hull hoped, the required mechanistic explanations for behavior.

Because Hull's mechanico-biologism is not formally expressed in his writing, we have to search for material regarding it in unpublished sources. His underlying biologism is clearly revealed in the following passages in a letter to Spence, written at about the time he formulated the diminution-of-drive hypothesis: "drive operates in some indirect way on the habit structure and the nervous system, somewhat as caffeine and benzedrine do" and "The action of the caffeine, it seems to me, can hardly be due to the activity of any particular stimulus, but must be due to the physiological or physical chemical action of the drug upon the portions of the nervous system in which the habit structure lies."[67]

Hull's biologism, it would seem, trumped his behaviorism. In a letter to Spence about secondary reinforcement, he wrote,

> may it not be that through the process of evolution certain receptor discharges which are closely related to needs, for example, smell and taste, are especially active when the need for food is great, and that at such times the stimulation of these receptors by certain chemical substances are reinforcing without more ado? That is rather a radical method of cutting the Gordian knot, though it seems to me quite credible.[68]

In sharp contrast to Hull, Spence remained consistently behavioristic in his thinking. For example, in September 1940 he wrote to Hull,

> I still am not quite able to accept the description of the reinforcing state of affairs in terms of a drop in the level of drive strength, but I suppose if you

put it forward as a hypothesis with the further statement that it is a function of the attainment and commerce with the goal stimulus, it is satisfactory.[69]

The rest of the paragraph in Spence's letter is devoted to an analysis of the term "instrumental"; he uses the example of salivation being instrumental in bringing food into the stomach. In the same way, in an earlier letter, Spence had interpreted Hilgard and Marquis's use of "instrumental" as referring to "acts learned in environmental confrontation, instrumental in bringing about the goal stimulus."[70] We can see that Spence avoided all reference to supposed inner states and limited himself entirely to the consideration of observable behavior.

Later, in December 1940, Spence wrote to Hull,

> Some of the boys have been reading your chapters; and, while they are very favorably disposed to the later chapters, they have often commented critically concerning the early ones, which they think emphasize too much the biological, evolutionary aspects. . . . Strangely enough, to them it appears teleological, which makes me worry somewhat because they are all very clear on the point that you do not favor such interpretations. When I take up the specific points and indicate that you are attempting to formulate the mechanisms lying behind this descriptively purposive type of behavior phenomenon, they withdraw their criticisms. But, if these boys, with their much more thorough background and specific knowledge of your theoretical formulations, make this mistake, I shudder to think how the naive psychologists and those not so familiar with your point of view will interpret this.[71]

And so we have the paradox that the creator of an all-embracing behaviorist system was not a strict behaviorist.

To sum up, my intention has been to demonstrate that Hull was driven by his need to meet the challenge set by the Gestalt psychologists. Although Hull and Spence never openly said so, even in their correspondence, they seem to have had a powerful urge to institute an American theory of psychology that would be as free as possible from European influences. Certainly their correspondence is full of questionings and speculations, sometimes anxious, sometimes aggressive, about the influence of Gestalt ideas on their native-born colleagues. The record indicates that the other forces operating on him were subordinate to this primary one.

Hull's subordination of other objectives to the goal of challenging the Gestalt psychologists could be manifested in remarkably simplistic ways. For example, the capacity of his theory to make quantitative predictions was used to differentiate the two on the level of mere appearance. Hull wanted the pages of *Principles of Behavior* to look physically different from the pages of *The Growth of Mind* or *Gestalt Psychology*, to make it immediately evident to his readers that they had in their hands a scientific, not a philosophical, work. What better way to make the point than to fill his book with equations?[72] Although that propaganda aspect of his endeavors certainly weighed heavily with Hull, there was also a deeper reason for his obsession with mathematical logic. During the academic year 1926–27 Hull listened while Koffka attacked Watson. His basic response was to accept Watson's dictum that "the theoretical goal of psychology is the prediction and control of behavior." He then sought for a way to achieve that goal and avoid the damaging criticisms of Koffka and the other Gestalt psychologists. His postulate system was his means to those ends; it appeared to have the capacity to generate reliable predictions to guide choices, and hence offer its own proof against criticism.

It is not surprising, then, that Hull set such a high value on his work in mathematical logic. But given that in a sense he was merely reacting against another theory rather than actively grappling with problems created from within his own system, it is also not surprising that it was precisely in the quantitative aspect that Hull's theory failed most deeply. A clear example of that failure is provided by Hilgard in his critique of predictions derived from the postulate of effective reaction potential.[73] The example discussed by Hilgard was derived from an experiment by Arnold, in which rats had to push a succession of buttons in order to secure either a food reward or release from shock. Hull's predictions were based only on the food condition. Hilgard showed that Hull's logic was consistent and coherent so that it was possible for him, in principle, to make quantitative predictions. In practice, however, he had no rational or empirical basis for assigning values to his constants, so that he could not make such predictions in fact. Furthermore, a scrutiny of Arnold's experiment shows that there was no learning in the shock condition, which strongly suggests that Hull's concept of reaction potential does not have the degree of generality that he believed it to have. At the same time, the concepts of reaction potential and the goal gradient hypothesis remained rather vague hypothetical constructs. Hull's metatheory demanded that they become intervening variables, in which case it would have been demonstrated that they applied to a broad range of empirical situations and were defined in terms of such situations. It is sad to record that one of those who passed an adverse judgment on Hull's quantitative work was Spence himself:

> I must confess that I have not been able to understand Hull's treatment of delay in his new book, *A Behavior System*. In fact, I am quite concerned about the many stupid things that appear in this book, and I guess that I tend to repress and forget what is in it. The treatment of J does not make any sense at all to me. So far as I can follow it, it certainly does not seem to involve behavioral summation of J and D, however, I may be wrong in this for I have simply not had the heart to follow through on the nonsense which appears in this chapter.[74]

The failure to generate quantitative predictions based on the postulate of reaction potential also illustrates the operation of the third influence, the drive toward theoretical unification. In Hull's conception of a unified theory, the theoretical elements (the postulates and theorems) played a purely functional role and were publicly and empirically defined. The latter aspect is an expression of Hull's positivism, whereby he set himself apart from the Gestaltists. Hull failed to see that if he had treated his postulates as heuristic devices, he would have been able to achieve his ultimate goal of prediction while possibly avoiding the fallacies resulting from the oversimplified and empirically untenable definitions given to his postulates. He arrived instead at a theoretical solution to his difficulties, a particular way of conceiving the relationship between structure and function. Although Hull's solution was personally fruitful, it has serious conceptual problems, which have been cogently analyzed by William Rozeboom.[75] Hull wanted the effect of each input variable to be direct and noninteractive. In that way, he hoped to gain direct evidence for the effect of each antecedent variable on response output. For example, he hoped to show that each minute increase in need- or drive-reduction would be accompanied by a proportionate increase in habit strength. This, then, was Hull's version of behaviorism. He believed that if there were pooling of inputs so that the direct effects of inputs were progressively lost, one would be left with an ambiguous situation and there would be room for emergentism, cognitivism, and Gestalt.

It is at this point in the theory that Hull's mechanistic form of biological speculation came into play. The required simple relationship between input and output could be achieved if one were to conceive of organisms as machines. Hull failed to see that conceptions have to be given full theoretical expression and their implications explored. Partly because he did not wish to draw public attention to his mechanico-biological speculations and partly because his positivism interposed barriers between his system and the realm of pure theory, Hull never undertook the necessary work. As a result, his theory has appeared to some commentators to be an enclosed deductive system, supported by unacknowledged premises.[76] I would like to suggest that Hull's most deeply felt speculations lacked a disciplining and restraining framework. Thus there was no opportunity for his loose speculations to become firm theory. A good firm theory gives full scope to the life and power of intuitions. It also provides a means whereby the speculations become publicly communicable and an opportunity to generate corollaries and implications. Hull never got his private speculations to the point where they became available to a scientific community. He was very much like a prophet or guru who needed the help of acolytes to publicize his ideas and present them in a palatable form. What was truly vital to Hull could appear only in a disguised or attenuated form. Hence the many puzzling features of both versions of his theory of learning. Nevertheless, once one has made the effort required to enter Hull's life-world, one has to see that to recognize the parameters within which he chose to work is to acknowledge a substantial intellectual achievement based on persistence in the face of many problems and the struggle to produce a theory that would be at once all-embracing and precise and that would meet his rather exacting standards of what it meant to be scientific.

5

The Behaviorist as Philosopher
B. F. Skinner

Behavioral science reached its highest and most complete development in Skinner's writings. No behavioral scientist had a greater influence (both direct and indirect) on the discipline than he. But even though nobody disputes the extent of his influence, assessing its nature is a different matter. To quote Winston Churchill, he was a riddle wrapped in a mystery inside an enigma. I will analyze three themes in Skinner's intellectual life: the conflict between his incorporation into animal science and his desire to be a technologist of behavior; the contrast between his self-presentation as a polemicist and his apparent wish to be taken seriously as a scholar, especially a philosopher of mind; and the disjunction between his love of art and culture and his apparent brusque, indeed crude, dismissal of humanistic values and virtues. My three themes did not control Skinner's thinking in some sort of determinative sense but should be seen as evanescent but recurring motifs in his work.

The first theme manifests itself in Skinner's career path. He showed psychologists what it meant to be a creative scientist. Working entirely on his own, he created a unique version of behaviorism that, within the rather stringent limits imposed by its presuppositions, solved the problems involved in generalizing work from the animal laboratory to human life. More to the point, Skinner's version of positivism appeared to be both scientifically satisfactory and also applicable to the concrete issues of life, whether animal or human. Yet Skinner himself seemed to have had a lowly estimation of his achievements as a scientist. No sooner had he expressed his ideas in the form of his first book than he launched himself into Project Pigeon, a lengthy piece of applied work. To Skinner, Project Pigeon was a chance to explore unrealized potentials, not a distraction from his true work. In part because Skinner neglected pure research from about 1950 onward one has to say that his endowment to scientific psychology is exiguous. The principles of operant conditioning, especially the various schedules of reinforcement, remain powerful methodological tools. But it is, in my view, impossible to give an instance of a substantive Skinnerian finding whose truth would not be seriously contested. Skinner might have acted the part of a creative behavior scientist perfectly, but the lines he delivered have been consigned to psychology's history.

In regard to the second theme, one has to say that as a theory of mind, Skinner's version of behaviorism has much to recommend it. According to Daniel Dennett, Skinner faced fairly and squarely the essential problem confronting anyone who wishes to generate a scientific account of mental life—namely, how to describe the life of the mind without using the language of mentalism.[1] In his polemics against cognitive psychology and in his book on language Skinner tried to demonstrate how his terminology could completely replace a mental language. In common with Wittgenstein, Skinner scornfully rejected the ultimate authenticity of the subjective. He insisted that all statements about mental events be publicly verifiable. He claimed that public verifiability could be assured only if private and public events or objects were placed on exactly the same footing. Hence his frequently reiterated statement that private events were merely public events occurring within the skin. He believed we should explain actions solely in terms of the history of past reinforcements. His philosophy of mind was intimately linked to his work as a scientist. Skinner and his colleagues demonstrated, over and over again, that seemingly cognitively controlled behaviors could be patiently shaped in the Skinner box.

These examples, however, have always been much more persuasive within the Skinnerian camp than outside it. Skinner's critics claim that in real-life situations we can seldom identify reinforcing events and give a precise, moment-to-moment account of how reinforcers shape behavior designed to achieve some specified goal. So, they say, Skinner's theory of action really amounts to no more than a propagandist exhortation to seek out plausible histories of reinforcement for any given action. It is certainly difficult not to characterize Skinner as a polemicist. He was fatuously coy about his sources. As a result, he could always claim that specific criticisms had no force because they applied to a position that he did not hold (although one has to turn to his expositors, rather than Skinner himself, to find out what his true position might be). Above all, he failed to meet the essential criterion for any philosopher; he did not submit his own conclusions to critical appraisal. Yet a candid critic of Skinner would have to admit that she is always left with the baffling feeling that, no matter how comprehensive and trenchant the criticism, some undetected essence has escaped.

The third polarity is complex and subtle. Skinner displayed a disjunction between potential knowledge and abilities, on the one hand, and the expression of those qualities in his writings, on the other. He was a cultured man with, it seems, high intellectual aspirations. He had a good working knowledge of various philosophical doctrines and he seemed to have a true love for art and literature. The humanistic virtues guided his professional life as a young man. His early articles were beautifully argued and were models of scholarship. But from the 1950s onward his writings consisted of a repetitive (and, it must be said, frequently rebarbative) stream of unsubstantiated, unscholarly platitudes.

Perhaps we see here the manifestation of unresolved conflicts welling up from the depths of Skinner's personality. We know that the young Skinner suffered anguish and humiliation as he sat alone in his parents' house struggling to express thoughts and emotions that failed to find form in the written word. When release did come and *Walden Two* emerged, surely Skinner, the reader of Proust, cannot have felt fulfillment or satisfaction. Perhaps, then, in dismissing the humane values so contumaciously the mature Skinner was trying to excise a part of himself that longed for fulfillment but could find none.

The post–*Walden Two* Skinner exiled more than the liberal, the humane, and the cultured values from the country of his mind. The professional and scholarly virtues were also displaced. There the unconscious motive might have been rebellion against his father. As a young man, Skinner was eager for parental approval, and a stream of articles following the accepted canons was a sure route to that goal. But Skinner did not want his fame and respect to be confined within the boundaries of the psychological profession. Hence his search for a unique means of expression of his beliefs. The unconscious message to his father's spirit might have been, "Love me as I truly am, not as society would like to see me."

In his autobiography Skinner has given us a full account of the origins of his behaviorism, and his biographer, the historian Robert

Bjork, has added little to it. Unlike his neobehaviorist peers, Skinner had no undergraduate training in psychology (his bachelor's degree, from Hamilton College, New York, was in English). Following his graduation from Hamilton, Skinner spent what he called a "Dark Year" (mostly at his parents' home in Scranton) in which he unsuccessfully tried to establish himself as a writer of fiction.[2] He first became interested in behaviorism when, in August 1926, he read Bertrand Russell's review of C. K. Ogden and I. A. Richard's book *The Meaning of Meaning* in a small (but fairly influential) intellectual magazine called *The Dial*. Russell mentioned Watson, so Skinner read *Behaviorism* and *The Ways of Behaviorism*. His commitment to behaviorism was heightened after he read Russell's *Philosophy* when it was published in America in 1927.[3] Later in 1927 Skinner wrote a review of Louis Berman's book *The Religion Called Behaviorism*.[4] He submitted his review to the *Saturday Review of Literature*, but it was not published.

But Skinner also claimed that along with this shift in mode of expression went a change of substance, a switch from humanism to science. For example, in his autobiography he claims that his behaviorism began with the realization that the Law of Effect could explain how one learns to pack a suitcase.[5] Since Skinner was relying on his recollection when he wrote that passage, one could accuse him of gilding the lily. Placed in the context of his intellectual development, however, it has the ring of truth. Skinner's behaviorism was very much his own, both in its inspiration and in its development, and that idiosyncracy informed Skinner's words. What I find striking, however, is the unacknowledged deductive element in Skinner's thought. Nobody learns to pack a suitcase the way Skinner described; we watch others do it and then we get help when we begin for ourselves. Our own mode of packing is a late, not an early, development. Skinner, however, had to make a place in his thinking for the Law of Effect. The only way to do that was to violate commonsense observation.

Skinner finally made up his mind to study psychology as a result of reading an article on Bernard Shaw and Ivan Pavlov by H. G. Wells in the *New York Times Sunday Magazine* on November 13, 1927, the title of which was, in part, "To Whom Does the Future Belong: The Man of Science or the Expressive Man?" Wells asked whose life one would save if forced to choose, and opted for Pavlov the scientist rather than Shaw the humanist without any hesitation. Skinner treated his own literary aspirations with similar ruthlessness. He started reading *Conditioned Reflexes* in April 1928 and enrolled in Harvard's graduate school in September of that year.

Skinner has given very full and, on the whole, accurate accounts of his graduate school career and of the way his unique version of behaviorism came into being.[6] All he knew about behaviorism (or, indeed, about psychology) on his arrival at Harvard was based on what he had learned about Loeb at Hamilton and his reading of two of Watson's books and of Pavlov's *Conditioned Reflexes*. Once at Harvard, he took a laboratory class, based on Titchener's text, from Carroll Pratt, a weekly seminar from Walter Hunter on animal behavior, and classes in experimental psychology, the theory of psychology, the history of psychology, perception, and the analysis of conduct (the last being a class in physiology offered by W. J. Crozier). On the whole he found the classes in psychology boring and did poorly in most of them.

Of all Skinner's graduate courses, Crozier's Analysis of Conduct had the greatest influence on him. Crozier was powerfully influenced by the biological mechanist Jacques Loeb, who, as Skinner wrote, "resented the nervous system." In his discussion of Crozier's influence on his thought, Skinner clearly showed his perfect grasp of the essence of behaviorism—the equation of theory with method. At the same time we see how, for the behaviorist, the banishing of mind entailed the banishing of the nervous system. Finally, we see the enterprise that Watson began brought to its highest level of development. When studying animal behavior, one ignored altogether the adaptive functions of the behaviors in question and expunged from one's mind any question about causal influences working from within the animal. Instead, one made a completely physicalist analysis of the relationships between observed variables, especially those that can easily be brought under experimental control.

As part of a requirement for a course in physiology Skinner did a study of geotropic behavior in ants under the supervision of T. Cunliffe Barnes.[7] Not surprisingly, he flirted with the idea of switching to physiology. What seems to have prevented him was being given a free run of the psychology workshop following the retirement of the departmental technician (who was not replaced). Thereafter, Skinner experimented in a very free-floating way with a number of projects. His claim that he stumbled on his research paradigms by happenstance has been critically discussed by Steven Coleman, who has examined the available archival material and concluded that Skinner's early research program was theory-driven.[8] Coleman believes that Skinner was impelled by a search for quantitative orderliness and that, in interpreting the results of his experiments or in planning new lines of research, Skinner moved away from abstract concepts and toward concrete interpretations. As we see from Skinner's own account of the progress of his early work, he eventually built pieces of apparatus and recording devices that allowed him to take continuous records of behavior. Skinner wrote that the advantage of such cumulative records lay in their production of what "is in effect . . . the description of a process [of satiation of 'the facilitating condition' of hunger]"[9] Coleman comments that "To someone seeking behavioral orderliness, an inspectable display of it must have been a powerful payoff."[10]

It is crucial to grasp the point that Coleman is making. Skinner believed he drifted from project to project in his early research and stopped his explorations only when he had hit upon techniques for automatically producing continuous records of behavior from free-moving animals. To criticize Skinner for passively following the path of least resistance toward that goal instead of trying to reach some theoretically motivated one is to make all the concessions that he asks for from his critics. Instead, Coleman is arguing that Skinner was guided by unacknowledged theoretical imperatives. As we will see, those imperatives imposed crippling constraints on the range of conclusions Skinner could draw from his research program.

Skinner's early research culminated in a theoretical paper on drive written during his postdoctoral fellowship.[11] In his autobiography he commented on the article as follows:

> Fortunately, my commitment to operationism saved the main point of the paper: An organism was *driven* by hunger or thirst. A drive was not a force. I would stick to my observations, as Bridgman had done with the concept of force in physics. "The problem of hunger presents itself . . . as a variation in the strength of certain reflexes, a variation which ordinarily appears haphazard." It could be solved by finding some connection (a "third variable" in the terminology of my thesis) of which the variation was a function. In my experiment, how fast an animal ate depended upon how long it had been eating.

The fact that "drive" seemed to refer to a thing was a verbal accident. The concept had no experimental usefulness. "That there are physiological conditions correlated with all aspects of behavior no one will be likely to question," and the present result no doubt had physiological significance, but no physiological cause of the variation in strength had been demonstrated. Significantly, I added: "The same criticism may, of course, be applied to the concept of reflex strength, if that term is taken beyond the simple operational definition that we have given it."[12]

Here, Skinner was saying that the strength of a drive in a laboratory animal, as observed by an experimenter, depended on operations performed by the experimenter. Since we can know only that which we can observe (where those observations include our own past actions), all we can discuss meaningfully are relationships between observed outcomes. Therefore, drive should be specified only in terms of antecedent manipulations and consequent outcomes.

In his appraisal of Skinner's Ph.D. thesis, Boring commented that Skinner's treatment of the concept of reflex demanded the creation of a new school of thought, combined with supporting propaganda.[13] Skinner established propaganda and a school, and Boring, as we have seen, joined the school. From the 1950s onward all American experimental psychologists defined their theoretical constructs as "facts-as-relational-correlations."

Skinner confronted, more forcefully than any other behaviorist, the issue of the seeming incorrigibility of the subjective. In order to do so, he created a particularly robust version of positivism, saying that we could accept as true only those statements meeting verifiable criteria. Skinner's positivism was intimately connected with his attitude toward a science of behavior. When we asked what it meant for actions to be meaningful or comprehensible, he said we had to be both clear-minded and hardheaded. He believed we could say that we understood something only when we could predict and control its occurrence.[14] Initially, I will advance Skinner's position as strongly as I can. Then I will show that, even in its most robust version, it fails on all fronts.

Many of Skinner's critics have failed to realize that even if he was listening to Watson's urgings respecting the centrality of prediction and control in a science of behavior, he was by no means following Watson's program. He saw very clearly that fine-grained predictions were impossible and futile.[15] As Zuriff argues, a behaviorist theory can hope to be viable only if it is based on a coherent positivist philosophy of science, while that philosophy derives its force from the enunciation of principles describing individuals' capacity to predict and control their environment.[16]

An immediate problem with a behaviorist philosophy of science is that the supporting reasoning appears to be circular, an issue that Zuriff addresses. To declare that a law-like statement is true if and only if it refers to actions that are useful or adaptive appears to solve the question of what we mean by "truth" or "theory" by stipulation. To deal with the problem, Zuriff applies the same reasoning psychologist Paul E. Meehl did when addressing the issue of the presumed circularity of the law of effect.[17] Behaviorists save themselves from circularity, Zuriff claims, by demonstrating that, using procedures based on the established research practices of behavioral science, they can make verifiable predictions about ordinary human life. Second, he claims that behaviorists can specify which environmental events actually exert control over people's action. In consequence, the findings of the laboratory can be extrapolated to the moment-to-moment control over human behavior, including self-directed human behavior.

Skinner dealt with the issue of extrapolation by devising an explanatory principle that could be brought to focus on particular behavioral episodes and have a high degree of concrete actuality but would also have the broadest possible scope. He defined a reinforcer as any stimulus that had an effect on the frequency of emission of any given response or class of responses. Like Meehl, he thought that he had saved himself from the accusation of circular reasoning by invoking the principle of trans-situationality. Then he could specify the precise outcomes of the application of any given reinforcer to any specified situation.

Skinner's theory of behavior had to be derived from or at least be consistent with some philosophical position. I will start by assuming that Skinner was that elusive beast, an analytic behaviorist. The most succinct definition of analytic behaviorism has been given by A. J. Ayer, who wrote, "If I know that an object behaves in every way as a conscious being must, by definition, behave, then I know that it really is conscious. This is an analytical proposition. . . . [One] must define the existence of other men in terms of the actual and hypothetical occurrence of certain sense-contents."[18] In many places in his writings, for example in certain passages in *About Behaviorism,* Skinner seemed to portray himself as an analytic behaviorist. If Skinner was indeed an analytic behaviorist then it is usually held that his position could be decisively refuted by what is known as the no-particular-behavior argument.[19] Put simply, the no-particular-behavior argument states that there is no necessary connection between belief and action. Although we can typically infer belief from action and reliably predict that certain actions will result in certain beliefs, we can always imagine cases where belief and action are totally unconnected. Therefore, analytical behaviorism is false.

However, Boyer has shown that the no-particular-behavior argument has no force against Skinner's version of analytic behaviorism.[20] He starts by asserting that Skinner created a general account of behavior. Boyer defines the statement "x is reinforced to y" as follows: "Any behavior which y emits in some circumstance c shortly before getting x as a stimulus will have its probability of occurrence increased in further occurrences of circumstance c."[21] Boyer shows that analytic behaviorists are not limited to the study of actually occurring physical behavior. He claims that two dimensions along which behavior can be classified are frequently confused. On the one hand we have a distinction between current and remote behavior, and on the other a distinction between actual and possible behavior. An example of actual, current behavior is the movements of my fingers as I type this sentence. An example of current possible behavior is the movements my fingers would have made if I had phrased the sentence differently. An example of actual remote behavior is any of the actions I have actually carried out in the past or that I will actually carry out at any time preceding the moment I die. An example of possible remote behavior is the behavior of some as yet unstudied creature, including creatures as yet unevolved or unknown. Because the principle of reinforcement is completely and meaningfully generalizable, it can be applied to all four categories of behavior.

Boyer's argument can be applied to Skinner's treatment of language.[22] Skinner took the sentence as the fundamental linguistic unit. By avoiding taking the word as the fundamental linguistic unit and by assuming that linguistic structure had to be given priority over content, he preempted criticisms that behaviorists misunderstood the nature of language. He also directly incorporated pragmatics into his theory. Even more to the point, he used his theory of language to deliver a frontal attack against mentalism; language's fundamental role was to serve not as the vehicle of expression for putative agents but as a means of controlling behavior, whether intra- or inter-individually.

Skinner's creation and deployment of a specifically linguistic operant, the autoclitic, allows us to appreciate the scope and depth of his critique of mentalism. He defined autoclitics as follows: "We shall refer to such responses [Skinner's examples include: 'I see that . . .,' 'I demand . . .,' or 'I am tempted to add . . .'], when associated with other verbal behavior effective upon the same listener at the same time, as 'descriptive autoclitics.' The term 'autoclitic' is intended to suggest behavior which is based upon or depends upon other verbal behavior."[23]

Skinner's examples of autoclitics are all examples of the operation of intentionality. As Daniel Dennett says, intention concerns *aboutness* (that is, intentions point to objects or events), while to talk about intentional states entails attributing rationality to the holder of those states. We express intentions by using phrases such as "believes that," "knows that," "expects (that)," "wants (it to be the case that)," and "understands (that)." The object of such assertions (expressed linguistically by sentences like "he is honest") is treated, it is assumed, as a mental state by both the speaker and the listener(s). Skinner, then, had to deal with the issues of agency and choice.

In addition, linguists such as Noam Chomsky maintain that Skinner's theory cannot deal with syntax.[24] In syntax we seem to see acts of deliberate creation. Moreover, the act of creation in its totality must, it seems, precede what is created. For example, in the sentence "All the people who live next door are unbearably noisy," the selection of *all* at the beginning of the sentence determines the choice of *are* rather than *is* near the sentence's end. Chomsky claims that, given the vast number of specific transitions from word to word occurring in segments of running speech, we cannot explain the acquisition and comprehension of grammatically correct speech by appealing to the processes of rote learning, reinforcement, and generalization. We therefore have to assume that language users are agents acting as the conduits for language-specific rule systems.

Skinner simply and elegantly disposed of the problems of intentionality and syntax. He treated speakers as interacting sets of dispositions. Within a speaker, one set of dispositions could influence another. In expressions of intentionality the phrase "I believe . . .," emerging from one dispositional set, acts on the sentence "He is honest," emerging from another. The primary function of the utterance "I believe . . ." is to show a listener that the sentence "He is honest" should be taken as a description of the types of relationship that have held and will hold between the speaker and the person referred to. Statements of intentionality have two secondary functions. An extra-individual secondary function is the triggering of expressions of agreement or disagreement with a proposition. An intra-individual secondary function is to differentiate self-directed statements or thoughts (like "Oh! So he's honest," which could be the expression of a sudden recognition of someone's honesty) from other-directed statements.

Initially I can illustrate the strength of Skinner's position on syntax by discussing his treatment of grammatical quantifiers (such as *the*, *a*, or *all*). To take one of his examples, in "All swans are white" it seems that *all* refers to *swans*. Since all possible swans cannot be the object of perception, we are forced to assume, apparently, that *swans* refers to some mental entity. Skinner answers the criticism by maintaining that *all* modifies the entire sentence, which is an object with physical expression. As in the case of intentionality, the speaker uses *all* to signal the activation of particular dispositions (to point to or discuss exemplars of various species of swan, to discuss the principle of induction, and so on). The same argument, *mutatis mutandis*, applies to all the grammatical quantifiers.

We can then generalize the argument to cover all syntax. Any language shows characteristic patterns of ordering the fundamental grammatical units: subject, verb, and object. A paradigm of the fundamental English sentence is "Doggie eat cookies." Young children learn progressively to expand and modify that elementary schema. It is easy to derive sentences that are grammatically correct and semantically precise from such core examples (for example, the difference between "That doggie eats cookies" and "Most dogs eat cookies"). One can also combine basic forms by using the appropriate grammatical markers. We can combine the three sentences "The dog likes cookies," "The dog is greedy," and "The dog lives next door" into "The greedy dog that lives next door likes cookies." We also know that caretakers deliberately simplify their speech to young children. At the same time, they massively model simple basic structures and key relationships such as subject-of and subject/predicate boundaries. Furthermore, caretakers and children work in close synchrony. Both in their speech and during self-initiated linguistic play children over-rehearse familiar forms and try out novel ones. In the latter case, they are signaling caretakers that they are ready to move up a step in linguistic complexity. In essence, therefore, the principles of reinforcement and generalization apply to the acquisition of linguistic structure.

The concept of the autoclitic demonstrated that Skinner could explain possible remote behavior. We start with Skinner's presumption that language was concerned with social control. Social control demands shared norms and devices; syntactical rules are examples of such norms or devices. A mentalist believes that the rules themselves, together with the basis for deriving the rules, have to be represented in the minds of speakers and listeners. In differentiating the form of the English relative pronoun in the two cases "I know the man who lives next door" and "A man whom I know lives next door," a Chomskyan supposes that native speakers of English all know that both complex sentences can be decomposed into two simple sentences (in the first case, "I know the man" and "The man lives next door"; in the second case, "A man lives next door" and "I know him [the man]"). Speakers, furthermore, supposedly recognize that in the first sentence, the relative pronoun refers to the subject of the subordinate clause, whereas in the second it refers to the object of the subordinate clause. So speakers choose *who* in the first sentence and *whom* in the second. Skinner neatly sidestepped any need to refer to supposed underlying mental states. As a consequence of extensive modeling, children in highly literate families learn by rote correlations between relative positions of words in a sentence (the chief way grammatical subjects and grammatical objects are designated in English), the form of the pronoun, and the form of the relative pronoun. Effective communication among that privileged group of speakers demands the maintenance of those correlations. Hence they will be observed. In summary, then, the autoclitic is a powerful philosophico-linguistic device. On the one hand, it is plastic and can be applied to any of the world's languages. On the other, it is tightly defined and can be given specific manifestations in those languages.

Elsewhere I have demonstrated that Skinner's theory of animal behavior was conceptually and empirically bankrupt.[25] However, here I will suggest, on a preliminary basis, that the theory could plausibly be applied to a tightly constrained area of behavior. I will then demonstrate that further consideration shows us we must deny even this very limited role to the theory.

I will start my analysis by referring to a curious passage in the second volume of Skinner's autobiography:

> The lever, as a discriminative stimulus, is important (we can take it away to prevent the occurrence of the behavior), but the control it exerts when present depends upon the deprivation. As an example, assume that a man smokes a pipe because of certain reinforcing consequences; how can we make him more or less likely to smoke? We can prevent smoking by taking the pipe away, but if there is any control when it is available, it will be through some kind of satiation or deprivation.[26]

Skinner seemed to be advancing a circular and absurd argument. Behavior, according to him, occurred only under the control of a drive. Therefore, whenever we saw an example of behavior we had to assert that it was controlled by a drive specific to that behavior. I think that we can save Skinner from circularity and absurdity by recalling that he defined drive in terms of operations set up by the experimenter. As a result, his theory of drive could not be applied to the actions of free-living animals or to those aspects of laboratory behavior that were powerfully controlled by natural sources of motivation. But experimenters could set up what Tolman called "demands" within an animal or a person. Once such a demand had been brought into being, I will assert, one could explain subsequent behavior in terms of operant behavior. Let me illustrate what I mean by referring to the work on experimentally induced communication in chimpanzees by Savage-Rumbaugh and her colleagues.[27] The study is crucial because it is the only one that shows, quite unequivocally, that apes can exchange information via symbols.

The study was divided into three stages. In the first, the chimpanzees learned to request tools; in the second they learned to name the tools; in the third they learned to exchange the roles of requester and observer. One chimpanzee (the observer) responded to symbols (the names for tools) keyed onto a computer screen by the other chimpanzee (the requester). Each tool was specific to a particular box, which contained a banana. The observer selected the named tool and passed it to the requester, who then opened the box.

I think that there is no doubt that Savage-Rumbaugh and her coauthors did demonstrate that the communication between their subjects was intentional. The demonstration led one of the commentators on their work to write, "the visual patterns used in the keyboard system had mental associations with the objects."[28] Intentionality, however, does not necessarily entail cognitions. On the contrary, a Skinnerian could argue that the behavior of the chimpanzees is fully consistent with a radical behaviorist analysis. When we say that the requester intended the observer to comply with his request for a tool we mean that the requester set in motion a chain of behavior that had the ultimate reinforcing consequence that the required tool was presented to him. In the particular case we are dealing with, it is crucial to note that each component of the chain had been mastered by each chimpanzee by a rigorously prescribed course of training. Thus it is not necessary to say that the requester used his newly acquired symbolic behavior to represent the desired end to himself before engaging in the behavior designed to secure that end. As Zuriff comments, "Just as not all behavior is rule-governed, so not all intentional behavior is preceded by a verbal statement of intention. Therefore, it is a mistake to extrapolate from prototype cases of human intentional action which include verbal responses to all cases of intentional action."[29] Any attempt to maintain that Savage-Rumbaugh and her associates induced cognitions in their subjects would have to use a version of the no-particular-behavior argument. That is, a cognitive psychologist would have to produce evidence that cognitions led some life independently of the behavior with which they are associated. The only source for such evidence is verbal reports, and it is unlikely that chimpanzees will ever reach the stage of describing their own cognitions. Even if they were to reach that stage it is likely that their verbalizations, whether overt or covert, would have the simple function of controlling ongoing behavior in the ways described by Staats.[30]

Here I have demonstrated that Skinner's theory can explain complex, symbolic processes in higher animals. My critique of his theory of animal behavior showed that, at best, it plays a subordinate role in offering explanations for the behavior of lower animals engaged in relatively simple behavior (trial-and-error learning).[31] In the case of lower animals it seems that response-reinforcer relationships controlled by the consequences of actions interact in a complex way with stimulus-reinforcer relationships. In general, any predictions the theory makes about particular sequences of behavior have to be placed in a broader theoretical context. The broader context is the field of animal behavior as a whole. Once the relationships between the specific domains in which the theory is effective and that broader context have been established, I argue, it should be possible for radical behaviorism to play an effective, but subordinate, role. To sustain that role, radical behaviorists would have to define the areas in which the theory operates effectively and collaborate with others in order to discover the relationships between the subordinate and the superordinate domains.

I can illustrate what I mean in principle by referring to my analysis of the study by Savage-Rumbaugh et al. I will suggest that there is a difference between the role of the reinforcement when it promotes the survival of a species and its role when it promotes the immediate benefit of an individual member of a species. In the latter case the principle can operate only via a prolonged process of trial and error. During that process the animal must be nurtured and protected from predation. The life cycle of all species of apes is characterized by a lengthy period of dependency on adults. It is precisely in such species that one would expect the evolution of brain mechanisms that monitor the progress of successful and unsuccessful sequences of behavior.

In contrast, what we would expect from lower-level species are repertoires of behaviors for the elicitation of drive-controlled behaviors controlled by physiological states. Once the thresholds of the physiological states are low enough, the behaviors are triggered by particular stimulus configurations (releasers). The drive-controlled behaviors are released in order to force animals to restore some state of equilibrium (the behavior is part of the states and activities designed to maintain homeostasis). In a natural environment, release of the behavior is typically sufficient to ensure that there is a return to homeostasis. The acquisition of new responses is almost entirely under the control of stimulus-reinforcer relationships. The role of those relationships is to allow animals to increase the range of releasers that will elicit those drive-controlled behaviors designed to promote survival. Once a new response has been acquired, it can be maintained by response-reinforcer relationships. The function of response-reinforcer relationships in lower animals is to maintain a response "on course" by monitoring response feedback. It must be stressed that the feed-back is into a system whose adaptive function has been preestablished.

To sum up, I seem to be claiming that Skinner's theory is highly effective. By taking an apparently clear-cut case of intentionality at the subhuman level I have shown that, precisely because the intentionality was instilled into the chimpanzees laboriously and step-by-step, a Skinnerian can, quite justifiably, conclude that one should apply Ockham's razor and explain the behavior in terms of rote learning and reinforcement. Previously I had made the case that Skinner's treatment of language abolishes the necessity to appeal to intentions or other mental constructs. However, I will now undercut my own position by arguing that the theory's strengths are purely schematic and formal. I will demonstrate, first, that we do have to appeal to intentionality in order to explain spontaneous behavior in free-living primates. If we must appeal to intentionality at that level we must appeal to it in humans. Finally, I will show that the theory is acceptable only if one makes several implausible assumptions.

Up to this point I have argued that radical behaviorism was a useful theory but only in a few strictly delimited domains. To say that actions are under operant control is to say that actions are controlled by response feedback.[32] There was no need to assume that such feedback was evaluated in any way, according to Skinner, because one could devise experimental situations in which such evaluation manifestly did not occur, as in "concept formation" in pigeons.[33] Since concept formation lies at the apex of human cognitive achievements and since the pigeons' behavioral end product was descriptively identical to that of humans, we should conclude, according to Skinnerians, that the same causes operated in the two cases. The same argument applied, *mutatis mutandis*, to all human cognitions. So we have no need for rationality or consciousness.

To dispose of Skinner's theory, one must argue that it cannot explain the actions of lower animals (because the principle of operant conditioning cannot explain instinctive behavior) and that it cannot account for human mental life (because human cognitions and actions are embedded in and controlled by a complex cognitive framework). But I also suggested that we might save Skinner's theory by applying it to complex, nonlinguistically controlled cognitive acts, especially the seemingly intentional and rational behavior that we see in monkeys and apes. At the heart of my argument lay the assertion that Skinner's theory works here because it is precisely in such cases that we are able to create and monitor the course of a particular set of reinforcers. The precise specification of what was done then becomes, as Skinner demanded, the sole satisfactory explanation for the outcome.

To understand Skinner's position, one has to see how it contrasts with the cognitive psychologists' explanation for action. Skinner appealed to the history of past reinforcements; a cognitivist appeals to representations, decisions, and intentions. A cognitivist assumes that the mental is ontologically distinct from the physical. Mind differs from body because mind has the power to represent physical reality and perform operations (intentions and decisions) on representations.[34] For the present argument, a crucial assumption is that operations can be performed on representations of representations. The assumption abolishes the need for feedback loops (reinforcers) connecting each action, however abbreviated, with the physical world. We can then describe situations in which actions can be contemplated, assessed, but never undertaken, and, more to the point, situations in which one mind assesses and endeavors to influence events in another mind.

The issue to be addressed, then, is how a rational being arrives at decisions. Radical behaviorists believe that those who say that human or animal actions are guided by wants, desires, intentions, or beliefs are mistaken. For a radical behaviorist, to want or desire something is to seek that which has secured positive reinforcement in the past; to intend to do something is to be guided by one's history of past reinforcements; and to believe something is to produce verbalizations (whether explicit or implicit) that reflect one's past history of reinforcements.

In order to evaluate Skinner's position, I will concentrate on animal examples. I will do that because we know that even chimpanzees cannot talk to themselves. So it cannot be the case that animals consciously evaluate the consequence of their decisions. But if we can conclude that effective decision making occurs even in the lowest animals and that a radical behaviorist can offer only unconvincing explanations for these actions, we can conclude that it is possible that nonconscious decision making not under the causal control of language occurs in human beings as well. Given the evolutionary continuity between animal and human cognitive processes, one can then argue that conscious control of decision making inevitably emerged at some stage in the evolutionary process.

Dennett has suggested that ethologists can ask penetrating and fruitful questions about decision making in animals.[35] In order to develop a nonbehaviorist theory of decision making we have to address the issue of intention. Dennett makes the extremely fruitful observation that the best support for intentionality in animals must come from anecdotal evidence that emerges from prolonged observation of the behavior of particular species. Only in this way can we overcome the endemic circularity of behaviorist arguments. The behaviorist insists that the only acceptable evidence is that derived from repeated observation of selected behaviors under controlled conditions. But it is precisely such behavior that is susceptible to behaviorist explanations and nothing other than behaviorist explanations. Conversely, any candid and intelligent observer of animal behavior knows that it is the unexpected and novel that gives one the most powerful insights into the nature of animal action systems, given that those insights arise from a context of observation of the banal and quotidian. Contemporary work on the social and mental life of nonhuman primates supports this view. For example, Barbara Smuts has shown, quite incontrovertibly, that baboons entertain mental states and that, more to the point, their actions are controlled by those states.[36] Dorothy Cheney and Robert Seyfarth have carefully analyzed both field and laboratory studies of cognitions in apes and monkeys. Again, they conclude that apes show intentionality and that monkeys possibly do.[37]

Skinner's approach to theory can be criticized on three points. First, he had no justification for generalizing from his particular research practices to behavior and systems of action in general. Second, he conflated a functional analysis with a causal analysis. Third, his values, although purportedly derived from his research practices, were primary and guided the research and theory in an unacknowledged and unrecognized way.

With respect to the first issue, Skinner wanted to apply his explanatory principles to specific situations. In order to do that, he had to closely specify the nature of the situations and the mode of application of the principles. Skinner designed the Skinner box because, if we are to believe his own account, it gave him very close control over the behavior of free-moving laboratory animals without subjecting them to the same constraints they suffered in conventional pieces of apparatus (such as mazes or discrimination chambers). What he then did was to apply principles derived from his data beyond the laboratory by arguing from analogy (for example, in the famous analogy between the behavior generated by fixed ratio schedules and piecework). But arguments from analogy are extremely weak. What Skinner needed was a theory that would have justified his extrapolations. But his approach denied him access to such a theory. Further reflection shows, moreover, that one can use the principle of operant conditioning as an explanatory principle only if one has created beforehand a situation in which operant principles must apply. Skinner's theory is thus corrosively constrictive.

With respect to the second issue, Skinner consistently criticized those who demanded theories of causality because, in his eyes, any appeal to causal principles involves one in an infinite regress. He failed to realize that reliance on nothing but functional relationships involves one in equally profound difficulties. Suppose, for example, that a biologist establishes a relationship between mean size of territory and the supply of nutrients in a particular species of bird. It is then reasonable to suppose that members of that species defend a territory in order to ensure an adequate food supply. But we are still no closer to understanding the processes of territorial defense (which signals trigger which forms of territorial defense, when the signals exert a triggering effect, by what mechanisms the signals exert their effect, and how the triggering mechanisms are related to one another). In the same way, a Skinnerian can easily generate relationships between particular schedules of reinforcement and particular patterns of behavior. But the issue of how and why a given schedule exerts its effect is left open. Furthermore, by proposing the principle of reinforcement as the universal and necessary explanation for behavior, Skinner committed the logical fallacy of affirming the consequent. The only explanatory constructs that Skinnerians have at their disposal are antecedent conditions, and that which is to be explained are behavioral outcomes. Skinnerians then assume that, given that particular outcomes are, in laboratory situations, inevitably correlated with particular antecedent conditions, the antecedent conditions suffice as explanations. What they fail to realize is that identical outcomes can, in principle, be produced by widely different causes. For example, a former colleague (a dedicated Skinnerian) once told me that he had one of his sons (then a preschooler) operating a Skinner box on a variable interval schedule. My colleague asked his son why he was doing what he was doing and the child replied, "Because I know I have to, Daddy." Of course, any Skinnerian would say that the child was mistaken and that really he was operating under precisely the same constraints as a rat or a pigeon. But the belief that the child was mistaken is open to verification, and Skinner's theory offers us no means of doing so.

Let me take a simple example to illustrate what I mean. If two humans were performing an experimental task, one might say to the other, "Wow! This is fun. I wonder what we'll get to do next?" No matter to what level of sophistication one brought a chimpanzee, I think it is clear from the available evidence that it would never make such an utterance. If it were to do so, the complex set of presuppositions that surround any human utterance would have to be available to it. Many of those presuppositions are nonlinguistic, but because they are shared between speaker and listeners, they help to determine particular meanings. Among the presuppositions lying behind the utterance I quoted is the understanding that the task is part of a program of research, so that it lies in a somewhat indefinite area halfway between play and work. In addition, the speaker and listener share the expectation that it is possible to devise similar tasks.

Human language, then, occurs within a highly complex self-induced and self-monitored cognitive network. Of course it is possible to argue that the network is set up and maintained by a process of reinforcement. But given the complexity of the context of the specific meanings of even simple utterances and the speed and accuracy with which humans assess and use those contexts, it seems preferable to appeal to modeling and other modes of internal representations for an explanation.

What is ultimately at stake, then, is the context of meanings in which actions take place. In the Skinnerian laboratory, the context of meaning is one of rigid control of carefully prespecified actions and settings for those actions. In free-living lower animals, the context of meaning is provided by the ecological niche to which any given species has become adapted and the instinctively controlled processes and mechanisms that mediate adaptation. In the higher primates the context for action is complex, subtle, fluid, and, ultimately, unique to each individual.

Finally, I will assert that Skinner's values were a set of pre-theoretical assumptions that were incorporated into unstated axioms from which the principles guiding his theory and his research practices were derived. The axioms were, first, a commitment to positivism (the data language had to be concrete and had to refer only to observable events) and, second, the belief that animals and humans were guided by a very narrowly focused form of individualistic utilitarianism. Skinner believed, in effect, that organisms would perform an act if and only if it brought immediate gain. Effectively, Skinnerians place laboratory animals under constraints that satisfy those principles. They then conclude that their data and their laws of behavior fully explain all human behavior, with no exceptions whatsoever. Above all, the research practices purportedly justify programs of social action. But the real basis for those programs lies in the unacknowledged values that controlled the research in the first place.

By adopting the role of a polemicist-technologist, Skinner actively promoted those values. With the publication of *The Behavior of Organisms* in 1938, Skinner's theory and attendant research practices had been fully worked out. Given his lack of interest in psychology's subject matter and his scornful attitude to its professional life, he had little desire to thrust his way to the discipline's commanding heights by expanding his paradigm. Furthermore, he had just completed a long applied project (Project Pigeon). There he had tried, unsuccessfully, to persuade the U.S. air force to use a guidance system for bombs operated by trained pigeons. In the second volume of his autobiography Skinner wrote of Project Pigeon that "The research that I described in *The Behavior of Organisms* appeared in a new light. It was no longer merely an experimental analysis. It had given rise to a technology."[38] In addition, he had been involved in attempts to market the Air-Crib (the baby-tending device in which his second daughter, Debbie, had been reared as an infant).

Skinner's values and his theory of society are most fully expressed in his novel, *Walden Two*. Although Skinner wrote *Walden Two* very quickly (it took him seven weeks), the actual writing was preceded by a fairly long and thorough preparatory period. The immediate impetus for writing the novel came from discussions with a group of friends at the University of Minnesota. Before that, Skinner had read Elizabeth Tyler's *Freedom's Ferment*, an account of ideologically driven communities in America.[39] He also read some utopian novels, especially Edward Bellamy's *Looking Backward*.[40]

Given that, by 1945, there is evidence that Skinner was beginning to place more value on the populist exposition of social technologies than on academic research, and given that he was preparing himself fairly thoroughly for that role, we have to set *Walden Two* in its intellectual framework. It is not just a utopian novel, but a utopian novel that can be situated within a very particular genre, which Howard Segal calls the technological utopia.[41] In America there is quite a long tradition of technological utopian writings (Segal lists over twenty works published between 1883 and 1933). He makes the point that only in America did one see an equation between the inevitability of progress and progress as technological. Segal's utopian authors saw technology as the sole panacea of social ills; Skinner was very firmly a part of that tradition.

Skinner was part of the American technological utopian tradition in a more important sense. All the technological utopian writers revered work and subordinated academic knowledge to knowledge directed to useful ends. In King Camp Gillette's *People's Corporation*, all the inhabitants of his utopia served in an industrial army, led by those whose merit earned them a place at the top of the social pyramid.[42] As in the case of *Walden Two*, this meritocratic structure mysteriously absolved the inhabitants of the necessity of engaging in political life.

Segal also makes an interesting point about the obscurity of the writers whose work he surveys.[43] He says that normally the writer of a utopian novel aims to radicalize his readers by displaying the defects of existing society and positing some alternative (as William Morris did in his *News from Nowhere*, for example). In American utopian novels, in contrast, we see the uttering of received truths in a slightly outré form, so that they attracted few readers. *Walden Two*, as we will see shortly, can also be interpreted as a vehicle for the expression of the commonplace.

Finally, Alan Elms persuasively argues that the writing of *Walden Two* involved a strong personal component. In 1945 Skinner was undergoing a fairly severe personal crisis. Project Pigeon had proved to be abortive, the sales of *The Behavior of Organisms* were extremely low, and Skinner had accepted the headship of the department of psychology at Indiana University, so that he and his wife would be leaving behind a large circle of friends.[44] Elms suggests that the writing of his novel allowed Skinner to exercise a series of wish fulfillments. In the novel he drew a portrait of an agreeable social environment characterized by low-key, pleasant social relationships (according to Elms, a disguised representation of the situation that the Skinners were about to leave).[45] According to Elms, the novel's central character, Frazier, is someone whose administrative achievements lie behind him and who is free both to contemplate his work and to leave day-to-day decision making to others (whereas Skinner was, for the first time, about to embark on an administrative phase in his life). Finally, Frazier controls human beings' lives, whereas up to that point, Skinner had supervised the lives of mere rats and pigeons.

Formally, *Walden Two* is a typical utopian novel. That is, it merely provides a vehicle for a central character (Frazier in this case) to discourse about the principles underlying the construction of an ideal community. The other characters react in various ways to what they hear and see. Even major novelists like H. G. Wells (in his *Men Like Gods*) have followed this format, which makes for rather dull fiction because there is little action of any interest, while the characters are mere cardboard cutouts.[46]

The major themes in Frazier's discourse are the following. First, he asserts that everything we know about human nature can be not just discovered but very clearly categorized and organized. Second, he claims that *all* human behavior can be modified, given the appropriate technology. As Frazier says, "It requires all the techniques of applied psychology, from the various ways of keeping in touch with opinions and attitudes to the educational and persuasive practices which shape the individual from the cubicle to the grave. Experimentation . . . not reason." For example, one of the visitors to Walden Two, Burris, asks, "How many geniuses can you expect to get from such a limited assortment of genes?" Frazier replies, "Is that a pun? Or do you really think that geniuses come from genes? Well, maybe they do. But how close have we got to making the most of our genes? That's the real question."

Third, the modifications should all be in the direction of making people more socially efficient and more productive, so that they become happier. One of Frazier's most proudly brandished achievements is the four-hour working day at Walden Two. Fourth, the principles of efficiency are applied to education. Frazier says,

> Since our children remain happy, energetic and curious, we don't need to teach "subjects" at all. We teach only the techniques of learning and thinking. As for geography, literature, the sciences—we give our children opportunity and guidance, and they learn them for themselves. In that way we dispense with half the teachers required under the old system, and the edu-

cation is incomparably better. Our children aren't neglected, but they're seldom, if ever, *taught* anything.[47]

Fifth, as Frazier's little speech implies, the emphasis in *Walden Two* is on applied, not pure, knowledge. Indeed, at one point Frazier says that pure science is merely a leisure activity. The technocratization of life extends to the organization of society in Walden Two and to the political sphere. The community is divided into four groups—Planners, Scientists, Managers, and Workers. Each group has clearly assigned functions. The Planners are people like Frazier who enunciate various principles of social technology but without specifying how those principles should be put into action. The Scientists test and modify the principles, the Managers put them into action, and the Workers actualize the principles. Each group, supposedly, recognizes and accepts its place in the hierarchy. There is no room for and no need for any political organizations or processes (or, indeed, for any feedback from the lower strata of society to the higher). Because the principles formulated at the apex of society guarantee the Good Life for all, any form of political discussion would interfere with the efficiency of society. In a truly efficient society, everyone will attain the good life, which Skinner defines as the gaining of health, the securing of the absolute minimum of physical labor, the chance to exercise talents and abilities, the possibility of having intimate and satisfying personal contacts, the abolishing of attitudes of domination and criticism, and the attainment of relaxation and rest.

The sixth and final theme of *Walden Two* is the distrust of emotion.[48] The distrust emerges in both minor and major ways. For example, one of the visiting group, Mary, demonstrates an embroidery stitch. Burris comments, "But as the group broke up, I was conscious of the fact that no one thanked her or expressed gratitude in any other way. This, I later discovered, was in accordance with the Walden Two code."[49] We see there a distrust of the expression of emotion, combined with an implicit suggestion that distance and formality are preferable to warmth and intimacy in social relations. In another passage Frazier expresses much more clearly his fear of the potentially disruptive power of emotion:

> "Surely that's going too far!" said Castle. "You can't be so godlike as that! You must be assailed by emotions just as much as the rest of us!"

"We can discuss the question of godlikeness later, if you wish," replied Frazier. "As to emotions—we aren't free of them all, nor should we like to be. But the meaner and more annoying—the emotions which breed unhappiness—are almost unknown here, like unhappiness itself. We don't need them any longer in our struggle for existence, and it's easier on our circulatory system, and certainly pleasanter, to dispense with them."[50]

Skinner seemed to view emotion as an irruption of untamed nature into his ordered social schemes.[51] That distrust shows the extent to which Skinner and his fellow technological utopians wanted to restructure human mental life. As the incident involving Mary's demonstration of the embroidery stitch shows, Skinner's suspicions extended to the benevolent emotions. It is as if he feared that to give oneself over to warmth, love, affection, or general feelings of benevolence was to weaken the barriers against the spontaneous and unexpected. If we take the example of the baby-tender in which Debbie was reared, Skinner, the well-meaning father, was providing an environment of his devising that would lower Debbie's threshold for action and dispositions of which Skinner could approve. That is, although Skinner had Debbie's interests in mind, it was he who decided what those interests should be. In the same way, we cannot doubt that Frazier was well disposed toward the inhabitants of Walden Two. But his kindliness did not extend to consulting them about their needs, especially their more deeply felt aspirations or yearnings.[52]

The distrust of emotions shows how theory and practice interacted in Skinner's thought. We can contrast his theory with Freud's. For Freud, the study of human emotional life was the core of his theory. The emotions were the source of energy for all human endeavors, provided a limitless source of data, and, given the inherent ambiguity of human emotions, engendered salutary humility in the theorist. Ambiguity and uncertainty were anathema to Skinner, largely because he placed practice and application above theory. One cannot found a program, especially a program that is to be largely carried out by subordinates, on ambiguity and uncertainty. As any good administrator knows, outbursts of emotion create situations that have to be managed on an ad hoc basis. Skinner's solution was to do away with the need for ad hoccery by controlling emotions at their source (that is, by socializing people appropriately from infancy onward).

The determination to control also showed itself in Skinner's treatment of the political fabric of Walden Two. Like the Progressives, he was extremely suspicious of politics; it was too haphazard but also too crucial to be left to the hazy intuitions of the populace and the manipulations of the politicians. As Kumar comments,

> [Skinner] is at once less political than many utopian writers, and at the same time a good deal more concerned with political control than most. Skinner's utopia is conveniently apolitical in rejecting government because government means coercion, and "you can't force a man to be happy." It is also apolitical, to a startling degree, in its innocent contemplation of the means by which utopia will be achieved. Most modern utopias assume a considerable degree of conflict and struggle in the achievement of utopian goals. . . . For Skinner, however, utopia in the form of Walden Two is to be had more or less for the asking. "Any group of men of good will can work out a satisfactory life with the existing political structures of half a dozen modern governments."
>
> Government can simply be ignored. "All we ask is to be left alone." This apolitical quietism as to means, however, by no means extends to the ends of Walden Two. It soon turns out that hostility to government is of a very qualified kind. Walden Two . . . is not anarchist. "I am not arguing for no government at all, but only for none of the existing forms." What [Skinner's spokesman] in fact objects to in current forms of government is not so much that they are coercive as that they lack proper control. That indeed is why they are coercive: "Governments which use force are based upon bad principles of human engineering." Their intervention is clumsy and haphazard. They cannot experiment, and so they never learn. Power is passed from one group to another which repeats the errors of its predecessor. The requirement is clear: "We want a government based upon a science of human behaviour."
>
> We have, therefore, to see that there is after all government in Walden Two: quite a lot of it, by conventional standards. But it is government reduced—or elevated—to the function of planning and management, such that to members of the community politics in the old sense has little meaning and virtually no existence. Walden Two carries into effect the Saint-Simonian slogan picked up by some nineteenth-century Marxists and anarchists: "from the government of men to the administration of things". But as critics . . . were quick to point out you do not remove politics or political power by calling it administration.[53]

Even in face-to-face communes, government (especially participatory democracy) is necessary. The point emerges clearly from the experiences of those who established Twin Oaks, a commune based directly on Skinnerian principles. Kathleen Kincade, one of the founders, writes,

> What keeps our system from turning into a tiresome bureaucracy is its simplicity—that decisions can be made by at most three people, and usually by a single manager, using his or her own judgment. What keeps it from being a dictatorship is that there is nothing to gain from dictatorial decisions. All decisions that are of interest to the group as a whole are discussed with the group as a whole. No legislation can be put across unless members are willing to go along with it. There is no police force here to carry out anybody's will. Our only technique is persuasion.[54]

What Kincade describes bears no resemblance to Walden Two, where all decisions were preplanned.

Control was the dominant force driving Skinner's theory and research. The animal laboratory was a precise simulacrum of society. Its work, Skinnerian views of society, and Skinnerian technologies were strictly controlled by prior unstated theoretical commitments. If we take two crucial types of fact, response and reinforcer, both had circular definitions in Skinner's theory. Thus "response" was defined in terms of frequency of output, that is, work carried out by the animal. That work, in turn, was meaningful only if it was under the control of a schedule of reinforcement. Schedules of reinforcement represented paradigm social situations. Social forms were incorporated into the foundations of the theory *ab initio*, not derived from it. The famous variable interval schedule, for example, where food or water is dispensed randomly to a rat or a pigeon, ensured prolonged and steady rates of responding. The human analogue for a Skinnerian would be any number of social situations in which reward is dispensed at widely spaced and unpredictable intervals of time (by teaching staff to students and by deans and department heads to their staff, for example). Skinner and his followers assumed that rewards impinged directly on actions. Nowadays we know that in animals, the rewards exert their influence via biologically determined brain or mental structures. In the same way, rewards influence human actions only within social structures that operate equally on the dispensers and the recipients of those rewards.

Skinner imposed the exigencies of his values on the animal scientists who applied his theory. The laboratory was a place where what one might call transitivity of docility was instilled into neophyte social scientists. In shaping animals in a Skinner box, the students learned patiently to extract the required behavior from their animal subjects. That process taught them, and those who applied the theory, techniques of teaching others (schoolchildren, convicts, or mental defectives, for example) to subjugate themselves to the imperatives of the social engineer and thereby to the needs of an imagined society.

The ultimate vacuity of Skinner's theory emerges starkly in this passage from Kathleen Kincade. Commenting on the concept of reinforcement as applied in social situations, she writes,

> We know that the approval of our peers is a powerful reinforcer. Also, peaceful and pleasant human relations are reinforcing. . . . That throws the area of behavioral engineering open to the consideration of all techniques that have ever been used for social control: law, admonition, persuasion, encounter groups. Under the general heading, "It is reinforcing to get along together," we can try anything that looks as if it might help and legitimately call it behavioral engineering. Thus, if we try some encounter techniques invented by Skinner's theoretical opponents, we are not thereby placing ourselves in some philosophical camp that is inconsistent with our admiration for behaviorism.[55]

There is no need to comment on that passage, beyond saying that the ultimate rebuttal of any theory is to have it consigned to oblivion by one of its supporters.[56]

The circularity in the definition of the key terms in the theory resulted from its deductive nature. All statements derived from the theory (especially descriptions of research findings and practices to be followed in applied settings) therefore had a merely internal justification. Only if he could make social reality conform to his theory of human nature could Skinner hope to present empirical justification for his social technology. So we can treat *Walden Two* as a prolonged wish fulfillment.

The novel was not a mere *divertissement*. If we assess it in terms of its public impact we can see that Skinner was struggling to resolve the ambiguity between the scientist/technologist and philosopher/polemicist roles. By disguising serious thoughts as fiction and by partitioning aspects of himself into fictional characters, he could allow the polemicist full rein and give untrammelled expression to his deepest convictions. He could also short-circuit the need to adduce the evidence for his beliefs, the most fundamental aspect of which was that whatever was happening in the animal laboratory had immediate implications for the amelioration of the human condition. The writing of *Walden Two*, furthermore, allowed Skinner to give simultaneous expression to a need for acceptance, a need to rebel, and a need to impose on the world the sort of unique vision that one finds in art. On the negative side, Skinner removed himself from the collective enterprise of science. Skinner the rebel could not operate within the collaborative, consensual social mores of science. On the positive side, he sought a means of affirming a personal vision of human nature and society that would have the force and authentication accorded to scientific truths. By writing a utopian novel he satisfied all his needs. As a writer of a novel, he was accorded the same treatment as other writers of fiction. But because *Walden Two* is a utopian novel, readers are free to assume that the various social devices to be found in it have scientific warrant.[57]

6

Behaviorists as Social Engineers
Behavior Modification Applied to Abnormal Psychology

Psychological behaviorism found its highest and most complete expression in the behavior modification movement. Behavior modifiers believed that psychological abnormalities or dysfunctions could be fully understood in terms of actions and that all actions could be brought under the control of external contingencies. Therapists (or experimentalists) fully controlled the nature and administration of those contingencies, which, behavior modifiers believed, could be applied to all aspects of human mental and social life. Like Watson, behavior modifiers believed that to understand is to predict and control. Their Watsonian treatment of explanation allowed them to convert ideology into science. The principles of behavior modification were not just derived from the principles of classical and operant conditioning, and not just (so it seemed) derived from "laws of behavior" formulated and tested in animal laboratories. Behavior modification had diffuse origins but a common body of theory and a common set of research practices; as in the case of "real science," the idiosyncrasies of the founders did not seem to be expressed in the activities of the large numbers of behavior modifiers working in many countries.

To study the history of behavior modification is to prove that ideology, not science, controlled the movement. The history of behaviorism's role in mental health parallels the history of behaviorism. In both cases, we find an early, frankly ideologically based phase, peaking in the mid-1920s, and a later phase, seemingly based on laboratory work (largely with rats and pigeons), well-formulated theories, and a positivist theory of science, reaching its apogee in the 1960s. The differences between the two phases are more apparent than real. A version of the Progressivist ideology controlled Watson's thinking and projected itself into Hull's and Skinner's thought. That same impulse, albeit in an attenuated and transformed version, pervaded the therapeutic interventions and educational programs of the behaviorists of the 1960s.

There is a conceptual link between early and mature behavior modification. All behaviorists are united in upholding an instrumental theory of value. To be a good citizen is to be an efficient and productive citizen. Watson's supporters and Skinner's followers shared the common belief that if all are efficient and productive then humanist goods (such as a healthy and well-balanced psychic life) will emerge as byproducts of the appropriate modes of socialization. Behaviorists combine an active distrust of humanism with their instrumentalism. They believe that humanism is misconceived because it is elitist and is trapped in traditional modes of thinking. It cannot deal with pressing social problems because its concepts are poorly conceived and lack explanatory or predictive power.

Throughout their history, behaviorists have been united in claiming that society needs concepts and values that are semantically transparent, that have an adequate inductive history (that is, are clearly derived from experience), and that yield definite predictions. Above all, our value system must be thoroughly pragmatic (truths must clearly lead to effective social interventions). Lying behind the behaviorists' contempt for humanism is a robust populism. They believe that all one's meanings should be immediately clear to someone who is reasonably intelligent and literate. They see humanists as those who have inducted themselves into cults (only those who are members can appreciate the full meaning of all the terms used).

In the field of mental health, behaviorists' distrust of humanism is linked to their distrust of and opposition to psychoanalysis. At the same time, behaviorists from Watson onward have recognized that psychoanalysis expresses certain indispensable truths about human nature. In particular, they share psychoanalysts' belief that character or personality is formed very early in life, largely as a consequence of interactions between children and their mothers. However, they strenuously reject the concept of the unconscious (those behaviorists who are prepared to take psychoanalysis seriously claim, like Watson, that unconscious merely means "unstatable") and even more forcefully reject the psychoanalytic belief that the mind is ultimately a *terra incognita*. Behaviorists have tried to "tame" psychoanalysis by defining concepts like regression or defense mechanism operationally and by converting psychoanalysis into a psychic technology.

Instead of espousing humanism, behaviorists adopt a version of scientism. In common with their Progressive forebears, they see science not just as technology but as a technology that must have social applications. Just as they despise humanism, so they despise any characterization of science as the pursuit of pure truth. In the realm of behavioral science, they believe that one can state psychic or social goals clearly, define those goals as objective outcomes, and clearly specify the means whereby those goals can be achieved. This chapter will be devoted to the application of those general goals to the field of mental health.

The origins of behavior modification are to be found in the attempts by American psychologists, mental hygienists, and educators to apply the principles of conditioning to social and psychological problems. These programs had a frankly ideological rationale; they were based neither on theories of conditioning nor on sustained programs of research. The leading proponents of conditioning at this time (William H. Burnham, his student Florence Mateer, and John B. Watson) were content to generalize their limited knowledge of Pavlov's, Bekhterev's, and Krasnogorski's work as widely as possible to human psychology. The ideological framework for the application of the techniques of conditioning to human problems in 1920s America can be construed as a version of scientific Progressivism, expressing itself through the mental hygiene movement. Burnham claimed that the problems of feeblemindedness and insanity could be completely overcome only if wholesome, life-enhancing habits were instilled early in life.[1]

Like Burnham, Watson had connections with the mental hygienists. He knew a wealthy member of the movement, Ethel Sturges Dummer, who sponsored a symposium on education in which Watson was one of the speakers.[2] Like other Progressives of that time, Dummer believed in science's power to create the social conditions leading to a cure for society's ills. "Only through science," she wrote, "may we secure a right public opinion and better procedure."[3]

Because the mental hygiene movement's only source of funding was the Laura Spelman Rockefeller Memorial, the movement eventually came under the latter's control. Those controlling the LSRM (especially Beardsley Ruml and Lawrence K. Frank) preferred a preventive rather than curative approach to social problems. Hence, children and their mothers constituted the target population for ameliorative measures.[4] At the same time, the leading figures in the LSRM, like others associated with late Progressivism, no longer saw the major source of social ills as feeblemindedness; rather, the major problem was the inadequate control of the emotions. Those best equipped to deal with society's ills were, for scientific Progressives, objective, dispassionate, scientifically trained experts.[5]

The mental hygienists' work would have been impossible without broad social support, and that support was certainly forthcoming. Public support in its most direct form came from the LSRM, which was a private charity.[6] At the same time, governments gave both the LSRM and the mental hygienists some assistance.[7] Indirect evidence for support comes from the publishing history of Burnham's book *The Normal Mind*, which was reprinted in 1925, 1926, 1927, 1929, and 1931, suggesting that it was widely read. Moreover, there were connections between the mental hygiene movement and the movement dedicated to the introduction of business methods into the administration of schools, spearheaded by Franklin Bobbitt and Frank Spaulding.[8] In 1903, Burnham wrote, "the same business principles adopted in modern industry should be applied here. . . . The director can buy in the cheapest market because he buys in large quantities and at the most favorable time."[9] Although he was referring solely to financial administration, Burnham (together with other mental hygienists) was dedicated to making the educational process more efficient in terms of cost-effectiveness in the classroom, standardized methods of teaching, and a standardized product. Techniques of conditioning, in principle, met those criteria.

The best-known advocate of conditioning in the 1920s, Watson, had the mental hygienists' support, as shown by the approving references to him in *The Normal Mind*. He also excited a high level of public interest. He wrote numerous articles in journals with a readership comprising a segment of the intellectual public, such as *Harper's*, and made numerous radio broadcasts. Kerry Buckley comments that Watson was America's first popular psychologist and that he brought what seemed to be scientific rigor to social problems.[10]

Another essential determining factor in the role of conditioning was the emergence of an explicitly American psychology that rejected German experimental psychology. It was also characterized by the central role given to comparative psychology, a concern to generate an objective, scientifically based psychology, and an implicit or explicit behaviorism. Crucially, that behaviorism was linked to a concern with practical psychological issues. Although early American psychologists, such as James and Hall, had what seem in retrospect rather florid theories of human instinct, by the 1920s American psychologists on the whole had relegated instincts to at best a peripheral role. Their environmentalism caused them to place the study of habits at psychology's center, while their objectivism and scientism made the conditioned reflex a highly viable candidate for the controlling mechanism in habit.

One can see those features in Frederic L. Wells's *Mental Adjustments*, published in 1913, one of the first books on abnormal psychology to appear in America.[11] With respect to the role of comparative psychology, Wells noted that much more depended on an animal's failure to respond correctly to a nutritionally related cue than on a failure to strike the correct telegraph key in a reaction-time experiment. A consequence of comparative psychology's central role was the stressing of the systematic ontogenetic study of children. The expected outcome of such studies was the tracing of the ontogeny of habits, especially maladaptive ones. Wells did not anticipate discovering any significant instinctive patterns; he argued that environment will almost inevitably overcome heredity.[12]

A behavioristic, objectivist, societally directed, pragmatic functionalism underpinned Wells's position. He wrote, "What distinguishes true ideas from false ones is simply that true ideas are represented in conduct by useful reactions, and false ideas by wasteful ones." At the same time, everything we do, no matter how trivial, must serve some social purpose.[13] Wells exploited the prevailing associationistic theory in psychology and advanced what amounted to a conditioning theory to explain phobias: "If an experience is associated with a pronounced affect or emotion, of whatever character, that affect or emotion will tend to become associated with other experiences themselves connected to the first experience," and "The essential thing is to conceive the emotional process as a *reaction*."[14] He also prefigured the concerns of the behaviorists in another respect. Throughout his book he propounded a behaviorist version of psychoanalysis that stressed the role of psychic mechanisms in producing both adaptive and maladaptive behavioral patterns. In that version Wells accepted without question Freud's belief that basic personality structures were established permanently very early in life. Given his objectivist stance, Wells had to avoid appealing to covert explanatory mechanisms, such as repression.[15]

Watson and Burnham took the new American psychology and directed it toward societal problems by making the mother the sole agent of socialization and by making the conditioned reflex the mechanism that she unwittingly used. Watson's views on the role of the mother as the involuntary creator of psychoneuroses needs to be seen in the context of his broader ontogenetic principles. Basing himself on William James, Watson claimed that human beings consisted of a mass of habits, some prepotent, others suppressed, and yet others vestigial or tentatively developed. He reduced the distinction between the conditioned and the unconditioned stimulus to the ability to state what we know about our behavioral tendencies and the inability to do so retrospectively. He wrote,

> The implication is clear that in the psychoneuroses I should look for *habit disturbances*—maladjustments—and should attempt to describe my findings in terms of the inadequacy of responses, of wrong responses, and of the complete lack of responses to the objects and situation in the daily life of the patient. I should likewise attempt to trace out the original conditions leading to maladjustment and the causes leading to its continuation.[16]

In that passage we can plainly see that Watson was positing an environmentalist ontogeny and giving behaviorism an ideological role. Both gave a scientific gloss (in the sense of a depersonalized objectivism) to psychologists' work, which was just what Ruml and Frank wanted. Furthermore, Watson (and Burnham) treated conditioning as a completely involuntary process, so that only experts could really understand its nature and its role in society.[17]

During what I have characterized as the frankly ideological stage of conditioning, its proponents were almost exclusively concerned with advancing conditioning's claims as a means of both understanding the human psyche and providing techniques for social control, rather than with generating sophisticated theories of conditioning and conducting research. Burnham wrote,

> The contribution of the conditioned reflex to education, mental hygiene, and psychiatry is fivefold: first, in giving an objective method for study; second, in showing the elements of one's problems; third, in showing the way

to develop healthful associations and to avoid pathological ones; fourth, in saving one from many erroneous interpretations; fifth, in showing the significance of inhibition, and a method by which injurious inhibitions can be removed.[18]

In chapters 4 and 5 of *The Normal Mind*, Burnham gave numerous examples of the ways beliefs, attitudes, and prevailing behavior patterns could have been induced by conditioning, but he gave no empirical evidence whatsoever. Watson was equally strenuous in advancing conditioning's preeminence as a mode of psychological explanation. In particular, he claimed that by the age of three, involuntary conditioning by caregivers had completely formed a child's personality.[19]

The intellectual basis for Watson's and Burnham's claims were astoundingly thin, comprising a large-scale study by Florence Mateer (one of Burnham's students), a series of studies by Watson and his associates, and Watson's clinical observations.[20] Mateer clearly operated in the tradition that Wells had established. That is, she accepted that the basis for all habit formation was the laying down of neural pathways as a consequence of associations between sensations and motor responses formed largely during childhood. She also uncritically accepted Krasnogorski's and Pavlov's theory of the neural basis for habit formation.[21] Mateer also accepted Krasnogorski's finding that speed of acquisition of conditioned reflexes was positively correlated with age. She modified Krasnogorski's procedure for conditioning the swallowing reflex in young children. She then correlated rate of acquisition of the reflex with scores on a battery of intelligence tests, hoping to demonstrate that measuring such rates of acquisition would be a more efficient and cheaper way of assessing intelligence than the administration of tests. Once again, Mateer was operating within Wells's tradition, in that she believed that the study of the ontogeny of habits would have practical consequences.[22]

Behavior modification and early work on applied conditioning developed in very different institutional settings. Ullmann and Krasner point out that the early researchers, such as Mateer, Watson, Guthrie, and Jersild and Holmes (together with Burnham and Hollingworth, who helped to publicize their work), worked in educational and medical settings.[23] Their intellectual support, therefore, came from scientific Progressivism, so that interest in their work died as a consequence of the decay of that movement.[24]

Had the earlier work been hardier it might have survived the desiccation of its environment. Studies such as Watson's, Mateer's, and Jones's were poorly conceived and simply did not constitute the research mass required to support applied programs. Furthermore, these early workers conceived of conditioning inadequately. It was not until the mid-1930s that American psychologists began to realize that conditioning followed two distinct paradigms, one instituted by Thorndike and the other by Pavlov. In effect, Watson and his contemporaries were attempting to apply the techniques of Pavlovian conditioning (in which one established an adaptive or meaningful relationship between an initially neutral and a "driving" or reinforcing stimulus) to situations requiring the use of the Thorndikian (instrumental) paradigm (in which one established an adaptive or meaningful relationship between a response and some benign or adverse consequence—that is, a reinforcer). Moreover, Pavlovian and instrumental conditioning could be differentiated, in part, by the belief that Pavlovian conditioned responses were inevitably built on preexisting reflexes, thereby automatically limiting the range of application of those techniques to human behavior. Further developments in the applications of conditioning to human problems had to await the creation of the requisite techniques of instrumental conditioning.

Those techniques were deployed in a social environment very different from that of the 1920s. In the thirty years following World War II, America went through a period of unparalleled economic growth and social optimism. Society entertained very friendly feelings toward the behavioral sciences. As the acknowledged experts on human beings, psychologists were given carte blanche to offer solutions to complex problems. One of the solutions was behavior therapy or behavior modification. Behavior modifiers, like other mental health professionals, especially those working in the community psychiatry movement, believed that they possessed the means to substantially reduce levels of mental illness. Furthermore, in the 1950s and 1960s behavior modifiers and humanists were, on the whole, allies. For example, Krasner has written that in the postwar years, humanists shared the behaviorist desire to shape a better world.[25] Krasner offered a further reason for the sympathetic interest granted to behavior therapy.

Concomitantly with social optimism, there was a break from authority, tradition, and history. The individual was no longer viewed as "the victim of a mechanically relentless historical process."[26] A highly deterministic, indeed fatalistic, theory such as psychoanalysis therefore became the object of suspicion. The conditions were right for a therapy that emphasized the role of the current environment of the individual in reinforcing behavior. Krasner also noted that the humanist, client-centered therapist Carl Rogers and Skinner shared a belief in individualism, resulting in the assertion of individual rights, especially the right to a happy and fulfilling life. Behavior therapy, with its emphasis on helping the individual, was in a natural position to take a prominent role in the realization of the full potential of the human personality.

The first step in realizing that potential entailed reformulating the problem of mental illness. Studies of mental illness among military personnel in World War II provided the means to achieve that goal. William C. Menninger's report on the role of psychiatry in the American military during World War II exerted a powerful influence.[27] Menninger drew the groundbreaking conclusion that very little mental illness resulted from genetic factors or from complexes induced during childhood (for example, he noted that only 7 percent of hospitalized psychiatric patients were psychotic). He wrote,

> We learned that the maintenance of mental health was largely a function of leadership which included the extremely important element of motivating the man to want to do his job and remain loyal to his associates and his unit. The absence or weakness of these supportive factors in the presence of many excessive stresses seems to account for many of the psychiatric casualties, a large number of which undoubtedly occurred in individuals with a minimal predisposition to mental illness.[28]

Menninger realized that a study of the nature and treatment of mental illness in the military had enormous implications for psychiatry's role in civilian life. For example, approximately 1,875,000 men were rejected for military service because of neuropsychiatric disorders. Even a superficial study of such a huge sample had to be significant. First, very short (three-month) training courses produced highly effective mental health personnel. Menninger drew a second conclusion:

if intensive treatment was provided early, in an environment in which the expectation of recovery prevailed, remarkable results were obtained. Even with streamlined treatment in a system that provided outlets in activity, along with personal and group psychotherapy, a phenomenal recovery rate occurred. This was true in combat treatment areas where 60% were returned to duty within a few days and an additional 30% within a few weeks. . . . *There is strong suggestive evidence to believe that if we could educate, if we could adequately staff our clinics and our hospitals and if above all we could emphasize and practice intensive early treatment, we could materially increase the present rate of recovery of mental illness.*[29]

Menninger exhorted psychiatrists

to turn up the road which leads us into the broad field of social interests; we can devote our efforts to the potential opportunities of helping the average man on the street. We can reorganize our front on the basis that we have just experienced an international psychosis and we are living in a world filled with its residual of grief and sorrow and suffering that have nothing to do with "dementia praecox" or the "oedipus conflict," but with individual struggles, community needs, state and national problems and international concerns.[30]

Well before Menninger published his article, the federal government of the United States, as part of the massive intervention in society and the economy that guaranteed American prosperity for many years to come, was starting to establish the institutions in which mental health personnel would be trained. Following Vanevar Bush's recommendations to President Roosevelt regarding the training of scientific personnel, including those in the mental health field, the National Mental Health Act became law in 1946. The National Institute of Mental Health (NIMH) was created in 1949.[31]

The establishment of the first fully developed programs for training clinical psychologists in the United States was part of the Veterans Administration.[32] The care of veterans created a form of socialized medicine. World War II produced sixteen million veterans, while in 1946 there were about four million left from previous wars. Thus the training of clinical psychologists was largely state-supported in the postwar era, while the state offered a major avenue of employment for newly graduated psychologists.[33]

Even though many practitioners of modern American behavior modification were drawn from the ranks of those psychologists, the origins of the movement lay elsewhere. Will Menninger and others had realized that short-term psychotherapy was exceedingly effective, and behavior modification was short-term therapy *par excellence*. However, traditional types of therapy maintained their allure among the newly trained VA psychologists. Psychoanalysis, in particular, had a very high prestige in America. Freud's training analysis was the first program expressly designed to train psychotherapists, and that very primacy assured the dominance of psychoanalysis over other forms of psychotherapy for decades. From the 1930s onward, many prominent European analysts, such as David Rapaport, Else Frenkel-Brunswick, Karen Horney, and Erich Fromm, emigrated to America and played a prominent role in the psychotherapy movement. America's sheer wealth assured them of a place in American society; many Americans could afford the heavy cost of an analysis, while there was sufficient surplus wealth in the country to support institutions such as the Menninger Foundation.

Psychoanalysis was, however, rapidly transformed and incorporated into a positivist, pragmatic framework derived from learning theory. A group working under Clark Hull's leadership at the Institute of Human Relations at Yale produced almost all the versions of behavior therapy or behavior modification having such a basis.[34] The group's thinking was thoroughly instrumentalist. First, the members believed that psychoanalysis provided all the concepts required to explain and describe mental illness.[35] Second, they believed that there was a body of accepted psychoanalytic practice of proven effectiveness.[36] They operated with what one might call a standardized model of normal mental life, in which a person's role was limited to adjustment to a predetermined social niche. The theorist's role was limited to the translation of psychoanalytic concepts into the language of learning theory. The researcher's role was limited to the operationalizing of those concepts and the discovery of the functional quantified relationships between them. The clinician's role was limited to the teaching of methods of adjustment leading to the restoration of "normality."

Societally, then, the IHR's work continued that of Watson and Burnham. It is especially noteworthy that members of the group, such as Hull, O. Hobart Mowrer, and John Dollard, fully accepted, like

Watson, the Freudian dictum that neuroses are familially generated in early childhood.[37] Hence they shared Watson's faith that appropriate techniques of socialization could eradicate abnormal psychological functioning. In terms of theory, research, and clinical practice, however, the IHR group was far more sophisticated than Watson.

The group seems to have started work in early 1936.[38] Hull began a series of seminars, involving people from several disciplines, in which psychoanalysis was seriously discussed and in which some members of the group tried to incorporate psychoanalysis into learning theory. These seminars resulted not only in a theory of psychopathology and versions of psychotherapy based on the principles of learning theory, but also in expansions of the power and scope of learning theory itself.

Of all the members of the Yale group, Mowrer made the strongest contributions. He began with a theoretical article published in 1939, "A Stimulus-Response Analysis of Anxiety and Its Role as a Reinforcing Agent," dealing with the role of secondary reinforcement.[39] For learning theorists working with animals and those working with humans, motivation was a serious problem. Animals, it would appear, were motivated only by biological needs, whereas such needs controlled only a minute fraction of human learning (and none of the human learning observed in laboratories). Basing himself on Freud's treatment of anxiety as a premonitory signal, Mowrer posited anxiety as a universal motivator. Moreover, by pointing out that the degree of anxiety was not necessarily commensurate with the extent of anticipated trauma, he established the basis for a learning-theory explanation for irrational fears (neuroses). In an immediately subsequent article, "Preparatory Set (Expectancy): Some Methods of Measurement," Mowrer demonstrated in detail how his principles could be applied to experimental findings.[40] He then proceeded to lay the foundations for a unified theory of learning. He pointed out that theories of habit formation, up to that point, had exceedingly disparate rationales. He showed that a unified theory of motivation could be deduced from the Freudian concept of anxiety. First, a theory of motivation demoted mere association to a secondary status (associations required explanations, while, were we to assume that animals had minds, the making of associations would be different in human and in animal minds, so that we could not generalize directly from animal to human experimental work). Second, we could assume that anxiety would be both benignly and threateningly aroused (the gifted athlete or schoolchild, although assured of success, is nevertheless aroused, and that level of arousal drops sharply to a resting state once a task is completed; in terms of quantity, the level of felt anxiety and the extent of restoration to the resting state are the same in the common herd). So drive reduction is the common source of all motivation.

Mowrer also showed his Yale colleagues and other learning theorists how to convert the language of psychoanalysis into the language of learning theory. Here Mowrer's most significant work was his 1940 article "An Experimental Analogue of 'Regression' with Incidental Observations on 'Reaction Formation.'"[41] Like the two articles I have summarized above, this had a dual function in that, besides operationalizing a psychoanalytic concept, it constituted one of the paradigm cases of what learning theorists came to call "escape learning" (a form of habit formation in which an animal has to learn to lessen the harmful consequences of unavoidable trauma). Finally, Mowrer, in collaboration with his wife, produced the first empirically justified version of behavior therapy: a treatment for childhood enuresis.[42] The Yale school did not follow up on this lead, however, and their contributions were almost exclusively at the theoretical level.

What Neal Miller called "liberalized S-R theory" remained relatively unchanged from the time the Yale group formulated it. That meant that nobody in the group raised questions about psychoanalysis as a basis for a theory of psychopathology. It was only as learning theory came close to its demise that anybody proposed using learning theory itself as a basis for psychotherapy. But psychologist Albert Bandura realized that in the quarter century since the Yale group began its work, the required developments had not occurred.[43] On the basis of a review of studies using the techniques of counterconditioning, extinction, discrimination learning, reward, punishment, and social imitation, he concluded that learning theory had only a slight impact on the practice of therapy, and suggested that a more concerted effort was needed to apply learning theory to therapy:

> [I have] suggested . . . that many of the changes that occur in psychotherapy derive from the unwitting application of well-known principles of learning. However, the occurrence of the necessary conditions for learning is more by accident than by intent and, perhaps, a more deliberate application of our knowledge of the learning process to psychotherapy would yield far more effective results.[44]

Technologies derived from operant conditioning dominated the behavior modification movement. Psychologist Paul R. Fuller, working under J. R. Kantor's influence, carried out the first experimental study in behavior modification's new phase.[45] The small number of Kantor's adherents, however, guaranteed that his role in the behavior modification movement would be slight. Skinner, with his large group of followers, exerted much more influence. Moreover, largely because of his early research work, Skinner contributed crucial theoretical insights. Early work in applied conditioning did not take root, in part, because its proponents failed to distinguish between operant and classical conditioning. Skinner's careful differentiation of these two forms of conditioning and his elaboration on the potential of operant conditioning led to increased interest in behavior modification in the psychological community. He also assigned himself a foundational role in the behavior therapy movement; Krasner claims that Skinner was the first person to use the term.

A study he carried out in collaboration with Ogden Lindsley and H. C. Solomon was the first fruit of Skinner's venture into behavior modification and marked the entry of the term "behavior therapy" into the psychological literature.[46] Lindsley also conducted a study with Azrin on the effects of reinforcement on cooperation between children.[47] They reported that cooperative behavior could be conditioned and extinguished without any verbal instruction regarding the tasks from the experimenters. Thus their study suggested that cooperation could be learned for the sake of reward, without recourse to more complex explanations of the behavior.

Operant principles found their most ample application in token economies. Token economies are staff-operated operant systems in which the delivery of tokens controls the target population's actions; these economies are designed for use in institutional settings such as mental hospitals, institutions for the mentally retarded, and schools.[48] Versions of token economies were also used in jails. These systems broke new ground in that the principles of behavioral science were applied directly to nonlaboratory situations. As Kazdin commented, "it is especially important to single out token reinforcement because it has permitted a larger extension of programs than ordinarily is the case with type [sic] of reinforcing events."[49] In institutions tokens are awarded for the performance of basic social tasks, such as getting dressed or helping to keep the ward tidy. In schools the usual "target behaviors" are the maintenance of an acceptable level of academic performance or maintaining acceptable social behavior. Tokens can be used to buy desirable items (e.g., cigarettes in mental hospitals) or to gain access to social privileges (e.g., going to the cinema or gaining a day pass in a mental hospital). Token economies provide us with a paradigm for studying the role of operant reinforcement in the institution and maintenance of acceptable patterns of social behavior.

Tokens were first used as rewards in experiments with chimpanzees in the 1930s.[50] Ferster and DeMyer (working with autistic children) and Lovaas (working with normal children) were the first to use tokens with humans.[51] Staats demonstrated that performance curves for complex behavior (learning how to read, in his case), when tokens were used as reinforcers, approximated those for simple behavior. More to the point, he also demonstrated that tokens sustained performance much better than social reinforcers.[52]

Token economies emerged independently from the Skinnerian (in Teodoro Ayllon and Azrin's pioneering study) and the Kantorian tradition (in the work of Birnbrauer and his collaborators).[53] Within three years of the appearance of the first work, forty-eight other token economies were operating in the United States.[54]

Ayllon laid the basis for his token economies while working at the Saskatchewan Hospital, Weyburn, Canada. His programs were based on a particular conception of the nature of mental illness, the social structures of mental hospitals, and the roles of the staff members in those hospitals. Ayllon also tried to train staff members such as psychiatric nurses to eschew psychodynamic interpretations of patients' speech and actions. That is, his work had a powerful ideological component. Ayllon and Michael wrote, "From the point of view of modern behavior theory, such strong behaviors, or behavioral deficits, may be considered the results of events occurring in the patient's immediate or historical environment rather than manifestations of his mental disorder."[55] In a famous study, Haughton and Ayllon induced seeming compulsive behavior in a severely regressed psychotic patient at Weyburn.[56] By using shaping and token reinforcement, they trained the patient, who previously had been totally inactive, to carry a broom around the ward. They then asked two psychiatrists, who did not know that the patient had been trained to do the task, to observe her and interpret the "symptom." The psychiatrists duly came up with interpretations, one of which was floridly psychoanalytic. Haughton and Ayllon commented, "The apparent uselessness and irrelevance of the patient's behavior is indeed the hallmark of behavior often clinically described as 'compulsive' or 'psychotic.' Yet, examination of some of the environmental conditions under which the response was developed, may make it easier to understand how similar classes of behavior are developed and maintained by environmental contingencies."[57]

In their work at Weyburn, Ayllon and his collaborators trained psychiatric nurses to function as dispensers of reinforcement. They defined reinforcement in simple, commonsense terms, telling the nurses,

> Reinforcement is something you do for or with a patient, for example, offering candy or a cigarette. Any way you convey attention to the patient is reinforcing. Patients may be reinforced if you answer their questions, talk to them, or let them know by your reaction that you are aware of their presence. The common-sense expression "pay no attention" is perhaps closest to what must be done to discourage the patient's behavior. When we say "do not reinforce a behavior," we are actually saying "ignore the behavior and act deaf and blind whenever it occurs."[58]

Ayllon and Azrin, working with a population of female chronic psychotics, created the classical token economy. Using the techniques he had used at Weyburn, Ayllon applied the principles of experimental design directly to the control of the behavior of entire groups of patients. He and Azrin demonstrated, without doubt, that the delivery of tokens, and only the delivery of tokens, controlled the target behaviors of their subjects. However, although the delivery of tokens necessarily controlled behavior, it is not clear that token delivery was sufficient to control behavior. We can solve the issue only by examining other token economies and analyzing the social forms characteristic of institutions.

The first question to ask is, "What could the patients at Anna State buy with tokens?" Ayllon and Azrin answer the question fully. Tokens could earn patients a choice of bedroom (and thereby choice of sleeping partners), eating group, personal chair, and room divider (which in effect gave a patient her own bedroom). Patients could buy the privilege of leaving the ward without an escort or a private meeting with a staff member. They could actively take part in a religious service of their choice. Tokens also gave access to various leisure activities—a personal radio or TV set, the opportunity to listen to a live band or go to dances. Or patients could purchase personal items (consumables, grooming equipment, extra clothing, reading and writing materials, and other special items on request). Taken together, the set of rewards constitutes a portrait of normal life.

Birnbrauer and his associates worked in a classroom of educably mentally retarded pupils at the Rainier School, Washington State. In one of their studies, they gave a detailed report of the effect of instituting, withdrawing, and reinstituting token reinforcements. The effects of the tokens on the academic performance of the pupils was at best ambiguous: the withdrawal had no effect on some, on others it had adverse effects only on the error rate, and it caused a decline in performance and an increase in error rate in a minority. As the researchers point out, academic performance had little relevance for the pupils' lives, and that lack of relevance could explain the academic ineffectiveness of the token economy program. Withdrawal of the tokens did, however, cause dramatic reversions to the behavior problems that were endemic before the token economy was introduced. So it would seem that token economies have the same effects on the behavior of institutionalized psychotics and on mental retardates who are forced to perform academic work. That is, the economies allow the introduction and maintenance of social behaviors acceptable to the staff.

Many of those who believe in the efficacy of operant techniques also believe that the underlying theory can provide us with an analysis of social forms and, above all, procedures for changing social forms and social practices. It is strange that only one person, R. C. Winkler, gave the word "economy" its literal meaning.[59] He wrote, "Token-earning behavior in a token economy can be regarded as patient output. Since this output by definition earns tokens, patient output is directly related to patient income and patient output may be regarded as patient income."[60] Winkler also commented that "Reinforcement principles do not make clear predictions about spending patterns in token reinforcement paradigms."[61]

Winkler first demonstrated that token and real economies were functionally equivalent. As in real economies, the expenditures of those with moderate earnings use up 90 to 110 percent of their income. The expenditures of low earners tend to exceed their income, while the expenditures of high earners fall below their income. He also showed that expenditure patterns in token economies follow

Engel's curves. That is, if income is low, most expenditure is on necessities; luxuries are bought only with surplus income.

Continuing his analogy between token and real economies, Winkler differentiated between economic balance and savings, where by economic balance he meant the ratio between expected income and expected expenditure. Winkler could manipulate economic balance and savings independently either by changing wages or by changing prices. So if wages fell or prices rose, someone could maintain the same level of savings by spending less. However, in his crucial manipulation he instituted a favorable economic balance by dropping prices while at the same time wiping out savings by issuing a new currency. He could assess the effect of savings by comparing behavior in two experiments. In the first, prices were dropped, while in the second they remained constant. Savings accumulated more rapidly in the first experiment. If savings were a crucial determinant of behavior, then performance should have dropped more sharply in experiment 1 than in experiment 2 (once someone had accumulated a certain amount of savings, performance should have ceased), and that is what Winkler found.

He tried to account for the finding by appealing to reinforcement theory. If savings were low, he argued, the person should feel deprived and would work harder. If savings were constant, people would work harder when prices were high than they would when prices were low. However, that was not the case. Furthermore, prices had no differential effect on primary consumption in the two experiments (once again, there was no deprivation effect).

Winkler ran a further experiment in which he differentially manipulated savings (he had a high savings and a low savings condition) but increased wages. He found that if savings were high, increased wages had no effect, whereas, if savings were low, increased wages did have an effect. Once again it was the level of savings (and only the level of savings) that controlled behavior in token economies.

Winkler demonstrated quite conclusively that savings have the same function in a token economy that they have in a real economy. He also demonstrated that the acquisition of individual tokens does not directly affect behavior in the same way that the acquisition of individual food items affects rats' or pigeons' behavior. In a real economy, savings afford individuals security and the means to escape from the constraints of the economy or achieve their own goals. If we combine Winkler's findings with Ayllon and Azrin's system of rewards, we can say that the token economies instituted in the mental hospitals of the 1960s, far from bringing patients under the control of the contingencies operating in those institutions, provided them with a means of escape, at least into a fantasy version of normal life.

Token economies are subject to three types of criticisms. First, the behavior modifiers' reasoning is characterized by certain logical flaws. Second, the principles of behavior modification cannot explain the social structure of mental hospitals or the actions, beliefs, and emotions of mental patients. Third, behavior modifiers believed that they could undertake an analysis of society as a whole; instead, one can say that the behavior modification was controlled by social forces that its adherents did not understand.

Logically, one can detect four flaws in the reasoning of behavior modifiers. First, they tend to confuse mere associative with causal relationships. Second, they are guilty of the inductive fallacy. Third, they fail to distinguish between necessary and sufficient causes. Fourth, they make the error of denying the antecedent. With respect to the first error, we can take Ayllon's early studies as our point of departure, especially as these constituted the foundation for his token economies. All were aimed at achieving direct improvements in individual behavior, with each program tailored to the idiosyncracies of the patient. Broadly speaking, one can say that Ayllon gave operant explanations not just for the change in his patients' behavior but also for the maladaptive behavior that was altered or suppressed. Thus, in one case a patient was taught to replace attacking the staff with squatting (Ayllon believed that the attack behavior had been instituted by operant contingencies and could be obliterated by alternative contingencies). But when Ayllon tried to train the patient to approach the staff, he attacked them once again (squatting was merely masking the propensity to attack). In another case Ayllon successfully taught a woman to suppress her complaints about bizarre bodily symptoms. But after a relative came in to ask her to sign over some property, the talk returned. Gerald Davison argued that the operant-controlled renunciation of the bizarre talk merely masked an underlying emotional state that was its real cause.

An analysis of the treatment of one of Krasner and Gericke's patients, Susan, raises the same issues.[62] She insisted on always wearing white clothes. The ward staff used that desire to control her in-ward behavior. They forced her to wear black and put her onto a token economy so that she could earn the right to wear white. Behaviorally, the program was successful. But Susan had a delusional system in which black represented sin and evil, white purity and goodness. Krasner and Gericke gave no evidence to show that the delusional system was changed. Using these examples, one can formulate a fundamental objection to operant explanations for actions and beliefs. I would argue that if delusions, irrational fears, and other psychological forces operate out of sight, we have no reason to assume that token economies will abolish them. Operant procedures may produce people who seem reasonably well socialized and relatively rational, or who operate in terms of generally accepted social norms and practices. There is, however, no reason to assume that social practices with a semblance of normality are controlled by the same forces operating in society at large.

Second, all Skinnerians are guilty of the inductive fallacy. To illustrate it we can return to the practical joke Ayllon and Haughton played on the psychiatrists at Weyburn. They argued that they had produced a *bona fide* symptom by using operant techniques (both psychiatrists interpreted the patient's behavior as a genuine symptom). By implication, they concluded that every symptom has an operant origin. But even if operant conditioners produced hundreds of symptoms, it would not follow that all symptoms were operants.

An example of the third logical error (the failure to distinguish between necessary and sufficient causes) occurs in Ayllon and Azrin's study. They left us with no doubt that the delivery of tokens, and only the delivery of tokens, controlled the in-ward actions of their patients at Anna State Hospital. But while we cannot deny the fact that token delivery controlled behavior, we cannot affirm that token delivery was sufficient as well as necessary. Behavior modifiers interpret tokens as mere reinforcers that automatically induce behavior. But that does not mean that patients interpret tokens in this way. That is, the patients could have been acquiring tokens and apparently complying with Ayllon and Azrin's demands to serve purposes of their own.

Fourth, we have the error of denying the antecedent. For example, the staff is ordered to stop paying attention to the manifestations of an eating disorder. The disorder stops. Behavior modifiers conclude that the same phenomenon that stopped the disorder (attention) caused it in the first place. But that, says Davison, is analogous to concluding that because aspirin cures headaches its absence causes them. As he puts it, *"knowledge about how to change a phenomenon is not tantamount to knowing how it originated."*[63] Behavior modifiers' refusal to engage in causal analysis renders their explanations nugatory. They follow Skinner in their belief that to explain is to produce phenomena under specified circumstances. But production is not equivalent to explanation; however carefully one controls all the overt or observable conditions in an experiment, undetected causal factors could be operating. Davison illustrates the point beautifully by referring to Rimland's theory of autism.[64] Rimland argued that because autistics are neurologically incapable of making connections between social input and socially appropriate actions, only overt reward will have any effect on controlling their actions. However, Rimland believed that behavior modification's role is limited to the control of action. The principles of behavior modification cannot, he claimed, explain why it is that those same principles have to be applied to autistics (i.e., knowing *that* the principles work does not, in itself, tell us *why* they work).

The four logical errors coalesce around the issue of causal explanation. Since we are dealing with human beings, we can ask what beliefs and feelings the patients had about token economies. Davison points out several times that behavior modifiers use statements by patients in a highly selective manner. In general, they discount the statements because they are made by irrational people (see, for example, the statements by patients in Ayllon and Azrin's study). They make no attempt to enter the patients' life-world (just as operant conditioners refuse to enter the life-space of their animal subjects).

Token economies could be justified in a purely technical sense. They benefited both patients and staff. Patients became more tractable and required less care and attention while, at the same time, they acquired tangible rewards. Staff had relatively genial relationships with patients and, above all, could feel that they were fulfilling professional functions in a very positive sense. However, the more thoughtful Skinnerians were not content to remain at this mundane level. Because they believed that operant principles explained all human functioning, they treated chronic wards or school classrooms as microcosms of society. Procedures controlling behavior in these environments, they believed, exerted the same degree and extent of control in society at large.

Only one person, it would seem, realized that if one wished to restore the societal functioning of chronic schizophrenics, one had to make a much more sophisticated analysis of societal forms than those to be found in the operant literature. I am referring to the work of George Fairweather and his associates.[65] This group, using impeccable operational terminology, described a mental patient as: "an individual who has not demonstrated the minimal behaviors required for assuming a community role which is rewarded by his social group."[66] No behaviorist would quarrel with that definition. Fairweather's first study resembled a token economy in that its aim was to improve adjustment to the life of a mental hospital, much of the responsibility for making the adjustment was assigned to the patients, and improvements in behavior were linked to an explicit system of rewards (money and passes). It differed from a token economy because Fairweather was explicitly attempting to prepare patients for their eventual release and, above all, because patients were given genuine autonomy. In his experimental wards Fairweather established what were in effect patient-run therapy groups. Groups as a whole set tasks for members and monitored progress in those tasks, reporting the results to weekly meetings with ward staff. As behavior improved, patients moved steadily toward their discharge.

In a later program, Fairweather's group successfully helped a group of chronic psychotics to work outside a mental hospital and to lead reasonably satisfying lives. Before their discharge, a group of patients planned what work they would do and assigned one another tasks within the organization (a janitorial and home- and garden-care firm). The results were conspicuously successful. However bizarre their work methods, the group obtained and held contracts for work such as janitorial contracts or house painting. As Fairweather wrote, "Mr. Smith, a person with six and one-half years of previous hospitalization, diagnosed as a 'chronic schizophrenic,' was now totally in charge of all aspects of work and life at the 'new lodge.'"[67]

Fairweather realized full well that if chronic psychotics were to survive in outside communities one could not apply normal community standards and expectations to them:

> a marginal person must have a sense of his own worth in order to identify effectively with his society. For this reason, many current social and economic programs for marginal persons which maintain them in subordinate social statuses by regulations pertaining to their eligibility or qualifications

for various forms of public assistance fail to enhance the substantive accomplishments of their segment of our society. . . .

This study has shown that, for certain persons, employment is possible only under specially designed supportive conditions in the community. Such persons are, at least initially, unable to assume the full employment responsibilities required by the ordinary work role in our society. This problem is critical not only for discharged chronic mental patients but also for other marginal groups, such as ex-prisoners and uneducated persons. If industry selects its employees solely on the basis of their ability to produce, what role is the larger society then willing to provide for those persons not only incapable of meeting such industrial role requirements but also not sufficiently disabled to require continuous care?[68]

In mental institutions, token economies collapsed not because of their intrinsic weaknesses but because of external social pressures. In America, starting in 1966, over a hundred legal cases revolving around the issue of the rights of those incarcerated by the state were brought before the courts, and a body of case law steadily accumulated.[69] Although the cases mostly concerned the rights of the mentally incompetent, in general they had a decisive impact on token economies.

In America from the 1860s onward, the state had been involved in the issue of mental health, but the involvement was limited to the legal control of commitment procedures.[70] The state left the care of the mentally incompetent to the relevant institutions. The civil rights cases of the 1970s were a new departure in that the courts involved themselves in the operation of institutions. Three forces contributed to this change. The first was Thomas Szasz's sustained attack on the professional competence and supposed objectivity of the psychiatric profession; the second was the work of the social scientists who created "labeling theory"; and the third was the growing realization that conditions in institutions were appalling.[71]

Bruce Ennis, a civil rights attorney, was one of those who spearheaded the attack on psychiatry.[72] Ennis concentrated his fire on the unreliability of psychiatric diagnoses (and the corresponding role of psychiatrists as instruments of coercive control) and on the abysmal lack of treatment for the chronically mentally ill. The consequence of the resultant court cases brought by Ennis and many other civil rights lawyers was the accumulation of a body of case law that, as Levine comments, "contributed towards deinstitutionalization and the necessity for community based care."[73] Legal doubts about efficacy of treatment led to judicial demands for the provision of services in the least restrictive alternative.[74] Such demands, once again, were a force influencing deinstitutionalization.

The case having the most direct consequences for token economies in mental hospitals was *Wyatt v. Stickney*.[75] Ultimately the court ruled that no involuntary work was permitted, even if the effects of the work were therapeutic. Voluntary work was permitted, provided that the patients earned the federal minimum wage. Lawyer David Wexler commented as follows on the *Wyatt* decision,

> The approach taken by the landmark *Wyatt* decision, if widely followed, would have an immense impact on traditional token economies. Patients could not be forced in any way to perform institutional labor assignments—and the force could not legitimately be exerted indirectly by making basic reinforcers "contingent" upon appropriate performance. Further, if patients should decide voluntarily to undertake institutional tasks, the minimum wage is the legally required "reinforcer." Under *Wyatt*, therapeutic assignments unrelated to hospital operations can constitute legitimate target responses that can be rewarded without regard to the minimum wage. But, perhaps most significant for token economies, *Wyatt* and related legal developments seem to have a great deal to say regarding the definition of legally acceptable reinforcers. *Wyatt*, together with an occasional piece of proposed or enacted legislation, has begun the process of enumerating the rights guaranteed to hospitalized mental patients. The crux of the problem, from the viewpoint of behavior modification, is that the items and activities that are emerging as absolute rights are the very same items and activities that the behavioral psychologists would employ as reinforcers—that is, as "contingent rights."[76]

Wexler continued his analysis by scrutinizing a principle enunciated by Bruce Ennis—if labor is therapeutic, then we will see it in private clinics.[77] In public institutions we will see cost-saving labor. Wexler argued that the principle would not bear scrutiny because patients in private and public institutions are very different. Those in private institutions are wealthier, have shorter stays, and are less stigmatized on discharge. Those in public institutions are poorer, older, have a longer history of mental illness, are less intelligent, and have limited work skills. Wexler believes that work is better than no work, especially if the work prepares people to work on discharge.

One way to avoid exploitation, Wexler suggested, would be to prevent patients from being indispensable in a job; he comments that Ayllon and Azrin applied the principle by insisting on job rotation. However, one still faces the problem of arriving at an adequate and legally sustainable level of reimbursement. If *Wyatt*'s minimum wage requirement were to be imposed, one would face the danger that outside labor would be brought in to perform most tasks (because outsiders would be more efficient), leaving the patients to molder. A way out of the difficulty would be to demonstrate that labor, even when reimbursed at a substandard rate, has a universal therapeutic effect. Regrettably for token economies, the evidence is negative.

First, even in the most successful token economy ever (at Anna State), Ayllon and Azrin reported that eight out of the forty-four patients failed to respond to the procedure. (Wexler commented that the success rate would be far lower in less well-conceived or well-managed programs.) Second, patients released from token economies have a higher relapse rate that most groups of chronic patients.[78] That finding is consistent with my discussion of Fairweather's work. I made the point that his procedures differed decisively from standard token economies in that his group specifically prepared patients for work in the outside world. If, as I have already suggested, token economies do little more than palliate conditions in mental hospitals, then given that the social life of mental institutions is drastically different from normal social life, those exposed to token economies are less, not better, prepared for return to the outside world.

Wexler did suggest that legal problems could be overcome if operant conditioners used idiosyncratic reinforcers (e.g., availability of truly soft-boiled as opposed to standard cafeteria-style boiled eggs, or being given the opportunity to pet kittens). Wexler commented, "In fact, the most fruitful combination might be to combine individualized treatment programs with an efficient, easy-to-administer general therapeutic system. If, however, the criteria for a successful system is [*sic*] efficacy with the least drastic deprivation possible, it appears that token economies for chronic psychotics may well finish no better than second best."[79]

Proponents of token economies have been denied the opportunity to put Wexler's suggestions into effect. As a consequence of the civil rights cases and because of the discovery of major tranquilizers for the "treatment" of schizophrenia and lithium chloride for the control of depressive psychosis, almost all psychotics are no longer held in long-term care institutions. In effect, the state has assigned the psychiatric profession a primary role in the management of psychosis, and psychiatry has chosen to use physical treatment almost exclusively. Behavior modification plays, at best, a minor role in that enterprise.[80]

With respect to mental health, the American lay public over the course of this century has consistently entertained two incompatible propositions. On the one hand, they believe that our lives are controlled by impalpable and unconscious forces that can be understood only by experts. On the other hand, they believe that mental dysfunction resembles physical illness in that its causes can be discovered and remedies instituted.[81] For decades, nobody disputed that psychoanalysts were the leading experts on the unconscious. By midcentury, however, the psychotherapeutic professions had lost their faith in psychoanalysis. It was helpless against the ravages of psychosis and, at best, inefficient, cumbersome, and, above all, costly as a means of dealing with neurosis. The response of the behavior modification movement to this professional crisis was rather like that of contemporary political and financial elites in the face of the current governmental fiscal problems in Western countries. They have used those problems as a stalking horse to implement policies drastically limiting the policy basis of the state's role, therefore ensuring that alternatives to their policies would be not just impractical but unthinkable. For both practitioners and patients, any successful therapy would, by definition and decree, be a form of behavior therapy, whereas any other form of therapy would be "useless and senseless."

In such a scheme, terms like *cure, normal,* or even *happy, contented,* or *fulfilled* lost their meaning. What counted was who controlled whom, by what means, and for what purpose. Chronic psychotics were not rendered normal in token economies; they were merely subjected to a set of contingencies other than those that operated in a regular ward. In the same way, a phobic patient merely exchanged a set of contingencies imposed during childhood for a set imposed during adulthood by a therapist. Neither psychotics nor neurotics, claimed behavior modifiers, were rational agents having free will or insight into their conditions. Even the therapists or the supervisors of token economies were the agents of reinforcement contingencies.

The America of the 1950s and 1960s offered behaviorists wide support. The behaviorist agenda matched America's societal and political agenda. As agents of their own society, behaviorists offered a program fully consistent with the desires and objectives of the host culture. A majority of thinking Americans of the day believed in what might be called "transcendent pragmatism." That is, they believed not just that the route to social change passed through the hearts and minds of those who were to be changed but that only overt, definable, and preferably quantifiable processes would lead to such change.

But beliefs, however strong and however diffuse, must ultimately be assessed against reality. Behaviorism's failure resides in its inadequate analysis of society. First, its view of human nature is extremely narrow. In particular, it fails to see that *society* and *human nature* are sociological concepts, that they have a history, and that their history determines their meaning. Second, its analysis of the nature of human nature is outcome-driven, which, third, leads to a failure to provide a causal account of human action. Fourth, it fails to analyze the nature of the social settings in which behavior modification is used. Scientism and instrumentalism control behaviorists' views of the nature of society. Societal and political institutions, they believe, are merely domains in which people seek instrumental gratification. We do not need to ask questions about society's nature or engage in analyses of social forms and institutions. Regrettably for behaviorists, the collapse of token economies and the restrictions that one must place on the use and interpretation of behaviorist therapies provide empirical disproof of their theories.

7

Faithful unto This Last
The Neobehaviorist Hegemony

There was once a time when an academic psychologist lived his or her professional life in a behaviorist world. Behaviorists set the agenda in departments of psychology, even for psychologists who did not belong to one of the neobehaviorist schools and who were not working in exclusively behaviorist areas (such as animal learning). This is not to say that all psychologists were behaviorists. But it is to say that academic psychologists concurred in the behaviorists' refusal to grant full citizenship to their opponents.

Neobehaviorism's dominance brought to fruition a particular philosophy of science whose origins I have found in Fechner's decision to arithromorphize all his data and in two of Ebbinghaus's innovations (characterizing all experiments as the discovery of functional relationships between independent and dependent variables and treating psychological outputs as work). Fechner's and Ebbinghaus's intellectual heirs (the operationists Boring, Stevens, Tolman, Skinner, and Spence) captured psychology's language and effectively robbed all nonbehaviorists of the power of speech. And, of course, the operationist says that those who cannot speak cannot think. Furthermore, the neobehaviorists completed the functionalists' reorganization of academic psychology's priorities. The study of sensation, perception, and cognition were pushed to psychology's periphery, and learning and motivation moved into center stage.

The neobehaviorists and their allies developed a body of knowledge—or perhaps one should say, given its ephemeral nature, a set of knowledge claims. Those knowledge claims were organized around certain assumptions concerning the determinants of thoughts, feelings, and actions. Just as the neobehaviorists and behaviorists treated knowledge itself instrumentally, so they treated all actions, mentations, and dispositions instrumentally, but in an exceedingly narrow sense. They assumed that all people and animals were automatically constrained to do that, and only that, which brought immediate benefits. If a creature did do something or entertain beliefs about doing something of no immediate benefit, then that something had to be a surrogate for or have direct connections with some immediate benefit. In that respect, neobehaviorists treated motives like hedonists or utilitarians would. However, both neobehaviorists and behaviorists believed that all creatures were automatically constrained to seek benefits and avoid harm or disadvantage. They claimed that no creature (including human beings) actively sought or foresaw benefits, advantages, or pleasures. Instead, they devised what psychologist Abraham Maslow characterized as deficit theories of motivation.[1] Maslow also pointed out that Freud's pleasure principle is, in fact, an "avoidance of pain" principle (Freud believed that the fundamental force driving human beings was fear of pain, not love of pleasure). In the same way, neobehaviorists such as Hull presumed that neither animals nor people were motivated, in any positive sense, to act in their own interest (and, most decidedly, motives like sympathy or altruism were at best secondary). Deficit theories of motivation were one-dimensional hedonistic theories in which pleasure had no intrinsic role (one sought pleasure, benefit, utility, or the good not for its own sake but merely to avoid deleterious consequences). Athletes compete in order to avoid the anxiety and misery resulting from losing, not from any intrinsic joy in using their skills; we acquire knowledge to avoid the anxiety aroused by our failure to do so and because knowledge is useful; young animals play not because they enjoy it but to learn certain skills.

Mowrer-style deficit theories of motivation unified psychology. If both humans and animals were driven into action rather than choosing actions, then humans and animals were essentially the same sorts of creatures, and one could generalize from animals to humans. I think it is far more significant that deficit theories of motivation also acted as a unifying force in psychology. They did so by affirming the value of certain basic approaches, which led psychologists to value certain subdisciplines above others. Within those subdisciplines essentially the same approach to knowledge claims prevailed. Specificity, concreteness, and difference were devalued. Neobehaviorism represented functionalism's apogee in psychology. What people thought, what people believed, what people felt did not matter. What mattered was the instrumental value of thoughts, beliefs, and feelings. Because developmentalists, learning theorists, those studying perception or the higher mental processes, social psychologists, personality theorists, and abnormal psychologists shared the same theory of human nature, all conducted their research in essentially the same way. Research, then, became programmatic rather than substantive. Because the assumptions underlying deficit theories of motivation were hidden from view and because the connection between such theories and neobehaviorism was tenuous and indirect, the unification appeared to have an objective rather than an ideological base.

Neobehaviorism's hegemony displayed itself in the treatment of psychology's subject matter. Certain specialities were thrust to the periphery and others elevated in importance. Those elevated were accorded essentially the same treatment. Physiological psychology and mental testing could not be engulfed within behaviorism, but their intrinsic status afforded them protection. Sensation, perception, language, and thinking were reduced to a secondary status, while learning and motivation became primary. Although the study of verbal learning and the study of memory were never behaviorist, both areas were taken over by exceedingly stark functionalists, and the same was true of personality and abnormal psychology.

Developmental psychology was ripe for the picking. Jean Piaget and, possibly, Freud are the only major theorists the field has ever had. American psychologists had ambivalent feelings about Freud and knew nothing of Piaget until John H. Flavell and Jerome Bruner introduced them to his ideas.[2] David Ausubel was the only major American contender as a theorist. But his influence was largely in education, and his ideas lay so far outside the form of empiricism and positivism that prevailed in his day that they were incomprehensible to most psychologists.[3] Otherwise, developmental psychology in the 1950s consisted of intelligence testing, the remorseless study of Arnold Gesell's developmental norms, and, in the case of language development, conducting surveys in vocabulary growth as a function of age. Behaviorists moved briskly into the vacuum. For example, in 1957 Robert R. Sears, Eleanor E. Maccoby, and Harry Levin published *Patterns of Child Rearing*, an influential and widely read developmental study.[4] Their title, in effect, summarized the book. They were not interested in patterns of endogenous mental growth but in familial patterns that predicted particular emotional and temperamental outcomes. They brought one of the projects of the Yale group to fruition by deploying a behaviorist version of Freudian theory.

In social psychology, Leonard Berkowitz's work on aggression provides a specific example of the introjection of ideas of a neobehaviorist origin into the field.[5] He deployed an emended version of the Yale group's frustration-aggression hypothesis.[6] Richard H. Walters and his associates used learning theory as an aid in explaining the process of socialization. Walters and Ross D. Parke summarized their position as follows: "reported relationships between such variables as social deprivation, dependency, self-esteem, and various measures of social influence can be largely understood in terms of (1) the eliciting and modification of orienting and responding responses, and (2) the behavioral effects of variations in emotional arousal."[7]

In the area of altruism, two theories deploying instrumentalist theories of motivation developed. Blau's social-exchange theory stated that individual rewards provided the basis for social associations.[8] Piliavin and his associates attempted to explain helping behavior in terms of a cost/benefit analysis driven by a selfish desire to rid oneself of an unpleasant emotional state.[9] Typically, the unpleasant state was not characterized in any way. The exclusive use of a self-regarding motive that was, at the same time, a negative drive was a classic use of a deficit theory of motivation.

Ultimately, deficit theories of motivation found their expression in social psychology in the theories of behavior exchange and equity theory, which thus played the same role as did drive-reduction theories of motivation in neobehaviorist animal science. In essence, behavior exchange stated that people strove to increase their degree of satisfaction relative to their degree of dissatisfaction.[10] Equity theory also postulated that the essence of human nature was to be selfish, but went on to maintain that societies were controlled by mechanisms ensuring that rewards and costs were assigned on a reasonably equitable basis.[11] Adherents of equity theory also differed from learning theorists in that they believed people undertook processes of rational comparison with one another in order to decide whether there had been an equitable sharing of particular rewards, whereas in almost all forms of learning theory it was assumed that both people and animals automatically strove to seek rewards, benefits, or advantages and to avoid pain, harm, or discomfort. Nevertheless, the assumption that the only or the overriding form of motivation was the desire to maximize benefits and minimize costs meant that the two types of theory were very similar. In terms of the shared beliefs of the protagonists regarding the nature of motivation, the two theories were identical.

Psychologists established their academic and intellectual priorities primarily via the course in experimental psychology that formed the essential core of any good undergraduate curriculum until perhaps twenty years ago. Benton J. Underwood, one of Spence's former doctoral students, wrote the most widely used text.[12] In combination with a required course in statistics, the experimental psychology course provided the means whereby undergraduate students learned the core content of psychology and the rudiments of scientific method. On the one hand, method rather than content was emphasized, so that the subject matter was of little intrinsic interest; its function was merely to elucidate the various principles of experimental design.[13] On the other hand, the content was not merely devalued; it was also highly circumscribed. The second edition of Underwood's text contains 591 substantive pages (that is, omitting the introduction, tables of random numbers, references, and index). Of this substantive portion, 46.2 percent was entirely or almost entirely devoted to method (Underwood did deal with perception and psychophysics, but he used those topics as means of illustrating various methodological principles), 7.78 percent to reaction time, 33.5 percent to conditioning and learning, 6.43 percent to memory, and 6.09 percent to thinking.

Underwood's text was not unified in terms of substance, even though his concentration on learning meant that he gave the impression that learning was the content of experimental psychology; but because substantive issues were so often used to illustrate some principle of method, methodological principles dictated content. Even more strikingly, the methods determined the choice of appropriate subject matter and the mode of solution of problems. In the natural sciences, we find the converse relationship; the subject matter controls methods of inquiry into its nature. But in psychology, operationism reigned supreme; form predominated over substance.

Neobehaviorism's dominance over subject matter was paralleled by an institutional dominance. For example, a survey of the editorship of the leading American journals of experimental psychology from 1945 to 1965 shows that the typical editor was either a behaviorist or a sympathizer. Langfeld, who was extremely sympathetic to Hull's views, edited the *Psychological Review* until 1948. Caroll C. Pratt, a strong advocate of operationism, took over until 1954, to be succeeded by the social psychologist Newcomb, who, even if he was not a behaviorist, was very much an empiricist. Richard L. Solomon, a neobehaviorist, was editor from 1960 to 1964, and was succeeded by Charles N. Cofer, who specialized in verbal learning. Samuel W. Fernberger was editor of the *Journal of Experimental Psychology* until 1946. From 1947 the editorship was held by two people prominent in the field of verbal learning: Francis W. Irwin (1947–49) and Arthur W. Melton (1950–62). David A. Grant, well known for his work on classical conditioning, was editor from 1963 onward. John F. Dashiell edited *Psychological Monographs* until 1947. Herbert S. Conrad was editor until 1957, when he was succeeded by the animal psychologist Norman L. Munn, who handed over to Gregory Kimble in 1963. Comparative psychologists edited the *Journal of Comparative and Physiological Psychology* until 1962 (Roy M. Dorcus until 1947, Calvin P. Stone from 1948 to 1950, and Harry F. Harlow from 1951 to 1962). The behaviorist W. K. Estes took over in 1962. Even when a comparative psychologist was editor, however, neobehaviorists like Frank Logan served as consulting editors.

A school of thought cannot be a school without acolytes. During neobehaviorism's period of ascendancy it was Spence, rather than Hull, who produced those acolytes. The graduate program at Iowa State University formed his operational base. According to Kendler,

> Iowa psychology in the early 1940s, despite the diversity of fields—learning, social, audition, personality, psychometrics, speech pathology, clinical, and intelligence—possessed a unity of purpose: to produce a reliable body of knowledge that could be theoretically integrated. An easy optimism reigned that the expected progress would be inevitable, and some even encouraged the dream that psychology would enter a new stage of development that would allow this discipline to take its rightful place among the hard sciences.[14]

Spence was appointed to Iowa State in 1938, and became head of the department of psychology in 1942; he retained that post until 1964, when he went to the University of Texas. Spence's chief rival at Iowa State was the Gestalt psychologist Kurt Lewin. Once Lewin had left to go to the Massachusetts Institute of Technology in 1944, Spence reigned supreme. In the mid-1940s he appointed two productive behaviorists, Judson S. Brown and Isadore E. Farber, to the Iowa faculty; another behaviorist, Charles Spiker, was appointed a little later.

In a book such as this, which deals with behaviorism at a very general level, it is impossible to do justice to Spence's contributions. Unlike equally creative and productive behaviorists (Tolman or Skinner, for example), he did not feel impelled to formulate a distinctive theory.[15] Instead he worked within the confines of Hull's theory. He was, however, a full collaborator in the enterprise and not a mere adjutant; the correspondence between Hull and Spence shows that Hull's theory should really be called the Hull-Spence theory.[16] As a Hullian, Spence never ceased to doubt that learning was psychology's fundamental area of study. Again following Hull, he also believed that Pavlovian conditioning provided the paradigm for theories of learning.

Spence's most significant contributions as a theorist were to operationism, and were therefore programmatic rather than substantial. Here he worked closely with his colleague at Iowa, Gustav Bergmann. Bergmann had been a member of the Vienna Circle; thus Spence's highly pragmatic and realistic operationism was much closer to logical positivism than that of his contemporaries.[17] Analogously, Spence was the most behaviorist of all the neobehaviorists. He believed, for example, that delay of reinforcement adversely affected performance because it induced frustration. Frustration in turn elicited responses that competed with goal-gaining responses.

In neobehaviorism Spence worked extensively on discrimination learning and, via his studies on eyelid conditioning, on motivation.[18] In discrimination learning animals are forced to make a choice. In the simplest cases, they must either respond or not; in slightly more complex cases they have to choose one action rather than another (e.g., turning left or turning right in a T-maze); in the most complex cases they have to base their choice on a cue (brightness, color, or size, for example). In the last case, it would appear that animals represent the experimental situation to themselves and respond to the relationship between the cues rather than to the cues themselves. This position (known as continuity theory) was, of course, anathema to an empiricist like Spence, who formulated a noncontinuity theory in which he asserted that the consistent association of reward with one cue elicited a tendency to approach it, whereas the consistent association of nonreward elicited avoidance tendencies. These tendencies, in turn, generated positive and negative gradients respectively. The algebraic sum of the two gradients controlled action and the outcome was seemingly relational choices. In a series of brilliant studies Spence demonstrated that his model could make many predictions and could overcome all the criticisms mounted against it during his lifetime. After his death his model was incorporated into a synthesis of the continuity and noncontinuity positions, but such an outcome would have pleased him.[19]

In motivation, Spence worked from the same assumptions as Hull but arrived at very different conclusions. Both were empirical environmentalists, animated by the belief that goal objects acquired their value or their significance as a result of detailed, moment-by-moment acquaintance. Both Hull and Spence, in common with most motivational theorists, assigned motivation a cue function and an arousal function. That is, animals were motivated to repeat past actions or habits, where habits were construed as inner forces established by learned associations between situations and actions. However, animals had to be propelled into action. Here the fundamental concepts were drive (psycho-physiological energy) and incentive (excitements or inhibitions acquired as a consequence of direct or remote experiences with goal objects). Hull gave habit a wide field of application (for example, initially he believed that the magnitude of reinforcement impinged directly on habit strength) and circumscribed that of arousal. In contrast, Spence restricted habit to the pairing of stimuli and responses. Conversely, he enlarged arousal's sphere of operation. Hull had assumed that drive and incentive exerted separate multiplicative effects on habit strength. Spence assumed that drive and incentive added their effects to each other and that the sum had a multiplicative effect on habit strength. If one did not question the assumptions of Hullian theory, Spence's formulation yielded superior predictions to Hull's.[20] Once one begins to question Hull's assumptions, however, Spence's theory collapses.[21]

Today very few authors of textbooks on learning and motivation assign even a section of a chapter to Spence. For the historian of behaviorism, however, he is a formidable figure because no other neobehaviorist could match his power and influence. Largely as a result of his efforts, Iowa psychology was extremely strong and therefore in a good position to benefit from the greatly increased funding that became available after World War II. Spence was solely responsible for obtaining the funding for a large research building, later named the Spence Laboratories of Psychology. The department of psychology at Iowa State led all other American universities in the production of graduate students and in the publishing of articles in the leading journals. In addition, Iowa led all other American universities in the publication of Ph.D. theses.[22]

Between 1940 and 1964 Spence graduated seventy-two doctoral students from Iowa State University, almost 50 percent of the total number of Iowa psychology doctorates for that period.[23] Furthermore, Farber (who got his Ph.D. under Spence in 1946) graduated eight doctoral students between 1951 and 1962. The first appointments of Iowa graduates spanned North America, from Toronto in the north to Tulane in the south, and from Washington in the west to New York University and Duke University in the east. Of Spence's Iowa students, nineteen had outstanding research careers. Eighteen achieved excellence in their supervisor's areas of expertise.[24]

Not unexpectedly, animal scientists comprise the largest group (ten people), nine of whom remained faithful to behaviorism to the end of their careers.[25] Of those nine, Gregory Kimble (Ph.D., 1945) was the dominant figure, not because of his research output but because he edited the second version of a classical text in learning, Ernest Hilgard's and Donald Marquis's *Conditioning and Learning*.[26] Kimble's version was an entirely new book rather than a revision and was also more than a synoptic view of what had become an extensive and variegated body of research. Kimble interpreted his material through Hull's and Spence's eyes. Other theorists (especially Guthrie and Tolman) were given a full and fair hearing. The purpose of that hearing was, however, to discount their views. Skinner received short shrift as a theorist (largely, I suspect, because his theory did not form a part of what Hull, Spence, or Kimble would construe as core or classical neobehaviorism). Like Hull, however, Kimble certainly conceded that Skinner had made invaluable methodological contributions. Kimble's book thus had all the formal characteristics of a scientific treatise. He deftly summarized the history of learning, marshaling his material so that it advanced toward a scientific consummation. He portrayed the acquisition and retention of all knowledge and all skills in terms of classical or instrumental conditioning. He set out the seemingly adamantine distinctions between the two forms of conditioning with exemplary clarity. The rest of the book consisted of a discussion of the various subfields of learning as interpreted by a convinced Hullian.

Frank Logan (Ph.D., 1951) developed a detailed syntax for the language of neobehaviorism. His micromolar theory treated each variant or form of a response (such as particular forces of speeds of responding) separately, and his research consisted of detailed studies of the relationships between relevant antecedent variables and specific response outcomes.[27] In principle, his work allowed neobehaviorists to explain certain puzzles and ambiguities. Most neobehaviorists followed Hull in defining response classes in terms of their outcomes (e.g., all bar-presses for food were placed in the same category). That led Hull to assume that all ways of assessing the same response class would automatically correlate, which is not the case. Logan demonstrated that different manifestations of the same goal-gaining class of responses are different responses and have specific and differing relationships to antecedent variables. For example, a near-satiated dog will respond weakly to a conditioned stimulus, but its ultimate level of learning may well be the same as that of a hungry dog, which will respond much more strongly.

Abram Amsel (Ph.D., 1948) followed in Spence's footsteps by giving a strictly behavioral account of the consequences of nonreinforcement.[28] Typically, neobehaviorists (including Hull) assigned nonreinforcement a merely passive role. Amsel, however, believed that nonreinforcement acted like punishment, thereby inducing frustration, which acted as a drive and elicited stronger and more forceful responses from frustrated than from nonfrustrated animals. The theory proved fruitful, and Amsel and his students produced a large body of work over a thirty-year period. But now the theory has run into the sand.[29] Amsel fought a vigorous rearguard action against the stolidly victorious cognitivists. Together with Michael Rashotte, he assembled a volume of Hull's theoretical articles with a commentary that unabashedly asserted the value of Hull's approach. His book *Behaviorism, Neobehaviorism, and Cognitivism in Learning Theory* was an equally vigorous defense of neobehaviorism as a whole.[30] Amsel played a role similar to Kimble's, but as the writer of a retrospective rather than a concurrent view of behaviorism.

Benton J. Underwood (Ph.D., 1942) bestrode the fields of memory and verbal learning like a colossus. Together with Leo Postman, he pushed the ill-fated interference theory of forgetting to its limits until it finally cracked. Interference theory is behaviorist in spirit in that it held that all forgetting results from interference at the time of recall. Memory was treated as nothing other than the obverse of forgetting, and forgetting was said to be exclusively under the control of processes that could be observed (and, of course, measured). Two more of Spence's Ph.D.'s (Arthur L. Irion, who graduated in 1947, and Clyde Noble, who graduated in 1951) had significant careers in the area.

Spence's students also played a significant role in the area of human learning and motivation. Howard H. Kendler (Ph.D., 1943) had an immensely productive career. He started by producing numerous studies on drive in which he attempted to demonstrate that Hull's position was superior to Tolman's. In the early 1950s he began to develop a behaviorist theory of thinking. Thereafter, using both humans and animals as subjects, he worked on such topics as memory, mediation, reversal shift, and discrimination. His wife, Tracy Seedman Kendler (Ph.D., 1943), often in coauthorship with her husband, worked on mediation learning (and on other topics) in children. Howard Kendler also wrote some significant theoretical articles, especially one in which he robustly defended what he called "S-R reinforcement theory" (the theory of Hull, Spence, and Neal Miller) against its detractors.[31] Toward the end of his life, however, he seemed to become disenchanted with neobehaviorism:

Although not as much confidence can be placed in historical conclusions as experimental data, a reasonable hypothesis can be offered that the dream of constructing a general behavior theory of the sort that Hull and Spence, and also Tolman and Lewin, envisioned was frustrated by an optimistic view known as behavioral determinism; behavior is a self-contained system that can be understood by reference only to environmental-behavioral relationships in the absence of neuropsychological processes. When theoretical controversies, such as latent learning . . . could be neatly resolved, we psychologists automatically assumed that the difficulty resulted from theoretical ambiguities, which, if eliminated, would result in theoretical resolutions by empirical means. In retrospect, perhaps another possibility should have been considered: Environmental-behavioral research is an open system in which many constant and fluctuating variables operate that are beyond the knowledge and control of the researcher. In essence, precise theories that have general implications cannot be formulated if based only on environmental-behavioral relationships.[32]

Irving M. Maltzman's (Ph.D., 1949) career was almost as productive as Kendler's. Like Kendler, he started to work on thinking in the mid-1950s, moving from there to semantic generalization. In 1970 he started work on human conditioning and worked on that topic for the rest of his career. Janet Taylor Spence (Ph.D., 1949) began her research career by working on anxiety and conditioning. In 1953 she constructed the Taylor Manifest Anxiety Scale, one of the most widely used scales in psychology. By the mid-1950s she was working on the influence of motivation on perception (a hot topic in those days), moving to response bias and recognition thresholds in the early 1960s.

It is usually said that neobehaviorism lost its power and influence because in the decade beginning in 1965, neobehaviorist animal science imploded, thereby destroying neobehaviorism's foundations and because, at about the same time, the so-called cognitive revolution occurred in experimental psychology.[33] Psychologists, in effect, returned to their roots and began to study taboo subjects such as consciousness, memory, or thinking, using human subjects.

The "cognitive revolution" is usually treated as a paradigm shift. One can apply that term, however, only if certain conditions are satisfied. First, the term can apply only to true sciences, and it is evident that the various forms of neobehaviorism were ideologies and not sciences. Second, a crisis must precede a paradigm shift. That condition does seem to be satisfied since there is no doubt that neobehaviorist animal science did fail. Many (probably most) American animal scientists working during the 1960s and 1970s, however, treated their findings and failures of prediction as what Kuhn would call "puzzles" rather than crises.[34] That is, they were confident that modifications to their theories would settle their problems; they did not feel obliged to abandon neobehaviorism altogether. Certainly, apart from the doubts that Kendler expressed, one sees no signs of regrets, no hints of wavering, no indications of weakening of resolve among Spence's ex-students, and they constitute by far the most significant group of neobehaviorists.[35]

Third, in a true paradigm shift we see a complete discontinuity. Thomas Leahey cogently demonstrates that we find continuities, not discontinuities, in experimental psychology. The major neobehaviorists, especially Tolman and Hull, believed passionately that the higher mental processes constituted the true object of psychological study and that "inner" or "mental" processes had no reality unless they found expression in action.[36] At the same time, the neobehaviorists knew that the forces determining action (especially dispositions) could not themselves become the objects of direct study. Hence their promulgation of operationism. Operationism provides the major connecting thread between neobehaviorism and cognitivism. Today's cognitive psychologists are as deeply committed to operationism, and thus to positivism, as the neobehaviorists were. As operationists, cognitive psychologists deploy fictional entities in exactly the same way as their forebears. Even though computer modeling has replaced the maze or the Skinner box as the analogy of choice, the former plays the same obfuscatory role as the latter. As Kendler realized, the worm in the neobehaviorist apple was its failure to discover genuine causal entities. Those committed to operationism can never overcome that problem. The fixation on physicalist analogies satisfies their longing for explanations with some solid basis but, like a neurotic symptom, does no more than provide them with secondary gain while simultaneously blocking the path to solutions to their deep-seated problems.

Both behaviorism and neobehaviorism were modernist in that their adherents strove to express timeless, universal, and all-inclusive truths. In the arts, modernist discourse was limited to the explication and application of unquestioned principles.[37] In exactly the same way, as Sigmund Koch has commented, behaviorism constituted psychology's philosophy of science.[38] The form of the typical journal article in an experimental journal during neobehaviorism's heyday embodied that worldview; the bulk of the article consisted of the method and the results sections, giving the impression that only technical questions required discussion.[39] Like modernism, behaviorism and neobehaviorism were programmatic (rather than substantive) and hierarchical (that is, their leaders had hero status in the profession, and most professionals were content to follow in their footsteps). Neobehaviorism was "cool." Publicly it expressed itself in a highly formal, neological, neomathematical language in which not a hint of emotion was to be found. Privately matters were different. The available archives are filled not just with emotions like joy, exaltation, foreboding, anger, and hatred but with strong intimations that Hull, Spence, and their colleagues felt the call of destiny. In that respect, neobehaviorists resembled abstract expressionist painters of the New York School; an Alex Colville or an early Frank Stella painting manifests detachment, self-confidence, and self-subsistence. There is no hint of the longing for power, fame, and glory that drove the abstract expressionists into their studios.[40]

Starting in the mid-1960s, the values, goals, and aspirations of the entire psychological profession changed insensibly but deeply and pervasively. Tough-minded, foundationist, positivist experimental psychology has endured but is no longer treated as the inescapable basis of all psychological knowledge. It has become a mere speciality in a practically oriented, pluralist profession. Neobehaviorism's dominance did not ensure its impregnability. Today it is a *terra incognita*. Contemporary psychologists no longer know the names of the leading neobehaviorists, let alone understand their concepts or follow their research practices.

Behaviorism unified the psychological profession, but at a heavy cost. By fusing American pragmatic, instrumental positivism with logical positivism, the behaviorist theorists of the 1950s provided psychologists with a language that was value-free both epistemologically and morally. By using that language to interpret data gathered by seemingly theory-neutral techniques, psychologists could conduct research in every realm of human life. Furthermore, by unknowingly pledging their alliance to methodological behaviorism, American psychologists hoped to avoid all prior theoretical commitments. The problem with value- and theory-neutrality is that it inhibits discussion of the grounds for one's beliefs. In the human sciences, where we must follow to its uttermost limits the discussion of what it means to be a knowing subject actively embedded in a rich and historically stratified social context, any form of positivism rapidly places crippling limitations on the enterprise. The limitations of methodological behaviorism impose a technological treatment of mind on empirical and theoretical outcomes before any specific investigations have begun. That technologizing of mind is a direct consequence of the research methods of psychology that, as Kurt Danziger has shown so convincingly, cannot possibly be theory-neutral.

Those who created the research practices of contemporary psychology believed very strongly that psychology's role was to create a socially useful technology of the mind. In the 1920s, when the basis for these practices was formulated, modernism was in full flood. The three great themes of modernism were the substitution of form for substance, the universalization of cultural, aesthetic, and metaphysical themes, and the exaltation of technology. Nature (including human nature) had, it seemed, been finally conquered. Those parts of it that were untamable could be experienced by travelers (and, at second hand, by those who read their books). Otherwise, the physical aspects of nature were subdued to human needs via agricultural technology, while the arts either celebrated nature in a purely formal sense or plundered the past in a search for a universal aesthetic. In that life-world, a technology of the mind seemed reasonable and realizable. It found expression in a richly imagined world that promised not just technological success and the ultimate means of understanding mental life but beauty and fulfillment. But now the sun of modernism, which nourished behaviorism and its seed, operationism, has sunk beneath the horizon. Bereft of its support, the psychological technologies of yesteryear are pale, limp, and etiolated.

Notes

NOTES TO THE INTRODUCTION

1. See Brian D. Mackenzie, *Behaviourism and the Limits of Scientific Method* (Cambridge: Cambridge University Press, 1977); John M. O'Donnell, *The Origins of Behaviorism: American Psychology, 1870–1920* (New York: New York University Press, 1985); Franz Samelson, "Struggle for Scientific Authority: The Reception of Watson's Behaviorism, 1913–1920," *Journal of the History of the Behavioral Sciences* 17 (1981): 399–425; idem, "Organizing for the Kingdom of Behavior: Academic Battles and Organizational Politics in the Twenties," *Journal of the History of the Behavioral Sciences* 21 (1985): 33–47; and Laurence D. Smith, *Behaviorism and Logical Positivism: A Reassessment of the Alliance* (Stanford: Stanford University Press, 1986).

2. See especially Mackenzie, *Behaviourism and the Limits of Scientific Method*.

3. See Willard D. Day, "On the Difference between Radical and Methodological Behaviorism," *Behaviorism* 11 (1983): 89–102; and Paul M. Churchland, *Matter and Consciousness* (Cambridge: MIT Press, 1984), 23–25, 54–55.

4. John B. Watson, "Behaviorism as the Psychologist Views It," *Psychological Review* 20 (1913): 158.

5. Samelson, "Struggle for Scientific Authority."

6. B. F. Skinner, "Why Are Theories of Learning Necessary?" *Psychological Review* 57 (1950): 193–216.

7. In Edward C. Tolman, *Drives toward War* (New York: Appleton-Century, 1942). Also see Nancy K. Innis, "Drives toward War" (paper presented at a Cheiron conference, Queens University, Kingston, Ontario, June 1989).

8. For a definitive account of the relationships between behaviorism and logical positivism, see Smith, *Behaviorism and Logical Positivism*.

9. See John B. Watson, *Psychology from the Standpoint of a Behaviorist* (Philadelphia: Lippincott, 1919), 322–33; and idem, *Behaviorism* (New York: People's Institute, 1924), chap. 10.

10. See Richard S. Peters and Henri Tajfel, "Hobbes and Hull: Metaphysicians of Behaviour," *British Journal for the Philosophy of Science* 8 (1958): 30–44; John A. Mills, "Hull's Theory of Learning as a Philosophical System: I. An

Outline of the Theory," *Canadian Psychological Review* 19 (1978): 27–40; idem, "Hull's Theory of Learning: II. A Criticism of the Theory and Its Relationship to the History of Psychological Thought," *Canadian Psychological Review* 19 (1978): 116–27; idem, "The Genesis of Hull's *Principles of Behavior*," *Journal of the History of the Behavioral Sciences* 24 (1988): 392–401; and Smith, *Behaviorism and Logical Positivism*, 155–62.

11. Finally, Tolman was a neorealist rather than a positivist. The neorealists were essentially materialists.

12. The behaviorists had two major antagonists in the field of animal science. In North America Frank A. Beach led one group. See Ernest R. Hilgard, *Psychology in America: A Historical Survey* (New York: Harcourt Brace Jovanovich, 1987), 415. The behaviorists' other antagonists were the European ethologists, led by Konrad Lorenz and Nikko Tinbergen. Lorenz vehemently attacked the behaviorists, especially in *Evolution and Modification of Behavior* (Chicago: University of Chicago Press, 1965). He also disapproved of American comparative psychology, although eventually there was a rapprochement between him and Lehrman. See Robert A. Hinde, *Ethology* (London: Collins, 1982), chap. 10.

13. See comments on the Milgram experiment in Henderikus J. Stam, Ian Lubek, and H. Lorraine Radtke, "Repopulating Social Psychology Texts: Disembodied 'Subjects' and Embodied Subjectivity," in *Reconstructing the Psychological Subject*, ed. B. Bayer and J. Shotter (London: Sage, in press). They state that the responses to Milgram's manipulations were more varied and ambivalent than he reported in published accounts of his work.

14. John A. Mills, "The Origins and Significance of Clark L. Hull's Theory of Value," in *Recent Advances in Theoretical Psychology*, vol. 2, ed. W. J. Baker, R. van Hezewijk, M. E. Hyland, and S. Terwee (New York: Springer-Verlag, 1990), 335–45; idem, "Some Observations on Skinner's Moral Theory," *Journal for the Theory of Social Behaviour* 12 (1982): 140–60; and idem, "Purpose and Conditioning: A Reply to Waller," *Journal for the Theory of Social Behaviour* 14 (1984): 363–67.

15. Watson, *Psychology from the Standpoint of a Behaviorist*, 10 (emphasis in original).

16. Woodworth's *Experimental Psychology* (New York: Holt, 1938) started life as a set of mimeographed notes that were modified from 1920 onward and known informally as the "Columbia bible." For an analysis of Woodworth's approach to experimental method, see Andrew S. Winston, "*Cause* and *Experiment* in Introductory Psychology: An Analysis of R. S. Woodworth's Textbooks," *Teaching of Psychology* 15 (1988): 79–83; and idem, "Robert Sessions Woodworth and the 'Columbia Bible': How the Psychological Experiment was Redefined," *American Journal of Psychology* 103 (1990): 391–401.

17. See Tim B. Rogers, "Operationism in Psychology: A Discussion of Con-

textual Antecedents and an Historical Interpretation of Its Longevity," *Journal of the History of the Behavioral Sciences* 25 (1989): 139–53.

18. See S. S. Stevens, "The Operational Basis of Psychology," *American Journal of Psychology* 47 (1935): 323–30; and idem, "The Operational Definition of Concepts," *Psychological Review* 42 (1935): 517–27.

19. Konrad Lorenz, "The Establishment of the Instinct Concept," in *Studies in Human and Animal Behaviour*, trans. R. Martin, vol. 1 (London: Methuen, 1970), 259–315. Original work published in 1937.

20. For example, see David Marr, *The Computational Investigation into the Human Representation and Processing of Visual Information* (New York: Freeman, 1982).

21. Kurt Danziger, *Constructing the Subject: Historical Origins of Psychological Research* (Cambridge: Cambridge University Press, 1990).

22. Rogers, "Operationism in Psychology."

23. See Harold Israel and B. Goldstein, "Operationism in Psychology," *Psychological Review* 51 (1944): 177–88.

24. See Neal E. Miller, "Effects of Drugs on Motivation: The Value of Using a Variety of Measures," *Annals of the New York Academy of Science* 65 (1956): 318–33.

25. Robert A. Hinde, *Animal Behaviour: A Synthesis of Ethology and Comparative Psychology*, 2d ed. (New York: McGraw-Hill, 1970), chaps. 8, 9, 12, 15.

26. See G. P. Baerends, "The Functional Organization of Behaviour," *Animal Behaviour* 24 (1976): 726–38; G. P. Baerends, R. Brouwer, and H. Tj. Waterbolk, "Ethological Studies on *Lebistes reticulatus* (Peters), I: An Analysis of the Male Courtship Pattern," *Behaviour* 8 (1955): 249–334; Hinde, *Animal Behaviour*, chap. 12; and David J. McFarland and R. Sibly, "The Behavioural Final Common Path," *Philosophical Transactions of the Royal Society of London*, Series B, 270, no. 207 (1975): 265–93.

27. For a theoretical explanation of instinctive drift and adjunctive behavior, see John E. R. Staddon and Virginia L. Simmelhag, "The Superstition Experiment: A Reexamination of Its Implications for the Principles of Adaptive Behavior," *Psychological Review* 78 (1971): 3–43.

28. For a balanced assessment of the role of operant conditioning, see Barry Schwartz and Steven J. Robbins, *Psychology of Learning and Behavior*, 4th ed. (New York: Norton, 1995).

29. Hinde, *Ethology*, 192; David McFarland, *Animal Behaviour*, 2d ed. (New York: Wiley, 1993), chap. 19.

30. Rogers, "Operationism in Psychology."

31. See Jacob Cohen, "The Statistical Power of Abnormal and Social Psychological Research: A Review," *Journal of Abnormal and Social Psychology* 65 (1962): 145–53; idem, "Some Statistical Issues in Psychological Research," in *Handbook of Clinical Psychology*, ed. B. Wolman (New York: McGraw-Hill,

1965), 95–121; and Graham M. Vaughan and Michael C. Corballis, "Beyond Tests of Significance," *Psychological Bulletin* 72 (1969): 204–13.

32. See Jan Smedslund, *Becoming a Psychologist: Theoretical Foundations for a Humanistic Psychology* (New York: Halsted Press, 1972); idem, "What Is Necessarily True in Psychology," in *Annals of Theoretical Psychology*, vol. 2, ed. J. R. Royce and L. P. Mos (New York: Plenum Press, 1984), 251–302; idem, *Psycho-logic* (New York: Springer-Verlag, 1988); and idem, "How Shall the Concept of Anger Be Defined?" *Theory and Psychology* 3 (1993): 5–33.

33. See Rogers, "Operationism in Psychology."

34. For a critique of current practices and alternatives to them, see the journal *Theory and Psychology*.

35. For an account of those doctrines, see Hamilton Cravens and John C. Burnham, "Psychology and Evolutionary Naturalism in American Thought, 1890–1940," *American Quarterly* 23 (1971): 635–57.

NOTES TO CHAPTER 1

1. Accounts of Progressivism can be found in John C. Burnham, "Psychiatry, Psychology, and the Progressive Movement," *American Quarterly* 12 (1960): 457–65; idem, "The New Psychology: From Narcissism to Social Control," in *Change and Continuity in Twentieth Century America: The 1920s*, ed. J. Braeman, R. H. Bremner, and D. Brody (Columbus: Ohio State University Press, 1972), 351–98; idem, "Essay," in *Progressivism*, ed. John D. Buenker, J. Burnham, and Robert M. Crunden (Cambridge, MA: Schenkman Books, 1977), 3–29; Eric F. Goldman, *Rendezvous with Destiny* (New York: Knopf, 1952); Lewis Gould, ed., *The Progressive Era* (Syracuse: Syracuse University Press, 1974); Samuel P. Hays, "Introduction: The New Organizational Society," in *Building the Organizational Society*, ed. J. Israel (New York: Free Press, 1972), 1–16; Richard Hofstadter, *The Age of Reform: From Bryan to F.D.R.* (New York: Knopf, 1955); R. Laurence Moore, "Directions of Thought in Progressive America," in Gould, ed., *The Progressive Era*, 35–43; David Noble, *The Paradox of Progressive Thought* (Minneapolis: University of Minnesota Press, 1958); Robert H. Wiebe, *Businessmen and Reform: A Study of the Progressive Movement* (Cambridge: Harvard University Press, 1962).

2. For an account of the emergence of the American social sciences from the American Social Science Association, see Thomas H. Haskell, *Emergence of a Professional Social Science: The American Social Science Association and the Nineteenth Century Crisis of Authority* (Urbana: University of Illinois Press, 1977).

3. For a full account of the history of American social science, see Dorothy Ross, *The Origins of American Social Science* (Cambridge: Cambridge University Press, 1991).

4. He devised a four-point scale, with the zero point represented by native-born Americans of Anglo-Saxon descent, the next point by white Americans born of foreign parents, the third by foreign-born white Americans, and the fourth by colored Americans.

5. Franklin Henry Giddings, "The Social Marking System," *Papers and Proceedings of the American Sociological Society* 4 (1909): 42–61.

6. Luther Lee Bernard, "The Objective Viewpoint in Sociology," *American Journal of Sociology* 25 (1919): 298–325.

7. Harold Laski, *The Dangers of Obedience and Other Essays* (New York: Harper, 1930), 152–53.

8. Robert E. L. Faris, *Chicago Sociology: 1920–1932* (San Francisco: Chandler, 1967), 41 (italics in original).

9. See Ernest W. Burgess, "The Growth of the City: An Introduction to a Research Project," in *The City*, ed. Robert E. Park, Ernest W. Burgess, and Roderick D. McKenzie (Chicago: University of Chicago Press, 1967), 47–62.

10. The institutionalists were a minority (albeit a powerful one) within American economics. The neoclassicists started a counterattack against them in the mid-1920s. The institutionalists met their Waterloo at a roundtable at the annual meeting of the American Economic Association in 1927, when seven neoclassicists confronted Mitchell. Following that episode, both Clark and Mitchell became subdued, and institutionalism lost its momentum. For an account of American economic theory in the late 1920s and the 1930s, see Ross, *Origins of American Social Science*, 415 ff.

11. Wesley Clair Mitchell, "Quantitative Analysis in Economic Theory," in *The Backward Art of Spending Money and Other Essays* (New York: McGraw-Hill, 1937), 27. Mitchell's article was his presidential address to the thirty-seventh annual meeting of the American Economic Association and was first published in the *American Economic Review* 15 (1925): 1–12.

12. See especially Charles C. Merriam, *New Aspects of Politics* (Chicago: University of Chicago Press, 1925). Albert Somit and Joseph Tanenhaus, in *The Development of American Political Science: From Burgess to Behavioralism* (New York: Irvington, 1982) claim that Merriam's article played a crucial role in the creation of the Social Science Research Council. Scientism was the dominant theme of the three National Conferences on the Science of Politics (1923–25). The most complete statement of the scientistic view is to be found in C. E. G. Catlin, *The Science and Method of Politics* (New York: Knopf, 1927), especially pt. 2, chap. 1.

13. Charles C. Merriam, "The Present State of the Study of Politics," *American Political Science Review* 15 (1921): 183–84.

14. See Merriam, *New Aspects*, 108 ff.

15. Merriam, "The Present State of the Study of Politics," 181.

16. Floyd H. Allport, "Political Science and Psychology," in *The Social Sci-*

ences and Their Interrelations, ed. William F. Ogburn and Alexander Goldenweiser (New York: Houghton Mifflin, 1927), 277.

17. Ibid., 268–69.

18. Somit and Tanenhaus briefly discuss this body of work *The Development of American Political Science*, 127–33.

19. For the New Realists' impact on psychology, see Thomas B. Leahey, *A History of Modern Psychology*, 2d ed. (Englewood Cliffs, NJ: Prentice Hall, 1994), 170–73; William M. O'Neill, "Realism and Behaviorism," *Journal of the History of the Behavioral Sciences* 4 (1968): 152–60; and idem, "American Behaviorism: A Historical and Critical Analysis," *Theory and Psychology* 5 (1995): 285–305.

20. Edwin B. Holt, Walter T. Marvin, Walter P. Montague, Ralph Barton Perry, Walter B. Pitkin, and Edward G. Spaulding, "The Program and First Platform of Six Realists," *Journal of Philosophy, Psychology and Scientific Methods* 7 (1910): 393–401; and idem, *The New Realism: Cooperative Studies in Philosophy* (New York: Macmillan, 1912).

21. See Ralph Barton Perry, "A Behavioristic View of Purpose," *Journal of Philosophy* 18 (1921): 85–105.

22. See Ralph Barton Perry, "The Cognitive Interest and Its Refinements," *Journal of Philosophy* 18 (1921): 365–75.

23. Of the six who wrote the New Realist Manifesto, only Holt, Perry, and Montague had fruitful philosophical careers. Spaulding became a professor at Princeton and described himself as an occasional contributor to scientific and philosophical periodicals. Marvin spent most of his career as dean of arts at Rutgers, publishing very little. Pitkin became a popular author, publishing forty-five books on an astonishingly wide range of topics.

24. See especially Edwin B. Holt, *The Concept of Consciousness* (New York: Macmillan, 1914).

25. See Edwin B. Holt, "Response and Cognition: II. Cognition as Response," *Journal of Philosophy, Psychology and Scientific Methods* 12 (1915): 393–409.

26. Behaviorism was a central problem for other American philosophers of the day. W. Heath Bawden, in "The Presuppositions of a Behaviorist Psychology," *Psychological Review* 25 (1918): 171–90, supported behaviorism. B. H. Bode criticized both behaviorism and the introspective method. See B. H. Bode, "What Is Psychology," *Psychological Review* 29 (1922): 250–58; idem, "The Method of Introspection," *Journal of Philosophy, Psychology and Scientific Methods* 10 (1913): 85–91; idem, "The Definition of Consciousness," *Journal of Philosophy, Psychology and Scientific Methods*: 232–39; idem, "Psychology as a Science of Behavior," *Psychological Review* 21 (1914): 46–61; and idem, "Intelligence and Behavior," *Journal of Philosophy* 18 (1921): 10–17.

27. Thomas Robischon, "Frederick James Eugene Woodbridge," in *Encyclo-*

pedia of Philosophy, vol. 8, ed. Paul Edwards (New York: Macmillan, 1967) summarizes Woodbridge's views very effectively on p. 345.

28. James E. Woodbridge, "The Nature of Consciousness," *Journal of Philosophy, Psychology and Scientific Methods* 2 (1905): 119–25. Woodbridge's thesis was clearly "in the air" at the time. W. Heath Bawden advanced it in "The Necessity from the Standpoint of Scientific Method of a Reconstruction of the Ideas of the Psychical and the Physical," *Journal of Philosophy, Psychology and Scientific Methods* 1 (1904): 62–68.

29. Walter P. Montague, "Confessions," in *Contemporary American Philosophy*, vol. 2, ed. G. P. Adams (New York: Russell and Russell, 1962), 144.

30. These articles, together with several others, are reprinted in Edgar Arthur Singer, Jr., *Mind as Behavior and Studies in Empirical Idealism* (Columbus, OH: R. G. Adams, 1924). Almost all the articles in the book were published or fully drafted before 1917.

31. According to Stevenson Smith and Edwin R. Guthrie, *General Psychology in Terms of Behavior* (New York: Appleton, 1921), 2, "The first systematic statement that mind could be described in terms of behavior was made by Dr. E. A. Singer, Jr."

32. Singer, *Mind as Behavior*, vii (emphasis in original).

33. James G. Taylor, *A Behaviorist Theory of Perception* (New Haven: Yale University Press, 1962).

34. Grace de Laguna, "*Dualism in Animal Psychology*," *Journal of Philosophy, Psychology and Scientific Methods* 15 (1918): 617–27. Washburn replied to de Laguna in "*Dualism in Animal Psychology*," *Journal of Philosophy, Psychology and Scientific Methods* 16 (1919): 41–44. De Laguna's rejoinder was published, in the same issue, as "Dualism and Animal Psychology: A Rejoinder," 296–300.

35. De Laguna, "*Dualism in Animal Psychology*," 620–21 (emphasis in original).

36. De Laguna, "Dualism and Animal Psychology: A Rejoinder," 297.

37. Ibid., 299.

38. De Laguna, "Emotion and Perception from the Behaviorist Standpoint," *Psychological Review* 26 (1919): 409.

39. Quoted in Robert S. Woodworth, *Contemporary Schools of Psychology*, 8th ed. (London: Methuen, 1951), 72–73 (all omissions from Cattell's text are Woodworth's).

40. William McDougall, *An Introduction to Social Psychology* (London: Methuen, 1908), 6. Also see a very similar passage in McDougall's *Physiological Psychology* (quoted in Woodworth *Contemporary Schools*, 73).

41. McDougall, *Introduction to Social Psychology*, 14.

42. Pillsbury did his undergraduate work at Nebraska under Harry Kirke Wolfe and his doctoral work at Cornell, graduating in 1896. His first teaching

post was at Michigan. From 1912 onward, he devoted his energies to writing textbooks. His most prominent works were *Essentials of Psychology* and *History of Psychology*. See the entry on him in Ludy T. Benjamin, Jr.'s, *Harry Kirke Wolfe: Pioneer in Psychology* (Lincoln: University of Nebraska Press, 1991) 154–56; and K. M. Dallenbach's obituary in the *American Journal of Psychology* 74 (1961): 165–76. Also see Paul Ballantyne's entry in the *American National Biography* (New York: Oxford University Press, in press). I am grateful to Dr. Ballantyne, who sent me the draft of that entry, and to Rob Wozniak for helping me find information about Pillsbury.

43. Walter B. Pillsbury, *Essentials of Psychology* (New York: Macmillan, 1911), vii.

44. Ibid., 5.

45. John Burnham comments that Woodworth tried to repudiate Watson's claim to the title "father of behaviorism." Woodworth buttressed his case by making selective quotations from Pillsbury's book. See Woodworth, *Contemporary Schools*, 73–74.

46. For an account of Meyer's life and career, see Erwin A. Esper, "Max Meyer: The Making of a Scientific Isolate," *Journal of the History of the Behavioral Sciences* 2 (1966): 341–56; and idem, "Max Meyer in America," *Journal of the History of the Behavioral Sciences* 3 (1967): 107–31. The only obituary I could find was by Ira J. Hirsch in the *American Journal of Psychology* 80 (1967): 644–45. Esper has written an excellent account of Meyer's contributions to behaviorism and linguistics in *Mentalism and Objectivism in Linguistics: The Sources of Leonard Bloomfield's Psychology of Language* (New York: American Elsevier, 1968). I am most grateful to Professor Roger Wales for acquainting me with Esper's book and for lending me his copy.

47. See Esper, *Mentalism and Objectivism in Linguistics*, 158. Meyer also said that in 1896 Watson was still a college freshman.

48. Esper, in *Mentalism and Objectivism in Linguistics*, said that Meyer was influenced by Geiger's *Der Ursprung der Sprache* (Stuttgart: Cotta, 1869; 2d ed., 1878).

49. Ibid., 118.

50. Max Meyer, "Frequency, Duration and Recency versus Double Stimulation," *Psychological Review* 41 (1934): 179.

51. Max Meyer, *The Fundamental Laws of Human Behavior: Lectures on the Foundations of Any Mental or Human Science* (Boston: R. G. Badger, 1911).

52. Max Meyer, *The Psychology of the Other-One* (Columbia: Missouri Books, 1921).

53. Quoted from Esper, *Mentalism and Objectivism in Linguistics*, 167.

54. See Willard Harrell's and Ross Harrison's comment on Weiss in "The Rise and Fall of Behaviorism," *Journal of General Psychology* 18 (1938): 367–421. Accounts of Weiss's life and work are to be found in Leonard Bloomfield, "Albert

Paul Weiss," *Language* 7 (1931): 219–21; R. M. Elliot, "Albert Paul Weiss: 1879–1931," *American Journal of Psychology* 43 (1931): 707–9; Esper, *Mentalism and Objectivism in Linguistics*; and my entry in the *American National Biography*. Weiss's most substantial piece of work was *A Theoretical Basis of Human Behavior* (Columbus: R. G. Adams, 1925; 2d ed., rev., 1929). For similarities between Watson's and Weiss's views, see Albert Paul Weiss, "Relation between Functional and Behavior Psychology," *Psychological Review* 24 (1917): 354; and idem, "Conscious Behavior," *Journal of Philosophy, Psychology and Scientific Methods* 15 (1918): 637.

55. Weiss, "Conscious Behavior," 637.

56. Weiss inveighed against mentalism in "The Mind and the Man-Within," *Psychological Review* 26 (1919): 327–34.

57. See B. F. Skinner *Verbal Behavior* (New York: Appleton-Century-Crofts, 1957).

58. See Charles F. Hockett, *A Course in Modern Linguistics* (New York: Macmillan, 1958). Hockett later renamed key features "design features."

59. Weiss, *A Theoretical Basis of Human Behavior*, 345.

60. Ibid., 353–54.

61. Albert Paul Weiss, "Behavior and the Central Nervous System," *Psychological Review* 29 (1922): 333–34.

62. Biographical information can be found in Paul T. Mountjoy and Jay D. Hansor, "Jacob Robert Kantor (1888–1984)," *American Psychologist* 41 (1986): 1296–97; Edward K. Morris, "Some Relationships between Interbehavioral Psychology and Radical Behaviorism," *Behaviorism* 10 (1982): 188–90; idem "Interbehavioral Psychology and Radical Behaviorism," *Behavior Analyst* 7 (1984): 197–99; and Edward K. Morris, Stephen T. Higgins, and Warren K. Bickel, "The Influence of Kantor's Interbehavioral Psychology on Behavior Analysis," *Behavior Analyst* 5 (1982): 160–63. Also see William S. Verplanck's preface to Noel W. Smith, Paul T. Mountjoy, and Douglas H. Ruben, *Reassessment in Psychology: The Interbehavioral Alternative* (Washington, DC: University Press of America, 1983). I received generous help from Ed Morris, Paul Mountjoy, Noel Smith, William Verplanck, and Brian Midgley. I published a draft of this section on Kantor in the *Interbehaviorist* 22 (1994): 8–13. Mr. Midgley's comment on my article (originally a letter to me) is on pp. 14–19 of the same issue.

63. For a discussion, see Brian D. Midgley and Edward K. Morris, "The Integrated Field: An Alternative to the Behavior-Analytic Conceptualization of Behavioral Units," *Psychological Record* 38 (1988): 483–500.

64. See, for example, Jacob Robert Kantor, "A Functional Interpretation of Human Instincts," *Psychological Review* 27 (1920): 50–72.

65. For accounts of the interbehavioral field, see Morris, "Some Relationships between Interbehavioral Psychology and Radical Behaviorism," 197 ff.

66. Ibid., 198–99.

67. Kantor enunciated his concept of the stimulus very early in his career. See "Suggestions toward a Scientific Interpretation of Perception," *Psychological Review* 27 (1920): 191–216.

68. Jacob Robert Kantor, *Interbehavioral Psychology: A Sample of Scientific System Construction* (Bloomington, IN: Principia Press, 1958), 16.

69. We have to bear in mind that Kantor treated "the brain" as a construct.

70. Those are Professor Verplanck's phrases (in my draft, I merely equated Kantor's setting factors with intervening variables, thereby eliciting criticism from all my Kantorian critics). They are taken, at his suggestion, from a letter to me dated January 27, 1994.

71. Nevertheless, Kantor influenced other behaviorists. For example, Skinner told Professor Verplanck that Kantor's views persuaded him to excise the concepts *drive* and *reflex reserve* from his theory.

72. Also see Midgley, "A Reply to Professor Mills," 16.

73. Letter to the author.

74. That passage is Whig history. I am attributing neobehaviorism's triumph solely to intellectual forces—theories that failed to fit the mold were destined to perish. In his letter to me, Professor Verplanck tells a much more subtle (and, I suspect, more truthful) story. In the 1920s and 1930s the faculty of the large eastern universities ran American psychology. Failure to gain a post there condemned academics to a peripheral status. Partly because he was Jewish and partly because he refused to play by the rules of the eastern WASP establishment, Kantor remained at Indiana. Verplanck hints that in principle, Kantor's ideas could have been influential; that is, had the psychological establishment been a little more socially and intellectually tolerant, American psychology would have had a different history.

75. Hunter derived his term from *anthropos* (man) and *nomus* (law). "The subject matter of anthroponomy is behavior. By *behavior is meant the muscular and glandular activity of the organism.*" Walter S. Hunter, *Human Behavior*, 4th ed. (Chicago: University of Chicago Press, 1932), 2. Biographical information about Hunter can be found in Walter S. Hunter, "Walter S. Hunter," in *A History of Psychology in Autobiography*, vol. 4, ed. E. G. Boring, H. S. Langfeld, H. Werner, and R. M. Yerkes (Worcester, MA: Clark University Press, 1952), 163–87; Leonard Carmichael, "Walter Samuel Hunter: 1889–1954," *American Journal of Psychology* 67 (1954): 732–34; Harold Schlosberg, "Walter S. Hunter: Pioneer Objectivist in Psychology," *Science* 120 (1954): 441–42; and my entry in the *American National Biography*.

76. See Walter S. Hunter, "An Open Letter to the Anti-Behaviorists," *Journal of Philosophy* 19 (1922): 307–8. In his autobiography Hunter states that his behaviorist creed is to be found in his articles "General Anthroponomy and Its Systematic Problems," *American Journal of Psychology* 36 (1925): 286–302; "Psy-

chology and Anthroponomy," *Journal of Genetic Psychology* 33 (1926): 322–46; and "The Subject's Report," *Psychological Review* 32 (1925): 153–70.

77. Walter S. Hunter, "The Delayed Reaction in Animals and Children," *Behavior Monographs* 2 (1913), no. 1; and idem, "The Delayed Reaction in a Child," *Psychological Review* 24 (1917): 74–87. Also see Wayne Dennis, "Thorndike, Hunter, and the Delayed Reaction," *American Psychologist* 10 (1955): 133–34.

78. Hunter, "The Delayed Reaction in Animals and Children," 73.

79. Hunter, "Psychology and Anthroponomy," 332–33.

80. Hunter, *Human Behavior*, 3d ed. (Chicago: University of Chicago Press, 1928).

81. Ibid., 119–20.

82. For an excellent account of Kuo's career, see Gilbert Gottlieb, "Zing-Yang Kuo: Radical Scientific Philosopher and Innovative Experimentalist, 1898–1970," *Journal of Comparative and Physiological Psychology* 80 (1972): 1–10.

83. Zing-Yang Kuo, "A Psychology Without Heredity," *Psychological Review* 31 (1924): 428.

84. Ibid., 427 (emphasis in original).

85. In "The Net Result of the Anti-Heredity Movement in Psychology," *Psychological Review* 36 (1929): 181–99, Kuo criticized Watson for maintaining the distinction between learned and unlearned reactions and said that he inconsistently admitted hereditary emotions while "denying the inheritance of instincts and 'mental traits'" (188–89).

86. Zing-Yang Kuo, "The Fundamental Error of the Concept of Purpose and the Trial and Error Fallacy," *Psychological Review* 35 (1928): 417.

87. Ibid., 420.

88. Ibid., 422 (emphasis in original).

89. Ibid., 425–26.

90. Ibid., 431.

91. See Karl S. Lashley, "The Behavioristic Interpretation of Consciousness," pts. 1 and 2, *Psychological Review* 30: 237–72, 329–53.

NOTES TO CHAPTER 2

1. See Willard Harrell and Ross Harrison, "The Rise and Fall of Behaviorism," *Journal of General Psychology* 18 (1938): 387, 388.

2. For example, see Edwin G. Boring, *A History of Experimental Psychology*, 2d ed. (New York: Appleton-Century-Crofts, 1950), 631; Edna Heidbreder, *Seven Psychologies* (New York: Appleton-Century-Crofts, 1933), 238. Also see David Murray, *A History of Western Psychology*, 2d ed. (Englewood Cliffs, NJ: Prentice Hall, 1988), chap. 10.

3. See Donald A. Dewsbury, *Comparative Psychology in the Twentieth Century* (Stroudsburg, PA: Hutchinson Ross, 1984), 56–82 passim; Robert Boakes, *From Darwin to Behaviourism* (Cambridge: Cambridge University Press, 1984), 143–48; and James T. Todd and Edward K. Morris, "The Early Research of John B. Watson: Before the Behavioral Revolution," *Behavior Analyst* 9 (1986): 71–88.

4. Robert Boakes, "John B. Watson's Early Scientific Career," in *Modern Perspectives on John B. Watson and Classical Behaviorism*, ed. James T. Todd and Edward K. Morris (Westport, CT: Greenwood Press, 1994), 145–50.

5. Watson's thesis was published as *Animal Education: An Experimental Study on the Psychical Development of the White Rat, Correlated with the Growth of Its Central Nervous System* (Chicago: University of Chicago Press, 1903); Allen's work was published as "The Associative Processes of the Guinea Pig: A Study of the Psychical Development of an Animal with a Nervous System Well Medullated at Birth," *Journal of Comparative Neurology and Psychology* 14 (1904): 293–359; Watson's work on terns is to be found in "The Behavior of Noddy and Sooty Terns," *Carnegie Institute Publication* 103 (1908): 197–255; the last study I referred to was published as Karl S. Lashley and John B. Watson, "Notes on the Development of a Young Monkey," *Journal of Animal Behavior* 3 (1913): 114–39.

6. For his chapter on the nature of habit (chap. 7) in *Behavior*, Watson relied entirely on Harvey Carr, "Principles of Selection in Animal Learning," *Psychological Review* 21 (1914): 157–65. Watson wrote that he had seen the manuscript and used it for his chapter, *Behavior: An Introduction to Comparative Psychology* (New York: Holt, 1914), 251.

7. For a good account of Baldwin's views, see Robert A. Richards, *Darwin and the Emergence of Evolutionary Theories of Mind and Behavior* (Chicago: University of Chicago Press, 1987), chap. 10.

8. See Watson *Behavior*, chap. 6.

9. "John Broadus Watson," in *A History of Psychology in Autobiography*, vol. 3, ed. C. Murchison (Worcester, MA: Clark University Press, 1936), 276.

10. Quoted in Kerry Buckley, *Mechanical Man: John Broadus Watson and the Beginnings of Behaviorism* (New York: Guilford, 1989), 71.

11. Herbert S. Jennings, *Reactions to Heat and Cold in the Ciliate Infusoria: Contributions to the Study of the Behavior of the Lower Organisms* (Washington, DC: Carnegie Institution, 1904). Watson's review was in the *Psychological Bulletin* 2 (1905): 144–47.

12. See his review of Jennings's *Behavior of the Lower Organisms* in *Psychological Bulletin* 4 (1907): 288–91.

13. Review of Loeb's *Dynamics of Living Matter*, in *Psychological Bulletin* 4 (1907): 293 (emphasis in original).

14. See John C. Burnham, "The Origins of Behaviorism," *Journal of the History of the Behavioral Sciences* 4 (1968): 143–51. Harrell and Harrison give Watson's behaviorism an even earlier origin. According to them, he began to discuss his ideas informally in 1903. His interlocutors told him that his ideas were applicable to animal, not human, work. Harrell and Harrison, "The Rise and Fall of Behaviorism," 372.

15. Watson to Yerkes, October 2, 1907, Yerkes Papers, Harvard University. Yerkes was commenting on Watson article "Kinesthetic and Organic Sensations: Their Role in the Reactions of the White Rat to the Maze," *Psychological Review Monograph Supplement* 8 (33) (1907): 1–100.

16. Burnham, "Origins of Behaviorism." Harrell and Harrison say that his Yale audience told Watson that behaviorism could merely describe, never explain.

17. *Behavior*, his text on comparative psychology.

18. Watson to Yerkes, September 18, 1909.

19. Watson to Yerkes, October 29, 1909.

20. Watson to Yerkes, February 6, 1910.

21. In a letter of January 14, 1910, Watson suggested to Yerkes that they arrange a "behavior dinner." Watson's suggested participants included Jennings, Yerkes, Harvey Carr, himself, M. E. Haggerty, Lawrence Wooster Cole, Fred S. Breed, S. O. Mast, and "the other Cole" (probably Leon J. Cole). He added "etc.," implying that his list was not complete. I must thank Don Dewsbury for identifying "the other Cole" for me.

22. Watson to Yerkes, July 21, 1912.

23. Watson to Yerkes, April 3, 1912.

24. Watson to Yerkes, January 30, 1912. Watson must be referring to "How Animals Find Their Way Home," *Harper's* 119 (1909): 685–89. He also wrote that he had agreed to write two further articles, one on the "modern trend of psychology" and one on "recent work on the homing sense." They were published as "The New Science of Animal Behavior," *Harper's* 120 (1910): 346–53; and "Instinctive Activity in Animals," *Harper's* 124 (1912): 376–82.

25. Watson, "The New Science of Animal Behavior," 348.

26. Ibid., 350–51.

27. For a contrary view, see Thomas B. Leahey, *A History of Modern Psychology*, 2d ed. (Englewood Cliffs, NJ: Prentice Hall, 1994); and David A. Murray, *A History of Western Psychology*, 2d ed. (Englewood Cliffs, NJ: Prentice Hall, 1988).

28. Roger Brown, *Words and Things: An Introduction to Language* (New York: Free Press, 1958), 93.

29. Watson to Yerkes, November 7, 1912 (emphasis added).

30. Watson to Yerkes, February 26, 1913.

31. Watson to Yerkes, March 12, 1913.

32. Watson to Yerkes, April 7, 1913 (emphasis added).

33. Published as John B. Watson, "Image and Affection in Behavior," *Journal of Philosophy, Psychology and Scientific Methods* 10 (1913): 421–28.

34. Franz Samelson, "John B. Watson in 1913: Rhetoric and Practice," in Todd and Morris, eds., *Modern Perspectives on John B. Watson and Classical Behaviorism*, 3–18.

35. Ibid.

36. Robert S. Woodworth, *Contemporary Schools of Psychology*, 1st ed. (New York: Ronald, 1931). Woodworth retained the same wording in his revised edition, published in 1948 (see p. 69). James T. Todd points out that no first-year psychology texts referred to the behaviorist manifesto until E. R. Hilgard's *Introduction to Psychology* appeared in 1953 (there was one oblique reference in a 1921 textbook). Todd implies that psychologists treated Watson as a revolutionary only with the appearance of courses on theories and systems from the 1950s onward. See Todd, "What Psychology Has to Say about John B. Watson: Classical Behaviorism in Psychology Textbooks, 1920–1989," in Todd and Morris, eds., *Modern Perspectives on John B. Watson and Classical Behaviorism*, 75–107.

37. A. W. Logue gives a full analysis in "Watson's Behaviorist Manifesto: Past Positive and Current Negative Consequences," in Todd and Morris, eds., *Modern Perspectives on John B. Watson and Classical Behaviorism*, 109–23. Leahey has a long summary in his *History of Modern Psychology*, 182–86. A. D. Lovie exhaustively compares the text of the article with Watson's version of it in his *Behavior*; see Lovie, "Ethnographic Discourse Analysis and J. B. Watson: The Behaviourist as Propagandist," in *Current Issues in Theoretical Psychology*, ed. W. J. Baker, M. E. Hyland, H. Van Rappard, and A. W. Staats (Amsterdam: North-Holland, 1987), 15–64.

38. See Samelson, "John B. Watson in 1913," 6–7.

39. John B. Watson, "Psychology as the Behaviorist Views It," *Psychological Review* 20 (1913): 169.

40. Ibid., 170.

41. Burnham, "Origins of Behaviorism"; and Albert E. Goss, "Early Behaviorism and Verbal Mediating Responses," *American Psychologist* 16 (1961): 285–98.

42. Harrell and Harrison have a useful discussion of the origins of Watson's theory of motor speech in "The Rise and Fall of Behaviorism," 379.

43. Watson, "Psychology as the Behaviorist Views It," 175.

44. Watson, "Image and Affection in Behavior."

45. Ibid., 427–28.

46. Burnham, "Origins of Behaviorism."

47. Franz Samelson, "Struggle for Scientific Authority: The Reception of Wat-

son's Behaviorism, 1913–1920," *Journal of the History of the Behavioral Sciences* 17 (1981): 399–425.

48. Edward B. Titchener, "On 'Psychology as the Behaviorist Views It,'" *Proceedings of the American Philosophical Society* 53 (1914): 1–17.

49. Fred L. Wells, "Dynamic Psychology," *Psychological Bulletin* 10 (1913): 434.

50. Samelson, "Struggle for Scientific Authority," 404.

51. Christian Ruckmich, "The Last Decade of Psychology in Review," *Psychological Bulletin* 13 (1916): 120. One does have to bear in mind that Ruckmich was a follower of Titchener. Nevertheless, he made his assertion largely on the basis of his content analysis of the literature.

52. Walter B. Pillsbury, "Definition and Method in Psychology" (paper presented at APA conference, 1914).

53. Mary Calkins, "Psychology and the Behaviorists," *Psychological Bulletin* 10 (1913): 288–91.

54. Watson, "Instinctive Activity in Animals."

55. Ibid., 380.

56. Ibid., 381.

57. Arthur O. Lovejoy reported that Knight Dunlap said, "The paternity, if true, was entirely inadvertent." Quoted in Harrell and Harrison, "The Rise and Fall of Behaviorism," 381n.

58. John B. Watson, "Behavior and the Concept of Mental Disease," *Journal of Philosophy, Psychology and Scientific Methods* 13 (1916): 589–97.

59. See Ruth Leys, "Meyer, Watson, and the Dangers of Behaviorism," *Journal of the History of the Behavioral Sciences* 20 (1984): 128–49.

60. Ibid., 131.

61. John B. Watson, "Content of a Course in Psychology for Medical Students," *Journal of the American Medical Association* 58 (1912): 916–18.

62. See Harrell and Harrison, "The Rise and Fall of Behaviorism," 382–83.

63. Watson, "Behavior and the Concept of Mental Disease," 590.

64. Ibid., 591.

65. In his article Watson said that Adolf Meyer had suggested these ideas to him in a conversation of 1912 or 1913.

66. Samelson, "John B. Watson in 1913."

67. The address was published as John B. Watson, "The Place of the Conditioned-Reflex in Psychology," *Psychological Review* 23 (1916): 89–117. The sources for Watson's knowledge of conditioning are not known. For histories of conditioning in America, see Gregory Razran, "Russian Physiologists' Psychology and American Experimental Psychology: A History and a Systematic Collation and a Look into the Future," *Psychological Bulletin* 63 (1965): 42–64; and Deborah J. Coon, "Eponymy, Obscurity, Twitmyer and Pavlov," *Journal of the History of the Behavioral Sciences* 18 (1982): 255–62.

68. John B. Watson and Rosalie Rayner, "Conditioned Emotional Reactions," *Journal of Experimental Psychology* 3 (1920): 1–14.

69. For a discussion of the circumstances in which the film was made and Watson's purposes in making it, see Benjamin Harris, "John B. Watson in the Director's Chair: Filmmaking as Behavioral Observation" (address at the annual meeting of the Association for Behavior Analysis, Philadelphia, May 1988).

70. For further discussion, see Benjamin Harris, "Whatever Happened to Little Albert," *American Psychologist* 34 (1979): 151–60; and Franz Samelson, "J. B. Watson's Little Albert, Cyril Burt's Twins, and the Need for a Critical Science," *American Psychologist* 35 (1980): 619–25.

71. The attempted replications were H. B. English, "Three Cases of the 'Conditioned Fear Response,'" *Journal of Abnormal and Social Psychology* 34 (1929): 221–25; C. W. Valentine, "The Innate Basis of Fear," *Journal of Genetic Psychology* 37 (1930): 394–420; and Elsie O. Bregman, "An Attempt to Modify the Emotional Attitude of Infants by the Conditioned Response Technique," *Journal of Genetic Psychology* 45 (1934): 169–98.

72. Ernest R. Hilgard and Donald G. Marquis, *Conditioning and Learning*, 1st ed. (New York: Appleton-Century, 1940). Gregory Kimble, *Hilgard and Marquis' Conditioning and Learning*, 2d ed. (New York: Appleton-Century-Crofts, 1961).

73. John B. Watson, "An Attempted Formulation of the Scope of Behavior Psychology," *Psychological Review* 24 (1917): 329–52.

74. Ibid., 37 (emphasis in original).

75. Kerry Buckley gives an excellent account of Watson's later career in *Mechanical Man*. David Cohen has a detailed account of the events leading up to Watson's forced resignation from Johns Hopkins in *J. B. Watson: The Founder of Behaviorism* (London: Routledge and Kegan Paul, 1979), chap. 6.

76. See Todd, "What Psychology Has to Say about John B. Watson"; and Steven R. Coleman, "Assessing Pavlov's Impact on the American Conditioning Enterprise," *Pavlovian Journal of Biological Science* 23 (1988): 102–6.

77. Franz Samelson has commented that initially nobody was willing to write Watson's obituary.

78. John C. Watson, *Behaviorism* (New York: People's Institute, 1924). The book was republished by Norton in 1925, and the University of Chicago Press published a revised edition in 1930.

79. For accounts of Guthrie's life and career, see Fred D. Sheffield's obituary of Guthrie in the *American Journal of Psychology* 72 (1959): 642–50; and Guthrie's comments about his career in "Association by Contiguity," in *Psychology: A Study of a Science*, vol. 2, *General Systematic Formulations, Learning and Special Processes*, ed. S. Koch (New York: McGraw-Hill, 1959), 158–95.

80. Guthrie published only two pieces of research: "Association as a Function

of Time Interval," *Psychological Review* 40 (1933): 355–67; and Edwin Guthrie and G. P. Horton, *Cats in a Puzzle Box* (New York: Rinehart, 1946).

81. Guthrie found the lecture so inspiring that he completed a Ph.D. on logic under Singer's direction at the University of Pennsylvania in 1912.

82. See especially Guthrie's late article, "Psychological Facts and Psychological Theory," *Psychological Bulletin* 43 (1946): 1–20.

83. Edwin Guthrie, *The Psychology of Learning* (New York: Harper, 1935), 4. Elsewhere Guthrie was even more explicit: "The possession of mind means the ability to learn." "Association by Contiguity," 174.

84. On this issue, see especially Guthrie, "Psychological Facts and Psychological Theory."

85. Guthrie, "Association by Contiguity," 161.

86. For example, see Guthrie, *The Psychology of Learning*, 5.

87. Guthrie, "Association by Contiguity," 161–62.

88. Ibid., 184.

89. Commenting on his and Horton's work on cats escaping from puzzle boxes, Guthrie wrote, "*The cat learns to do in the circumstances what it has been caused to do in the circumstances.*" *Cats in a Puzzle Box*, 39 (emphasis in original).

90. For example, see Edwin Guthrie, "On the Nature of Psychological Explanations," *Psychological Review* 40 (1933): 124–25.

91. Conrad G. Mueller and William N. Schoenfeld, "Edwin R. Guthrie," in Sigmund Koch, Kenneth MacCorquodale, Paul E. Meehl, William S. Verplanck, William K. Estes, Conrad G. Mueller, and William N. Schoenfeld, *Modern Learning Theory* (New York: McGraw-Hill, 1954).

92. The same argument, *mutatis mutandis*, applies to stimuli. For example, Mueller and Schoenfeld point out that Guthrie's maintaining stimuli, which play an irreplaceable explanatory role in his theory, are explanatory fictions.

93. Edwin Guthrie, "Conditioning: A Theory of Learning in Terms of Stimulus, Response and Association," *Yearbook of the National Society for Studies in Education* 41 (1942): 18, 30.

94. A. A. Roback, *Behaviorism at Twenty-five* (Cambridge, MA: Sci-Art Publishers, n.d.).

95. Ibid., 8. Roback agreed with that assessment: "I venture to predict . . . that in less than ten years, many students in psychology will not have heard [Watson's] name; and his books which now command prices of $1.25 or $1.00 in college book stores, will be at best on the 25 cents counter" (ibid., 15). Horace English was a little less forthright: "Behaviorism is dead without lineal descendant, yet it has left us an important legacy." "Psychology with Soul: Reviews of Richard Muller-Freienfels, *The Evolution of Contemporary Psychology* and Gardner Murphy, *A Briefer General Psychology*," *New Republic* 86 (1936): 53.

96. Harrell and Harrison, "The Rise and Fall of Behaviorism."

97. Ibid., 401–2.

98. Ibid., 380.

99. See Wilson D. Wallis, "Behavior and Purpose," *Journal of Philosophy, Psychology and Scientific Methods* 19 (1922): 580–82; idem, "Does Behaviorism Imply Mechanism?" *American Journal of Psychology* 35 (1924): 387–95; and idem, "Is Purpose Only Mechanism Imperfectly Understood?" *Journal of Philosophy* 22 (1925): 94–98.

NOTES TO CHAPTER 3

1. See Robert S. Woodworth, *Experimental Psychology*, 1st ed. (New York: Holt, 1938). Apart from the two editions of Benton J. Underwood *Experimental Psychology* (New York: Appleton-Century-Crofts, 1949, 1966), Woodworth's was the only text that covered a wide range of subject matter as well as dealing with experimental method.

2. Robert S. Woodworth and Harold Schlosberg, *Experimental Psychology*, 2d ed. (New York: Holt, Rinehart, and Winston, 1954).

3. See Woodworth and Schlosberg, *Experimental Psychology*, 2d ed., 530–33. Intriguingly, Underwood used the same example. See his 2d ed., chap. 8.

4. Woodworth and Schlosberg, *Experimental Psychology*, 531–33; also see Underwood, *Experimental Psychology*, 2d ed., 299–310.

5. Percy W. Bridgman, *The Logic of Modern Physics* (New York: Macmillan, 1927).

6. John A. Mills, "Operationism, Scientism, and the Rhetoric of Power," in *Positivism in Psychology: Historical and Contemporary Problems*, ed. C. W. Tolman (New York: Springer-Verlag, 1992), 67–82.

7. Kurt Danziger, *Constructing the Subject: Historical Origins of Psychological Research* (Cambridge: Cambridge University Press, 1990), 142–46.

8. Edwin G. Boring, "Intelligence as the Tests Test It," *New Republic* 35 (1923): 35–37.

9. Tim B. Rogers, "Antecedents of Operationism: A Case History in Radical Positivism," in Tolman, ed., *Positivism in Psychology*, 47–66.

10. For a comprehensive account of the dispute, see Dale A. Stout, "Statistics in American Psychology: The Social Construction of Experimental and Correlational Psychology, 1900–1930" (Ph.D. diss., University of Edinburgh, 1987). Also see idem, "A Question of Statistical Inference: E. G. Boring, T. L. Kelley, and the Probable Error," *American Journal of Psychology* 102 (1989): 549–62.

11. See Stout, "A Question of Statistical Inference," 558.

12. Edwin G. Boring, "Facts and Fancies of Immigration," *New Republic* 34 (1923): 245–46. For a full discussion of the background to Boring's writing of the review, see Stout, "Statistics in American Psychology," 277 ff.

13. See Stout, "Statistics in American Psychology," 290.

14. Carl Murchison and R. Gilbert, "Some Marital Concomitants of Negro Men Criminals," *Pedagogical Seminary* 32 (1925): 652–56.

15. The address was published as Edwin G. Boring, "The Physiology of Consciousness," *Science* 75 (1932): 32–39.

16. Helen Peak and Edwin G. Boring, "The Factor of Speed in Intelligence," *Journal of Experimental Psychology* 9 (1926): 71–94.

17. That is, the data showed that those with relatively high overall intelligence test scores completed both the items and the test overall relatively quickly, whereas the reverse was true for those with relatively low intelligence test scores.

18. Boring to Calkins, November 3, 1923, Boring Correspondence, Harvard University Archives.

19. Boring to Carmichael, November 16, 1927.

20. See letters of May 15 and June 11, 1928, and October 15, 1934, in the correspondence between Boring and Carmichael. Also see Boring to Tolman, February 27, 1928, in which Boring wrote, "Perry and I are keen for some kind of a behavioral-physiological-infrahuman psychologist."

21. Boring to Hull, April 28, 1938.

22. S. S. Stevens, "The Operational Basis of Psychology," *American Journal of Psychology* 47 (1935): 323–30; and idem, "The Operational Definition of Concepts," *Psychological Review* 42 (1935): 517–27. For discussions of the various types of operationism, see Tim B. Rogers, "Operationism in Psychology," *Journal of the History of the Behavioral Sciences* 25 (1989): 139–53; and idem, "Antecedents of Operationism."

23. Stevens, "The Operational Basis of Psychology," 323.

24. Ibid., 327.

25. Stevens, "The Operational Definition of Concepts," 521 (emphasis in original).

26. Boring to Langfeld, October 29, 1934. Boring spelled Carnap's name "Karnap," a clear indication that he knew him only by reputation. McGregor's article was published as "Scientific Measurement and Psychology," *Psychological Review* 42 (1935): 246–66. Others did not seem to share Boring's exuberant enthusiasm for his own and McGregor's work, whereas Stevens's articles continue to be widely cited. In terms of content I cannot see that Boring and McGregor added anything to what Stevens had already written.

27. See Edward C. Tolman, "Operational Behaviorism and Current Trends in Psychology," *Proceedings of the 25th Anniversary Celebration of the Inauguration of Graduate Studies at the University of Southern California* (Los Angeles: University of Southern California Press, 1936), 116. Tolman's lecture is reprinted in *Psychological Theory: Contemporary Readings*, ed. M. H. Marx (New York: Macmillan, 1951), 87–102.

28. The articles were "An Operational Analysis of 'Demands,'" *Erkenntis* 6 (1936): 383–92; "Operational Behaviorism"; "Demands and Conflicts," *Psycho-*

logical Review 44 (1937): 158–69; and "The Determiners of Behavior at a Choice Point," *Psychological Review* 45 (1938): 1–41.

29. Tolman, "Operational Behaviorism," 101.

30. Ibid., 89.

31. Ibid., 90.

32. All Tolman's intervening variables are listed in Kenneth MacCorquodale and Paul E. Meehl, "Edward C. Tolman," in Sigmund Koch et al., *Modern Learning Theory* (New York: McGraw-Hill, 1954), 189–90.

33. Edward C. Tolman, "Principles of Purposive Behavior," in *Psychology: A Study of a Science*, vol. 2, ed. S. Koch (New York: McGraw-Hill, 1959), 93.

34. See Tolman, "Demands and Conflicts," 158.

35. Described in C. J. Warden, *Animal Motivation* (New York: Columbia University Press, 1931).

36. Tolman, "An Operational Analysis of 'Demands'"; and idem, "Demands and Conflicts."

37. Edward C. Tolman, "The Intervening Variable," in *Psychological Theory: Contemporary Readings*, ed. M. H. Marx (New York: Macmillan, 1951) 90.

38. Tolman, "Principles of Purposive Behavior," 108 ff.

39. See Kenneth MacCorquodale and Paul E. Meehl, "On a Distinction between Hypothetical Constructs and Intervening Variables," *Psychological Review* 55 (1948): 95–107.

40. Edward C. Tolman, "Discussion: Interrelationships between Perception and Personality," *Journal of Personality* 18 (1949): 48–50. Also see idem, "Principles of Purposive Behavior." It should be noted that Tolman was extremely vague about what he meant by model: "As I see it, the word 'model' is merely a sloppy synonym used, when one gets tired of some more specific term, to designate the specific type of theoretical organization that one is proposing." "Principles of Purposive Behavior," 96.

41. Tolman, "Principles of Purposive Behavior," 131 ff.

42. See Edward C. Tolman, "There Is More Than One Type of Learning," *Psychological Review* 56 (1949): 144–55.

43. Edward C. Tolman, "The Nature and Functioning of Wants," *Psychological Review* 56 (1949): 364.

44. Tolman, "Principles of Purposive Behavior," 138.

45. In vicarious trial and error, an animal, when faced with an unfamiliar or difficult problem, pauses and, in human terms, appears to be trying out various alternatives "in its head."

46. Sir Ronald A. Fisher, *The Design of Experiments* (Edinburgh: Oliver and Boyd, 1935); and idem, *Statistical Methods and Scientific Inference* (New York: Hafner Press, 1956). For discussions of Fisher's role in psychological statistics, see Michael Cowles, *Statistics in Psychology: An Historical Perspective* (Hillsdale, NJ: Erlbaum, 1989). For accounts of the introduction of analysis of variance into

psychology, see Anthony J. Rucci and Ryan D. Tweney, "Analysis of Variance and the 'Second Discipline' of Scientific Psychology: A Historical Account," *Psychological Bulletin* 87 (1980): 166–84; and A. D. Lovie, "The Analysis of Variance in Experimental Psychology: 1934–1945," *British Journal of Mathematical and Statistical Psychology* 32 (1979): 151–78.

47. Edward C. Tolman and C. H. Honzik, "Degrees of Hunger, Reward and Non-reward, and Maze-Learning in Rats," *University of California Publications in Psychology* 4 (1930): 241–56. Tolman summarized the study in *Purposive Behavior in Animals and Man* (New York: Century, 1932), 60–61.

48. See Tolman, *Purposive Behavior,* 401–6.

49. See R. S. Crutchfield and Edward C. Tolman, "Multiple Variable Design for Experiments Involving Interaction of Behavior," *Psychological Review* 47 (1940): 38–42.

50. Crutchfield and Tolman's silence on theoretical questions is puzzling because Tolman's fundamental distinction between learning and performance cries out for treatment by experimental designs involving analysis of variance. However, the advantages conferred by hindsight are seldom available to pioneers in a field of study. Lovie ("Analysis of Variance in Experimental Psychology," 162) points out that in the first explicit treatment of the learning/performance distinction, Crespi used a design that was in effect factorial but used analysis of variance only to test for homogeneity of variance between the scores of his groups. See L. P. Crespi, "Quantitative Variation of Incentive and Performance in the White Rat," *American Journal of Psychology* 55 (1942): 467–517.

51. Lovie, "Analysis of Variance in Experimental Psychology," 164.

NOTES TO CHAPTER 4

1. Clark L. Hull, *Principles of Behavior: An Introduction to Behavior Theory* (New York: Appleton-Century-Crofts, 1943). Hull began to refer to the book as his magnum opus from January 1928 onward.

2. Clark L. Hull, *Essentials of Behavior* (New Haven: Yale University Press, 1951).

3. B. F. Skinner, *Science and Human Behavior* (New York: Macmillan, 1953).

4. See Hull's diary entry for September 9, 1934, in Ruth Hays, "The Psychology of a Scientist: IV. Hull's Idea Books," *Perceptual and Motor Skills* 15 (1962): 856. Tolman demanded that Hull grant him his place in history. Accordingly, Hull also had proof changes made in *Principles of Behavior.* See "Historical Notes Concerning the Concept of Molar Behavior and of the Intervening Variable," in *Principles of Behavior,* 31.

5. The complete Idea Books (Hull's name for his diary) are at the Sterling Library, Yale University, and are available on microfilm. Ruth Hays published numerous passages from the diaries in "Psychology of a Scientist: IV. Hull's Idea

Books." For Hull's correspondence with Spence, see the Spence Papers in the Archives of the History of American Psychology, Akron, OH.

6. *Psychological Research Memoranda, 1940–1944.* Copies of these memoranda are to be found in Yale University Library, in the Spence Papers at the Archives of American Psychology, University of Akron, at Duke University, and at the University of Saskatchewan.

7. The articles have been reprinted in Abram Amsel and Michael E. Rashotte, *Mechanisms of Adaptive Behavior: Clark L. Hull's Theoretical Papers, with Commentary* (New York: Columbia University Press, 1984). In his diary Hull said that he tried to publish a theoretical article each year during this time.

8. Clark L. Hull, "Mind, Mechanism, and Adaptive Behavior," *Psychological Review* 44 (1937): 1–32.

9. The book on rote verbal learning was Clark L. Hull, Carl I. Hovland, Robert T. Ross, Marshall Hall, Donald T. Perkins, and Frederic T. Fitch, *Mathematico-Deductive Theory of Rote Learning* (New Haven: Yale University Press, 1940). For a discussion of the place of the book on rote learning in Hull's general theoretical approach, see Laurence D. Smith, *Behaviorism and Logical Positivism* (Stanford: Stanford University Press, 1986), 316–30.

10. See especially Smith, *Behaviorism and Logical Positivism*, 307–16. For a speculative discussion of the possible role of Hull's fascination with machines in his learning theory, see John A. Mills, "Hull's Theory of Learning: II. A Criticism of the Theory and Its Relationship to the History of Psychological Thought," *Canadian Psychological Review* 19 (1978): 116–27.

11. Smith, *Behaviorism and Logical Positivism*.

12. Clark L. Hull, "The Conflicting Psychologies of Learning: A Way Out," *Psychological Review* 42 (1935): 491–516.

13. See Hull, *Principles of Behavior*, 23–24.

14. For a discussion, see Smith, *Behaviorism and Logical Positivism*.

15. See, for example, Sigmund Koch, "Clark L. Hull," in *Modern Learning Theory*, by W. K. Estes and others (New York: Appleton-Century-Crofts, 1954): Ernest R. Hilgard in Hilgard and Gordon H. Bower, *Theories of Learning*, 3d ed. (New York: Appleton-Century-Crofts, 1966); and Smith, *Behaviorism and Logical Positivism*.

16. Hull, "Conflicting Psychologies of Learning," 496.

17. Hays, "Psychology of the Scientist," 858.

18. See Smith, *Behaviorism and Logical Positivism*, 182.

19. Gregory Kimble, *Hilgard and Marquis' Conditioning and Learning*, 2d ed. (New York: Appleton-Century-Crofts, 1961), 140.

20. Clark L. Hull, "A Review of Some Behavior Mechanisms" (unpublished manuscript, filed in *Psychological Research Memoranda, 1940–1944*).

21. Margaret F. Washburn, *The Animal Mind: A Textbook of Comparative Psychology*, 3d ed. (New York: Macmillan, 1926), 331–32.

22. We know that he was aware of Thorndike's earlier work. In a *Psychological Memorandum* of November 13, 1941, Hull wrote that Washburn and Thorndike formulated the gradient of reinforcement hypothesis independently, referring specifically to p. 173 of Thorndike's *Work and Fatigue*, the title of vol. 3 of Thorndike's *Educational Psychology* (New York: Columbia University Press, 1913). However, the material on p. 173 has no relevance to the curve of work. I therefore presume that Hull was referring to Thorndike's article "The Curve of Work," *Psychological Review* 19 (1912): 165–94. On p. 173 of that article Thorndike referred to the "end-spurt." It was plausible to believe, he said, that the knowledge that a period of work is about to end could lead to an increase in performance. Although he could find no evidence for the presence of the end-spurt in mental work, we could presumably find it in a physical task like maze running.

It has been suggested to me that Hull derived the hypothesis of the goal gradient in part from Thorndike's notion of "readiness," which can be interpreted, according to my informant, as "something like 'differential associablity'" (the term appeared in *Educational Psychology*). Also see Robert C. Bolles, *Learning Theory* (New York: Holt, Rinehart and Winston, 1978), 16–17.

23. See Edward L. Thorndike, "A Proof of the Law of Effect," *Science* 77 (1933): 173–75; and idem, "An Experimental Study of Rewards," *Teachers College Contributions to Education*, no. 580 (1933). For a discussion of Thorndike's concept of spread of effect, see Gordon H. Bower and Ernest R. Hilgard, *Theories of Learning*, 5th ed. (Englewood Cliffs, NJ: Prentice Hall, 1981).

24. For a discussion of that phase of Hull's work, see Amsel and Richotte, *Mechanisms of Adaptive Behavior*; Hilgard and Bower, *Theories of Learning*, 3d ed.; and John A. Mills, "Hull's Theory of Learning as a Philosophical System: I. An Outline of the Theory," *Canadian Psychological Review* 19 (1978): 27–40.

25. See Clark L. Hull, "The Goal-Gradient Hypothesis and Maze Learning," *Psychological Review* 39 (1932): 25–43.

26. J. G. Yoshioka, "Weber's Law in the Discrimination of Maze Distance by the White Rat," *University of California Publications in Psychology* 4 (1929): 155–84.

27. Clark L. Hull, "The Rat's Speed of Locomotion Gradient in the Approach to Food," *Journal of Comparative Psychology* 17 (1934): 393–422.

28. It is possible that in following up this analogy, Hull shows us how far he was from developing his mature views on the relationship between reinforcement and incentive in 1934. One of the reviewers of a manuscript that I sent to *Behaviorism* commented that Washburn and Thorndike used the term "readiness" in different senses. Washburn used it in the sense of "motivationally aroused" (that is, being in a state of preparedness to benefit from reinforcement). Thorndike defined readiness as follows: "When any conduction unit is in readiness to conduct, for it to do so is satisfying. When any conduction unit is not in readiness to con-

duct, for it to conduct is annoying." *Educational Psychology*, vol. 2, 1–2. It is possible that Hull conflated Washburn's and Thorndike's meanings, hence his choice of a physiological preparation as the basis for an analogy with the behavior of freely moving animals.

29. For a review of those studies, see Norman L. Munn, *Handbook of Psychological Research on the Rat: An Introduction to Animal Psychology* (Boston: Houghton Mifflin, 1950), 376–96. Buel's and Drew's studies were J. Buel, "A Criticism of Hull's Goal Gradient Hypothesis," *Psychological Review* 45 (1938): 395–413; and G. C. Drew, "The Speed of Locomotion Gradient and Its Relation to the Goal Gradient," *Journal of Comparative Psychology* 27 (1939): 333–72.

30. Buel, "A Criticism of Hull's Goal Gradient Hypothesis," 400.

31. Drew, "The Speed of Locomotion Gradient," 368.

32. Hull to Spence, November 29, 1938.

33. Published as J. Buel, "A Correction to 'A Criticism of Hull's Goal Gradient Hypothesis,'" *Psychological Review* 46 (1939): 86–87.

34. Clark L. Hull, "Goal Gradient, Anticipation, and Perseveration in Compound Trial-and-Error Learning," *Journal of Experimental Psychology* 25 (1939): 566–85.

35. The work took two forms. There were studies of the form of the gradient, such as two by G. R. Grice, "An Experimental Study of the Gradient of Reinforcement in Maze Learning," *Journal of Experimental Psychology* 30 (1942): 475–89; and idem, "The Relation of Secondary Reinforcement to Delayed Reward in Visual Discrimination Learning," *Journal of Experimental Psychology* 38 (1948): 1–16. Both studies were carried out in Spence's laboratory. There were also studies in which Hull was able to use his theory to predict the pattern of progressive elimination of errors in complex mazes. (Clark L. Hull, "Reactively Heterogeneous Compound Trial-and-Error Learning with Distributed Trials and Terminal Reinforcement," *Journal of Experimental Psychology* 37 (1947): 118–35; and A. J. Sprow, "Reactively Homogeneous Trial-and-Error Learning with Distributed Trials and Terminal Reinforcement," *Experimental Psychology* 37 (1947) 197–213.

36. The requisite data were obtained in an experiment by W. J. Arnold, "Simple Reaction Chains and Their Integration: I. Homogeneous Chaining with Terminal Reinforcement," *Journal of Comparative and Physiological Psychology* 40 (1947): 349–63. Hull presented the mathematical work in *A Behavior System: An Introduction to Behavior Theory Concerning the Individual Organism* (New Haven: Yale University Press, 1952).

37. See Koch, "Clark L. Hull" and Hilgard's chapter on Hull in Hilgard and Bower, *Theories of Learning*, 3d ed.

38. Hays, "Psychology of a Scientist," 865.

39. Ibid., 867.

40. Hull, "Conflicting Psychologies of Learning," 492.

41. For an example of such attempts, see the discussion of what is meant by "observation" and "experience" in Wolfgang Köhler, *Gestalt Psychology* (New York: Liveright, 1947). Also see Köhler's critical discussion of the problem of quantification in psychology in his chapter 2.

42. Hull wrote in his diary, "My negative reactions are better than my positive ones." Hays, "Psychology of a Scientist," 824.

43. Another diary entry reads, "I was roused to violent activity by contact with Koffka, at Madison during the year 1926–1927." Hays, "Psychology of a Scientist," 836. For an account of the way Hull and Koffka reacted to each other, see J. A. Gengerelli, "Graduate School Reminiscences: Hull and Koffka," *American Psychologist* 31 (1976): 685–88.

44. The first quoted passage comes from a letter from Hull to Spence of July 2, 1942, while the second is from a letter of November 23, 1942.

45. For example, Hull described a confrontation with Köhler:

apropos of the general argument that I was putting forward to the effect that scientific matters should be settled on a scientific and logical basis rather than by some kind of warfare . . . [Köhler] came out with this remark: he said that he was willing to discuss most things in a logical and scientific manner, but when people try to make man out to be a kind of slot machine, then he would fight! And when he said the word "fight," he brought his fist down on the table with a resounding smack, and he did not smile when he did it, either. (Hull to Spence, May 20, 1941)

46. Kurt Lewin's most important general theoretical work was *Principles of Topological Psychology*, trans. Fritz Heider and Grace Heider (New York: McGraw-Hill, 1936).

47. John A. McGeoch (1897–1942) was head of the department of psychology at the State University of Iowa at the time of his death. His most comprehensive work was *The Psychology of Human Learning* (New York: Longmans, Green, 1942). His most enduring contribution was the creation of the interference theory of forgetting, especially in "Forgetting and the Law of Disuse," *Psychological Review* 39 (1932): 352–70.

48. See "Remarks to Mr. Hull's Supplementary Note, by Kurt Lewin," appended to Clark L. Hull, "The Problems of Intervening Variables in Molar Behavior Theory," *Psychological Review* 50 (1943): 390–92.

49. See Ralph K. White, "The Case for the Tolman-Lewin Interpretation of Learning," *Psychological Review* 50 (1943): 157–86. Ironically, on April 11, 1939, Hull sent Spence a list of thirty-five American psychologists who, he thought, could form a "behavioristic" group opposed to Gestalt psychology; White was one of those listed. Another American psychologist whom Spence considered to be strongly under the influence of Gestalt ideas was Claude E. Buxton. See Buxton, "Latent Learning and the Goal Gradient Hypothesis," *Contributions to Psychological Theory* 2 (1940), no. 2.

50. Others have made essentially the same suggestion. For example, see Donald T. Campbell, "A Tribal Model of the Social System Vehicle Carrying Scientific Knowledge," *Knowledge: Creation, Diffusion, Utilization* 1 (1979): 181–201; Franz Samelson, "On Behaviorism and Its Competitors, 1930–1950: The Case of the Conflict Model" (paper presented to Cheiron Conference, Philadelphia, June 1985); and idem, "On Behaviorism and Its Competitors, 1930–1950. 2: Stability and Turbulence in 1935" (paper presented to Cheiron Conference, Guelph, June 1986).

51. For discussion of Hull's approach to quantification, see Ernest R. Hilgard's chapter on Hull in Hilgard and Bower, *Theories of Learning*, 3d ed., 149–50, 169–82 (later editions have less material on the topic); and Amsel and Rashotte, *Mechanisms of Adaptive Behavior*, 97–102. For an extended criticism, see Koch, "Clark L. Hull," 63–86.

52. See entries in the Idea Books for May 24, 1945 (p. 871 in published version) and September 2, 1947 (pp. 875–76 in published version).

53. For a modern discussion of the form of acquisition curves, see Nicholas J. Mackintosh, *The Psychology of Animal Learning* (New York: Academic Press, 1974), 8–13, 147–50. In the case of respondent conditioning, Mackintosh concludes that although the curves are all S-shaped, there is as yet no theoretical model to explain this form. In the case of instrumental learning, he says that in different types of instrumental training we see a wide variety of pretraining procedures, and "Until the exact effects of these different procedures have been examined, the quest for a typical or true learning curve will be of questionable value." Hull's derivation of a negatively accelerated acquisition curve is a puzzling feature of his 1943 theory. For discussions, see Koch, "Clark L. Hull," 72–78; and Mills, "Hull's Theory of Learning: II," 125–26.

54. See Clark L. Hull, "Learning: II. The Factor of the Conditional Reflex," in *A Handbook of General Experimental Psychology*, ed. Carl Murchison (Worcester, MA: Clark University Press, 1934), 424–26; and Hull et al., *Mathematico-Deductive Theory of Rote Learning*, 158–65.

55. Shortly after the publication of *Principles of Behavior*, Hull had to concede that the connection between amount of reinforcer and strength of habit was less close than he had previously assumed. This change of position accompanied his willingness to consider seriously the distinction between learning and performance. Drive or motivation is involved in both cases, but it was said that drive helped to induce a permanent change in behavior in the first case, whereas it produced changes of only short duration in the latter case. Amount of reinforcer came to be seen as almost a paradigm case of a performance variable, largely as a result of studies, using rats in the straight alley, by L. P. Crespi, "Amount of Reinforcement and Level of Performance," *Psychological Review* 51 (1944): 341–57; and D. Zeaman, "Response Latency as a Function of the Amount of Reinforcement," *Journal of Experimental Psychology* 39 (1949): 466–83. The stud-

ies showed that changing the magnitude of a reinforcer had an immediate effect on the latency of responding and the speed of locomotion. In *Principles of Behavior* (129–33) Hull briefly considered the consequences of changing the amount of reinforcement delivered; he concluded that animals' performance would show a progressive change rather than an immediate response to the changed circumstances. In part he must have felt that to say that animals would make an immediate response to the new situation (as they typically do in the case of latent learning) would be to concede that some sort of "mentalistic" factors entered into the situation (the animals "knew" what response to make but modulated their effort in accordance with the available reward). In part the refusal to take the distinction between learning and performance seriously was a consequence of Hull's and Spence's positivism, as shown by the following passage from a document in the Spence Papers:

> The distinction between learning acquisition and performance or utilization is misleading in that there is no such distinction as far as behavior is concerned. The only thing we have is behavior or performance in a stimulus situation. Learning is what the psychologist sees by putting down on a graph the successive performances of the animal to the stimulus situation. As far as the animal is concerned there is only one thing performance or what is to say the same thing—response.
>
> Their [*sic*] performance or act, however, depends not only upon the external stimulating factors but also the internal stimuli also [*sic*]. When we change the latter, such as by eliminating the SD, it is not surprising that the response changes.

The above passage seems to have been written while Spence was at Iowa. It comes from a folder marked "Tolman's Theory of Learning." The preceding sheet of paper has some references to punishment and response strengthening, dated 1937.

56. Spence to Hull, January 13, 1941.

57. The studies are W. Horsley Gantt, "The Nervous Secretion of Saliva: The Relation of the Conditioned Reflex to the Intensity of the Unconditioned Stimulus," *American Journal of Physiology* 123 (1938): 74; and G. C. Grindley, "Experiments on the Influence of the Amount of Reward on Learning in Young Chickens," *British Journal of Psychology* 20 (1929–30): 173–80.

58. Hull to Spence, February 8, 1941. In *Principles of Behavior*, Hull presents the data from only one of Gantt's dogs (fig. 27, p. 125).

59. Hull, "Conflicting Psychologies of Learning," 511.

60. For a cogent criticism of Hull's position, see Donald K. Adams, "A Note on Method," *Psychological Review* 44 (1937): 212–18. Adams argued that Hull had committed the logical error of affirming the consequent. I am indebted to an anonymous reviewer for the *Journal of the History of the Behavioral Sciences* for clarifying that issue.

61. Ernest R. Hilgard, *Theories of Learning* 3d ed. (New York: Appleton-Century-Crofts, 1948), 57.

62. See Hull to Spence, October 28, 1939.

63. See Hull to Spence, December 26, 1940.

64. See Fantino and Logan, quoted at length in Amsel and Rashotte, *Mechanisms of Adaptive Behavior*, 14–15.

65. Clark L. Hull, "The Place of Innate Individual and Species Differences in Molar Behavior Theory," *Psychological Review* 52 (1945): 55–60.

66. See Smith, *Behaviorism and Logical Positivism*, 307–16, 482–87.

67. Hull to Spence, January 10, 1941.

68. Hull to Spence, April 2, 1941.

69. Spence to Hull, September 27, 1940.

70. Spence to Hull, September 9, 1940. For Hilgard and Marquis's use of "instrumental," see their *Conditioning and Learning*, 1st ed. (New York: Appleton, 1940).

71. Spence to Hull, December 20, 1940.

72. I am indebted to Kurt Danziger for that observation.

73. In Hilgard and Bower, *Theories of Learning*, 3d ed., 169–74.

74. Spence to Neal Miller, May 1954 (in Spence Papers).

75. William W. Rozeboom, "The Art of Metascience, or, What Should a Psychological Theory Be?" in *Toward Unification in Psychology*, ed. J. R. Royce (Toronto: University of Toronto Press, 1970), 54–163 (esp. 56–59).

76. See Louis Carini, "The Aristotelian Basis of Hull's Behavior Theory," *Journal of the History of the Behavioral Sciences* 4 (1968): 109–18; Mills, "Hull's Theory of Learning as a Philosophical System: I"; idem, "Hull's Theory of Learning: II"; and Richard S. Peters and Henri Tajfel, "Hobbes and Hull: Metaphysicians of Behavior," *British Journal for the Philosophy of Science* 8 (1958): 30–44.

NOTES TO CHAPTER 5

1. Daniel C. Dennett, "Skinner Skinned," in *Philosophical Essays on Mind and Psychology* (Montgomery, VT: Bradford Books, 1978).

2. See Burrhus F. Skinner, *Particulars of My Life* (New York: McGraw-Hill, 1976), 262–87; Steven R. Coleman, "B. F. Skinner, 1926–1928: From Literature to Psychology," *Behavior Analyst* 8 (1985): 77–92; A. Elms, "Skinner's Dark Year and *Walden Two*," *American Psychologist* 36 (1981): 470–79.

3. Bertrand Russell, *Philosophy* (New York: Norton, 1927).

4. Louis Berman, *The Religion Called Behaviorism* (New York: Boni and Liveright, 1927).

5. Skinner, *Particulars of My Life*, 299–300.

6. See B. F. Skinner, *The Shaping of a Behaviorist: Part Two of an Autobiography* (New York: Knopf, 1979), 3–102; idem, "A Case History in Scientific

Method," *American Psychologist* 11 (1956): 221–33; reprinted in B. F. Skinner, *Cumulative Record* (New York: Appleton-Century-Crofts, 1959), 76–100, and in *Psychology: The Study of a Science*, vol. 2, ed. S. Koch (New York: McGraw-Hill, 1959), 359–79.

7. This was published as T. Cunliffe Barnes and B. F. Skinner, "The Progressive Increase in the Geotropic Response of the Ant *Aphaenogaster*," *Journal of General Psychology* 4 (1930): 102–12.

8. Steven Coleman, "Quantitative Order in B. F. Skinner's Early Research Program, 1928–1931," *Behavior Analyst* 10 (1987): 47–65.

9. B. F. Skinner, "On the Conditions of Elicitation of Certain Eating Reflexes," *Proceedings of the National Academy of Sciences* 16 (1930): 430.

10. Coleman, "Quantitative Order," 63.

11. B. F. Skinner, "Drive and Reflex Strength," *Journal of General Psychology* 6 (1932): 22–37.

12. Skinner, *The Shaping of a Behaviorist*, 81–82.

13. Quoted in ibid., 73.

14. Skinner's dominance of behaviorist theorizing is evident from G. E. Zuriff's scholarly and comprehensive *Behaviorism: A Conceptual Reconstruction* (New York: Columbia University Press, 1985). Throughout the book Zuriff insists that behaviorist theorizing can be successful only if behaviorists can in fact predict and control behavior.

15. For a clear discussion of that issue, see Richard J. Herrnstein, "The Evolution of Behaviorism," *American Psychologist* 32 (1977): 593–603. I must thank Tamara Goranson for helping me clarify my thinking on that issue.

16. Zuriff, *Behaviorism*, 262. Zuriff quotes two passages from Skinner illustrating the pragmatic positivism of the behaviorist philosophy of science. Skinner wrote, "Scientific knowledge . . . is a corpus of rules for effective action, and there is a special sense in which it could be 'true' if it yields the most effective action possible" (*About Behaviorism* [New York: Knopf, 1974], 235); and "Empirical research . . . is a set of practices which are productive of useful behavior. . . . An important part of scientific practice is the evaluation of the probability that a verbal response is 'right' or 'true'—that it may be acted upon successfully" (*Verbal Behavior* [New York: Appleton-Century-Crofts, 1957], 428).

17. See Burrhus F. Skinner, "On the Circularity of the Law of Effect," *Psychological Bulletin* 47 (1950): 52–75.

18. Quoted by D. L. Boyer in "A Widely Accepted but Nontheless [*sic*] Astonishingly Flimsy Argument against Analytic Behaviorism," *Philosophia* 14 (1984): 153 (Boyer is quoting Ayer's *Language, Truth, and Logic*).

19. For statements of the no-particular-behavior argument, see C. C. Canfield, "Criteria and Rules of Language," *Philosophical Review* 83 (1974): 70–87; Roderick Chisholm, "Sentences about Believing," *Proceedings of the Aristotelian Society* 56 (1955–56): 125–48; M. Ginsberg, *Mind and Belief* (New York: Hu-

manities Press, 1972), 13–16; H. H. Price, *Belief* (New York: Humanities Press, 1969), 253–60; Alisdair MacIntyre, *Against the Self-Images of the Age* (New York: Shocken, 1971); and G. Sher, "Armstrong and the Interdependence of the Mental," *Philosophical Quarterly* 27 (1977): 227–35.

20. Boyer, "A Widely Accepted but Nontheless Astonishingly Flimsy Argument against Analytic Behaviorism."

21. Ibid., 167.

22. Skinner, *Verbal Behavior*.

23. Ibid., 315.

24. See especially Chomsky's review of Skinner's *Verbal Behavior* in *Language* 35 (1959): 26–58.

25. In John A. Mills, "An Assessment of Skinner's Theory of Animal Behavior," *Journal for the Theory of Social Behaviour* 18 (1988): 197–218.

26. Skinner, *The Shaping of a Behaviorist*, 182.

27. E. S. Savage-Rumbaugh, D. M. Rumbaugh, and S. Boysen, "Symbolic Communication between Two Chimpanzees (*Pan troglodytes*)," *Science* 201 (1978): 641–44; and idem, "Linguistically Mediated Tool Use and Exchange by Chimpanzees," *Behavioral and Brain Sciences* 4 (1978): 539–54.

28. Stephen Walker, *Animal Thought* (London: Routledge and Kegan Paul, 1983), 369.

29. Zuriff, *Behaviorism*, 130.

30. Arthur W. Staats, *Learning, Language and Cognition: Theory, Research, and Method for the Study of Human Behavior and Its Development* (New York: Holt, Rinehart, and Winston, 1968), 109.

31. See Mills, "An Assessment of Skinner's Theory of Animal Behavior."

32. See Nicholas J. Mackintosh, *The Psychology of Animal Learning* (New York: Academic Press, 1974), chap. 5.

33. See Robert Epstein, R. P. Lanza, and B. F. Skinner, "Symbolic Communication between Two Pigeons (*Columba livia domestica*)," *Science* 207 (1980): 543–45.

34. See David Premack and Guy Woodruff, "Does the Chimpanzee Have a Theory of Mind?" *Behavioral and Brain Sciences* 4 (1978): 515–26. The authors characterize mind in the same way I have.

35. Daniel C. Dennett, "Intentional Systems in Cognitive Ethology: The 'Panglossian' Paradigm Defended," *Behavioral and Brain Sciences* 6 (1983): 343–90.

36. Barbara B. Smuts, *Sex and Friendship in Baboons* (Hawthorne, NY: Aldine de Gruyter, 1985).

37. Dorothy L. Cheney and Robert Seyfarth, *How Monkeys See the World: Inside the Mind of Another Species* (Chicago: University of Chicago Press, 1990).

38. Skinner, *The Shaping of a Behaviorist*, 274.

39. Elizabeth Tyler, *Freedom's Ferment: Phases of American Social History to 1860* (Minneapolis: University of Minnesota Press, 1944).

40. Edward Bellamy, *Looking Backward, 2000–1887* (New York: Houghton Mifflin, 1889). There were at least twenty editions and numerous reprints, the last being in 1951.

41. See Howard P. Segal, *Technological Utopianism in American Culture* (Chicago: University of Chicago Press, 1985). I am deeply indebted to Larry Smith for drawing my attention to this invaluable reference.

42. Skinner seems to have derived his ideas on the organization of work from Bellamy's *Looking Backward*. Bellamy treated all types of work as qualitatively equal and accepted the principle that, within limits, one can do what one wants. However, he assigned different numbers of credits to different kinds of work.

43. Initially *Walden Two* was as obscure as other books in this tradition; sales were very low at first and the book went out of print. See Krishan Kumar, *Utopia and Anti-Utopia in Modern Times* (Oxford: Blackwell, 1987). I suspect that sales became good because, from the late 1960s onward, determinedly unconventional university teachers used the book, among others, to persuade students to discuss various social issues. In 1981 about two million copies were in print, according to Alan Elms.

44. Franz Samelson examined the sales records and told me that from 1939 to 1945 inclusive, three hundred copies were sold (about a hundred in 1939). In contrast, Hull's *Principles* sold over a thousand copies in its first year and 3,400 from 1946 to 1950 inclusive.

45. In the same vein, Krishan Kumar, in *Utopia and Anti-Utopia in Modern Times*, believes that in *Walden Two* Skinner re-created the atmosphere of the small-town America in which he grew up.

46. Skinner frankly admitted that there are major autobiographical elements in *Walden Two*. The name Frazier was a combination of Fred and Crozier. Castle, who serves as the unconvincing spokesman for conventional liberalism, was based on a friend, Aubrey Castell.

47. B. F. Skinner, *Walden Two* (New York: Macmillan, 1948), 110.

48. As in Watson's case, there may well have been a personal element in Skinner's distrust of emotion. Elms comments that Skinner was deeply upset by the emotional turmoil and uneasy social relationships of his "dark year."

49. Skinner, *Walden Two*, 75.

50. Ibid., 92.

51. My contention gets some support from a passage in which Frazier is talking about childless couples: "No sensible person will suppose that love or affection has anything to do with blood. One's love for one's wife is required by law to be free of a close blood connection. . . . Love and affection are psychological and cultural, and blood relationships can be happily forgotten." *Walden Two*, 133.

52. Elms comments on the restricted emotional range within which Walden Two's inhabitants were compelled to operate: "Walden Two's inhabitants do

have their pleasures. . . . But by stressing the avoidance of unpleasantness as a major goal of the society, Skinner has withdrawn from the residents much of the variety of behavioral choices, the range of emotional responses, and the introspective richness of which human beings are capable." "Skinner's Dark Year," 478–79.

53. Kumar, *Utopia and Anti-Utopia in Modern Times*, 366.

54. Kathleen Kincade, *A Walden Two Experiment: The First Five Years of Twin Oaks Community* (New York: William Morrow, 1973), 55.

55. Ibid., 150.

56. In his foreword to Kincade's book, Skinner responded with his typical bland evasiveness.

57. Perhaps we can say that Skinner's life was Watson's without the divorce and the expulsion from academe. Both of them, ultimately, appealed to the public at large and bypassed professional modes of communication.

NOTES TO CHAPTER 6

1. William H. Burnham, *The Normal Mind: An Introduction to Mental Hygiene and the Hygiene of School Instruction* (New York: Appleton, 1924), 18.

2. Papers given at the symposium were published in Herbert S. Jennings et al., *Suggestions of Modern Science Concerning Education* (New York: Macmillan, 1917).

3. Quoted in Kerry Buckley, *Mechanical Man* (New York: Guilford, 1989), 116.

4. For an account of the LSRM's work in child study and parent education, see Christine M. Shea, "The Ideology of Mental Health and the Emergence of the Therapeutic Liberal State: The American Mental Hygiene Movement, 1900–1930" (Ph.D. diss., University of Illinois at Urbana-Champaign, 1980), 215 ff. I am most grateful to Mark Flynn, who lent me his copy of the thesis.

5. Ibid.

6. By the end of the 1920s the LSRM was contributing $600,000 per year to the running costs of about thirty institutions involved in child care and in parental education.

7. For example, the Iowa Child Welfare Station was established by a bill in the state legislature in 1917. See Shea, "The Ideology of Mental Health," 212.

8. For accounts of that movement, see Raymond E. Callahan, *Education and the Cult of Efficiency: A Study of the Social Forces That Have Shaped the Administration of the Public Schools* (Chicago: University of Chicago Press, 1962); and David Tyack and Elisabeth Hansot, *Managers of Virtue: Public School Leadership in America, 1820–1980* (New York: Basic Books, 1982). I am most grateful to Mark Flynn for telling me about these two books.

9. William H. Burnham, "Principles of Municipal School Administration," *Atlantic Monthly* 92 (1903): 109.

10. Buckley, *Mechanical Man*, 148.

11. Frederic L. Wells, *Mental Adjustments* (New York: Appleton, 1917). Watson's associate Mary Cover Jones and her fellow students at Vassar were attracted to Watson's *Psychology from the Standpoint of a Behaviorist* because it downplayed the role of the standard experimental psychology of the day and stressed the importance for psychology of everyday problems of mental adjustment. See Jones, "A 1924 Pioneer Looks at Behavior Therapy," *Journal of Behavior Therapy and Experimental Psychiatry* 6 (1975): 181–87.

12. Wells, *Mental Adjustments*, 24.

13. Ibid., 29; the quotation comes from p. 46.

14. Ibid., 125 and 130 respectively (emphasis in original).

15. He postulated a mechanism called siphoning as a replacement for repression. Ibid., 130 ff.

16. John B. Watson, "Behavior and the Concept of Mental Disease," *Journal of Philosophy, Psychology and Scientific Methods* 13 (1916): 591.

17. It is intriguing that Burnham's only observation on Twitmyer's accidental discovery of the conditioned reflex (Edwin B. Twitmyer, *A Study of the Knee Jerk* [Philadelphia: John C. Winston, 1902]) was to note that the conditioned responses Twitmyer elicited from his subjects were involuntary.

18. Burnham, *The Normal Mind*, 145.

19. Watson believed that emotional patterns, especially irrational fears, resulted from conditioned reflexes. In his casual observation of children at the Harriet Lane Hospital in Baltimore between 1916 and 1920 he saw numerous examples of well-established irrational fears by age three. Apparently he concluded that the basic personality patterns were established by that age. See John B. Watson, "Studies on the Growth of Emotions," in *Psychologies of 1925: Powell Lectures in Psychological Theory*, ed. Carl Murchison (Worcester, MA: Clark University Press, 1928), 37–57.

20. Florence Mateer's study is reported in *Child Behavior: A Critical and Experimental Study of Young Children by the Method of Conditioned Reflexes* (Boston: Richard G. Badger, 1918). In her foreword Mateer states that she worked under Burnham's close supervision.

21. Ibid., 81–82.

22. In *The Normal Mind*, Burnham claimed that Mateer had succeeded in measuring intelligence by her method when her findings were, at best, tentative.

23. Leonard P. Ullmann and Leonard Krasner, *Case Studies in Behavior Modification* (New York: Holt, Rinehart, and Winston, 1965), 50 ff.

24. The Watsonian tradition did not die out altogether, however. See G. R. Pascal, *Behavioral Change in the Clinic: A Systematic Approach* (New York: Grune and Stratton, 1959).

25. Leonard Krasner, "The Future and the Past in the Behaviorism-Humanism Dialogue," *American Psychologist* 33 (1978): 800.

26. Ibid., 801.

27. William C. Menninger, "Psychiatric Experience in the War, 1941–1946," *American Journal of Psychiatry* 103 (1947): 577–86.

28. Ibid., 580.

29. Ibid., 581 (emphasis added).

30. Ibid., 583.

31. See Ellen Herman, *The Romance of American Psychology: Political Culture in the Age of Experts* (Berkeley: University of California Press, 1995), 245 ff.

32. See James G. Miller, "Clinical Psychology in the Veterans Administration," *American Psychologist* 1 (1946): 181–89.

33. By 1948 the Veterans Administration and the U.S. public health service were spending two to three million dollars a year on fellowships, hospital and clinical positions, research funds, and grants to universities. See Donald G. Marquis, "Research Planning at the Frontiers of Science," *American Psychologist* 3 (1948): 430–38.

34. The members of the group were Hull, the social scientist John Dollard, psychologists Neal E. Miller, Robert Sears, and O. Hobart Mowrer, psychiatrists Earl Zinn, Harry Stack Sullivan, and Erik H. Erikson (all of whom were either practicing psychoanalysts or very sympathetic to psychoanalysis at that time), and an anthropologist, Edward Sapir. For an excellent account of the influence of psychoanalysis on American psychology, see David Shakow and David Rapaport, "The Influence of Freud on American Psychology," *Psychological Issues* 4, Monograph 13 (New York: International University Press, 1964).

After completing his Ph.D. in sociology under William F. Ogburn at Chicago in 1931, Dollard studied psychoanalysis in Germany on a Science Research Fellowship. He was analyzed by Hanns Sachs and performed a control analysis under Abram Kardiner, Karen Horney, and others. Sapir brought him to Yale. His first publication was *Criteria for the Life History* (New Haven: Yale University Press [published for the Institute of Human Relations], 1935). His next publication was *Caste and Class in a Southern Town* (New Haven: Yale University Press [published for the Institute of Human Relations], 1937), a groundbreaking study of the role and consequences of racial prejudice in America. His next book, as a junior author with the black sociologist Alison Davis, was *Children of Bondage: The Personality Development of Negro Youth in the Urban South* (Washington, DC: American Council on Education, 1949). The major fruits of his collaboration with the IHR group were John Dollard, L. W. Doob, N. E. Miller, O. H. Mowrer, R. R. Sears, C. S. Ford, C. I. Hovland, and R. T. Sollenberger, in collaboration with Clellan S. Ford, *Frustration and Aggression* (New Haven: Yale University Press, 1939); John Dollard and Neal E. Miller, *Personality and Psychotherapy: An Analysis in Terms of Learning, Theory, and Culture* (New York:

McGraw-Hill, 1950); and N. E. Miller and John Dollard, *Social Learning and Imitation* (New Haven: Yale University Press [published for the Institute of Human Relations], 1941). As the most interdisciplinary member of the group, Dollard suffered the typical consequences in terms of his academic career. Even though he was one of America's most distinguished social scientists, he was a mere research worker at Yale from 1932 to 1952; he was eventually appointed full professor at age fifty-two.

Robert Sears did his graduate work at Yale under Hull's supervision in 1929–32 (studying visual conditioning in goldfish). He produced a number of studies on psychoanalytic themes in 1936 and 1937 and wrote to Hull during those two years. Sears's paper on projection at the APA conference in 1934 impressed Hull. Hull was so excited by a later article on repression that he ordered a hundred reprints (the article was Robert Sears, "Initiation of the Repression Sequence by Repeated Failures," *Journal of Experimental Psychology* 20 [1937]: 570–80). Sears joined the Yale staff in 1936 as a research assistant professor, becoming an assistant professor in 1937. In 1942 he resigned to go to the University of Iowa as professor and as director of the Child Welfare Research Station.

O. H. Mowrer began his professional career as an experimental psychologist. In 1934 he was appointed a postdoctoral fellow at Yale, working under Raymond Dodge. He met the IHR group there and became simultaneously interested in learning theory and psychoanalysis. From 1936 to 1940 he was an instructor in psychology and a research associate at the IHR; he resigned in 1940 to take up a post at the Harvard Graduate School of Education.

Neal Elgar Miller completed his Ph.D. at Yale in 1935. He was a social science research fellow at the Institute of Psychoanalysis, Vienna, in 1935–36. He was an instructor, assistant professor, and research psychologist at the IHR from 1936 to 1941, associate professor and research associate at Yale from 1941–42 to 1946–50, professor from 1950 to 1952, and James Rowland Angell Professor at Yale from 1952 to 1966; he resigned from Yale to end his career at Rockefeller University.

35. In February and March 1936 Hull wrote at length about psychoanalysis in his *Research Memoranda*. Nowhere did he express any dissatisfaction with or disquiet about psychoanalytic theory. For a published example of the IHR group's thinking here, see Dollard and Miller, *Personality and Psychotherapy*, 9–11. Hull and his colleagues fully accepted the reality of all the major psychoanalytic concepts such as cathexis (although Hull had to wrestle with its meaning), repression, regression, and transference.

36. I have already noted that Dollard was analyzed by Hanns Sachs. Neal Miller went even further. He was so persuaded of the effectiveness of psychoanalysis that he paid for an analysis at Vienna in 1935 with his social science research fellowship (the analyst was Heinz Hartmann). Mowrer shared his enthusiasm: "there was a time when I read [Freud's] works fervently and *in extenso*."

"O. Hobart Mowrer," in *A History of Psychology in Autobiography*, vol. 6, ed. Kenneth MacCorquodale, Gardner Lindzey, and Kenneth E. Clark (Englewood Cliffs, NJ: Prentice Hall, 1974), 329. Mowrer undertook a three-year psychoanalysis in an attempt to overcome his recurrent depressions. He became disenchanted with psychoanalysis in 1944–45 following an analysis with Hanns Sachs.

37. For example, see Dollard and Miller's forthright statement: "neurotic conflicts are taught by parents and learned by children." *Personality and Psychotherapy*, 127.

38. Hull's interest in psychoanalysis predated his systematic work on it. In his Idea Books he made some notes on a proposed book on the higher mental processes. One topic was to have been "Psychopathology and Freudian psychology, the emotional and instinctive life" (entry for June 4, 1933).

39. The article was originally published in the *Psychological Review* 46 (1939): 553–65 and was republished in O. H. Mowrer, *Learning Theory and Personality Dynamics: Selected Papers* (New York: Ronald, 1950), 15–27.

40. The article was originally published in *Psychological Monographs* 52 (1940), no. 2 and republished in *Learning Theory and Personality Dynamics*, 28–64.

41. Originally published in the *Journal of Abnormal and Social Psychology* 35 (1940): 56–87 and republished in *Learning Theory and Personality Dynamics*, 361–89.

42. First published as O. H. Mowrer and Willie May Mowrer, "Enuresis: A Method for Its Treatment and Study," *American Journal of Orthopsychiatry* 8 (1938): 436–59, republished in *Learning Theory and Personality Dynamics* (without the attribution to Mrs. Mowrer, whose name was also removed from the citation of the original article in the list of references, 390–417). Also see O. H. Mowrer, "Apparatus for the Study and Treatment of Enuresis," *American Journal of Psychology* 51 (1938): 163–66.

43. See Albert Bandura, "Psychotherapy as a Learning Process," *Psychological Bulletin* 58 (1971): 143–59.

44. Ibid., 155.

45. Paul R. Fuller, "Operant Conditioning of a Vegetative Human Organism," *American Journal of Psychology* 62 (1949): 587–90.

46. See Ogden R. Lindsley, B. F. Skinner, and H. C. Solomon, *Studies in Behavior Therapy: Status Report* 1 (Waltham, MA: Metropolitan State Hospital, 1953). In this study, the behaviors of psychotic (acute and chronic) patients were compared with the behaviors of "normal" individuals on an operant conditioning task. The subjects were placed in a monitored room for an hour a day for several days. If the subject pulled the plunger or lever on the apparatus his behavior was reinforced according to the reinforcement schedule. The reinforcements used included candy, cigarettes, or projected pictures. The researchers found that the behaviors of the psychotic patients seemed to be shaped by the reinforcement

schedule. This finding provided support for the theory that even psychotic behavior had been learned and that psychotic individuals could learn alternative behaviors. Also see Ogden R. Lindsley, "Operant Conditioning Methods Applied to Research in Chronic Schizophrenia," *Psychiatric Research Reports* 5 (1956): 118–53.

Krasner states that Lindsley and his coauthors were the first to use the term "behavior therapy," but that Arnold Lazarus independently used the same term to describe Joseph Wolpe's procedure.

47. N. H. Azrin and O. R. Lindsley, "The Reinforcement of Cooperation between Children," *Journal of Abnormal and Social Psychology* 52 (1956): 100–102.

48. For accounts of token economies, see Alan E. Kazdin, *The Token Economy: A Review and Evaluation* (New York: Plenum Press, 1977); and Teodoro Ayllon and N. H. Azrin, *The Token Economy: A Motivational System for Therapy and Rehabilitation* (New York: Appleton-Century-Crofts, 1968). For an excellent critical review of token economies in mental institutions, see Gerald C. Davison, "Appraisal of Behavior Modification Techniques with Adults in Institutional Settings," in *Behavior Therapy: Appraisal and Status*, ed. Cyril M. Franks (New York: McGraw-Hill, 1969), 220–78.

49. Kazdin, *The Token Economy*, 39.

50. For example, by J. T. Cowles, "Food Tokens as Incentives for Learning by Chimpanzees," *Comparative Psychological Monographs* 14 (1937), no. 71; and J. B. Wolfe, "Effectiveness of Token-Rewards for Chimpanzees," *Psychological Monographs* 12 (1936), no. 60.

51. See C. B. Ferster and M. K. DeMyer, "The Development of Performances in Autistic Children in an Automatically Controlled Environment," *Journal of Chronic Diseases* 13 (1961): 312–45; idem, "A Method for the Experimental Analysis of the Behavior of Autistic Children," *American Journal of Orthopsychiatry* 1 (1962): 87–110; and O. Ivar Lovaas, "The Control of Operant Responding by Rate and Content of Verbal Operants" (paper presented at Western Psychological Association meeting, Seattle, June 1961). Ferster and DeMyer's tokens gave access either to a vending machine that released food, candy, and so on or to events such as a thirty second performance by a pigeon. Lovaas's tokens allowed children to "buy" toys. Sidney W. Bijou and Donald M. Baer, in "Operant Methods in Child Behavior and Development," in *Operant Behavior: Areas of Research and Application*, ed. W. K. Honig (New York: Appleton-Century-Crofts, 1966), 718–89, used the same system as Lovaas.

52. See Arthur W. Staats, "A General Apparatus for the Investigation of Complex Learning in Children," *Behavior Research and Therapy* 6 (1968): 45–50. Staats's article is a progress report on research that he started in 1959.

53. Ayllon and Azrin started a token economy in a female ward at Anna State Mental Hospital, Illinois. See Teodoro Ayllon and N. H. Azrin, "The Measure-

ment and Reinforcement of Behavior in Psychotics," *Journal of the Experimental Analysis of Behavior* 7 (1965) 8: 357–83. Birnbrauer worked at Ranier School in Washington. See Jay S. Birnbrauer, Sidney W. Bijou, Montrose M. Wolf, and J. D. Kidder, "Programed [*sic*] Instruction in the Classroom," in Ullmann and Krasner, eds., *Case Studies in Behavior Modification*, 358–63; and Jay S. Birnbrauer, Montrose M. Wolf, J. D. Kidder, and Cecilia E. Tague, "Classroom Behavior of Retarded Pupils with Token Reinforcement," *Journal of Experimental Child Psychology* 2 (1965): 19–35.

54. John M. Atthowe and Leonard Krasner, "Preliminary Report on the Application of Contingent Reinforcement Procedures (Token Economies) on a Chronic Psychiatric Ward," *Journal of Abnormal Psychology* 73 (1968): 37–43.

55. Teodoro Ayllon and Jack Michael, "The Psychiatric Nurse as a Behavioral Engineer," *Journal of the Experimental Analysis of Behavior* 2 (1959): 323.

56. Eric Haughton and Teodoro Ayllon, "Production and Elimination of Symptomatic Behavior," in Ullmann and Krasner, eds., *Case Studies in Behavior Modification*, 94–98.

57. Ibid., 98.

58. Ayllon and Michael, "The Psychiatric Nurse as a Behavioral Engineer," 325.

59. R. C. Winkler, "Management of Chronic Psychiatric Patients by a Token Reinforcement System," *Journal of Applied Behavior Analysis* 3 (1970): 47–55; idem, "Reinforcement Schedules for Individual Patients in a Token Economy," *Behavior Therapy* 2 (1971): 534–37; idem, "The Relevance of Economic Theory and Technology of Token Reinforcement Systems," *Behavior Research and Therapy* 9 (1971): 81–88; idem, "A Theory of Equilibrium in Token Economies," *Journal of Abnormal and Social Psychology* 79 (1972): 169–73; idem, "An Experimental Analysis of Economic Balance, Savings, and Wages in a Token Economy," *Behavior Therapy* 4 (1973): 22–40.

60. Winkler, "A Theory of Equilibrium in Token Economies," 170.

61. Winkler, "The Relevance of Economic Theory and Technology to Token Reinforcement Systems," 88.

62. I am relying on Davison's account in "Appraisal of Behavior Modification Techniques with Adults in Institutional Settings."

63. Ibid., 272 (emphasis in original).

64. See Bernard Rimland, *Infantile Autism* (New York: Appleton-Century-Crofts, 1964).

65. See George W. Fairweather, ed., *Social Psychology in Treating Mental Illness: An Experimental Approach* (New York: Wiley, 1964); and George W. Fairweather, David H. Sanders, Hugo Maynard, and David L. Cressler, with Dorothy S. Bleck, *Community Life for the Mentally Ill: An Alternative to Institutional Care* (Chicago: Aldine, 1969). I find it ironic that I learned of Fairweather's work from the legal literature.

66. Fairweather, *Social Psychology in Treating Mental Illness*, 24.

67. Fairweather et al., *Community Life for the Mentally Ill*, 115.

68. Ibid., 338.

69. The first such case was *Baxtrom v. Herold*, 383 U.S. 107. Baxtrom was a convicted criminal who had been transferred from jail to a mental institution for the criminally insane but had been denied access to the procedures for civil commitment. The case eventually went to the Supreme Court, which ordered a review of his sanity, together with that of 967 others who were in the same legal category. Four years after the decision, less than 3 percent of the group were in either a jail or an institution for the criminally insane, but about 50 percent were in a mental hospital.

70. The most comprehensive review of these matters that I have found is Murray Levine, *The History and Politics of Community Mental Health* (New York: Oxford University Press, 1981).

71. Ken Kesey's novel *One Flew over the Cuckoo's Nest*, for example, had a powerful impact on public opinion. Kesey's fictional portrayal of the institutional culture had its academic counterpart in Erving Goffman, *Asylums: Essay on the Social Situation of Mental Patients and Other Inmates* (Garden City, NY: Anchor Books, 1961). Szasz had his most profound effect on legal issues in his book *Law, Liberty, and Psychiatry: An Inquiry into the Social Uses of Mental Health Practices* (New York: Macmillan, 1963). He continued his attack on the scientific pretensions of psychiatry he had developed in a previous book, especially by casting doubt on the objectivity of psychiatric nosology. More to the point, however, was his treatment of commitment as a means of social control. A good example of a labeling theorist is Thomas Scheff, *Being Mentally Ill: A Sociological Theory*, 2d ed. (New York: Aldine, 1984), 12–13. Other influential works on labeling theory were E. M. Lemert, *Social Pathology* (New York: McGraw-Hill, 1951); and H. S. Becker, *Outsiders: Studies in the Sociology of Deviance* (New York: Free Press of Glencoe, 1963). Also see a widely quoted study by D. L. Rosenhan, "The Contextual Nature of Psychiatric Diagnoses," *Journal of Abnormal Psychology* 84 (1975): 462–74.

72. See especially Bruce Ennis, *Prisoners of Psychiatry: Mental Patients, Psychiatrists and the Law* (New York: Harcourt Brace Jovanovich, 1972).

73. Levine, *The History and Politics of Community Mental Health*, 121.

74. The legal rule requiring provision of services in the least restrictive alternative was proposed by the trial judge in *Lake v. Cameron* (364 F.2d [D.C. Cir. 1966]). Mrs. Lake was a sixty-year-old woman who wandered, day or night, whatever the weather, so she was committed to St. Elizabeth's Hospital in Washington for her own protection. The judge suggested that the least restrictive alternative compatible with both the state's duty to protect Mrs. Lake and her right to live as normal a life as possible was a requirement that she carry an identification card so that police could return her to her home. For a discussion of the conse-

quences of applying the rule, see Levine, *History and Politics of Community Mental Health*, 125–29.

75. 325 F. Supp. 781, 784 (M.D. Ala. 1971) and 344 F. Supp. 373, 387 (M.D. Ala. 1972).

76. David Wexler, "Token and Taboo: Behavior Modification, Token Economies, and the Law," *California Law Review 61* (1973): 93–94.

77. Ennis propounded the principle in "Civil Liberties and Mental Illness," *Criminal Law Bulletin* 7 (1971): 101 ff.

78. Atthowe and Krasner, "Preliminary Report on the Application of Contingent Reinforcement Procedures (Token Economies) on a Chronic Psychiatric Ward."

79. Wexler, "Token and Taboo," 104.

80. I am grateful to Harley Dickinson for giving me that analysis of the situation. See Andrew Scull, *Decarceration: Community Treatment of the Deviant—A Radical View* (Cambridge: Polity Press, 1984).

81. I owe that insight to Harley Dickinson.

NOTES TO CHAPTER 7

1. For a discussion of the implications of Maslow's doctrine for Hull's theory, see John A. Mills, "Hull's Theory of Learning: II. A Criticism of the Theory and Its Relationship to the History of Psychological Thought," *Canadian Psychological Review* 19 (1978): 116–27.

2. John H. Flavell, *The Developmental Psychology of Jean Piaget* (Princeton: Van Nostrand, 1963); Jerome S. Bruner, "Inhelder and Piaget's *The Growth of Logical Thinking*: A Psychologist's Viewpoint," *British Journal of Psychology 50* (1959): 363–70; and idem, "The Course of Cognitive Development," *American Psychologist* 19 (1964): 1–16.

3. Ausubel's most important works were *Theory and Problems of Adolescent Development* (New York: Grune and Stratton, 1954); and *Theory and Problems of Child Development* (New York: Grune and Stratton, 1958). There were at least three editions of the latter.

4. Robert R. Sears, Eleanor E. Maccoby, and Harry Levin, *Patterns of Child Rearing* (New York: Harper and Row, 1957).

5. Berkowitz gave an overview of his work on aggression in "The Concept of Aggressive Drive: Some Additional Considerations," in *Advances in Experimental Social Psychology*, vol. 2, ed. L. Berkowitz (New York: Academic Press, 1965), 301–29 and a full account of his position in *Roots of Aggression: A Re-Examination of the Frustration-Aggression Hypothesis* (New York: Atherton Press, 1969).

6. See John Dollard et al., *Frustration and Aggression* (New Haven: Yale University Press, 1939).

7. Richard H. Walters and Ross D. Parke, "Social Motivation, Dependency, and Susceptibility to Social Influence," in *Advances in Social Psychology*, vol. 1, ed. L. Berkowitz (New York: Academic Press, 1964), 271. Also see Albert Bandura and Richard H. Walters, *Adolescent Aggression* (New York: Ronald, 1959).

8. Peter M. Blau, "Social Exchange," in *The International Encyclopaedia of the Social Sciences*, vol. 7, ed. D. L. Stills (New York: Macmillan, 1968), 452–57.

9. Irving M. Piliavin, Judith Rodin, and Jane A. Piliavin, "Good Samaritanism: An Underground Phenomenon," *Journal of Personality and Social Psychology* 13 (1969): 289–99.

10. See Kenneth Gergen, *The Psychology of Behavior Exchange* (Reading, MA: Addison-Wesley, 1969).

11. See Elaine Walster, Ellen Berscheid, and G. William Walster, "New Directions in Equity Research," in *Advances in Experimental Social Psychology*, vol. 9, ed. L. Berkowitz and E. Walster (New York: Academic Press, 1976), 1–42. The rest of vol. 9 was devoted to equity research.

12. Benton J. Underwood, *Experimental Psychology* (New York: Appleton-Century-Crofts, 1949). A second edition came out in 1966. In his foreword Underwood says that he could find no suitable text in 1946 when he began to teach experimental psychology.

13. I used Underwood's text when I taught experimental psychology at the University of Saskatchewan and felt obliged to add a series of lectures on various aspects of psychology.

14. Howard H. Kendler, "The Iowa Tradition," *American Psychologist* 44 (1989): 1126.

15. By the same token, Spence did not produce books comparable to Hull's *Principles of Learning* or Tolman's *Purposive Behavior in Animals and Men*. He did produce two books, but these are collections of articles rather than coherent texts. They are *Behavior Theory and Conditioning* (New Haven: Yale University Press, 1956); and *Behavior Theory and Learning: Selected Papers* (Englewood Cliffs, NJ: Prentice Hall, 1960). Spence gives an overall presentation of his position in the last chapter of the former. There is an excellent review of Spence's position in Ernest R. Hilgard and Gordon G. Bower, *Theories of Learning*, 4th ed. (Englewood Cliffs, NJ: Prentice Hall, 1975), 182–92.

16. See especially Hilgard's comments and his references to some of the relevant archival material in his and Bower's *Theories of Learning*, 3d ed. (New York: Appleton-Century-Crofts, 1966).

17. Bergmann gave a course on the philosophy of science at Iowa for many years and so must have disseminated these views to Iowa graduate students.

18. Spence established an eyelid conditioning laboratory.

19. See Gordon H. Bower and Ernest R. Hilgard, *Theories of Learning*, 5th ed. (Englewood Cliffs, NJ: Prentice Hall 1985).

20. Hilgard and Bower, *Theories of Learning*, 4th ed.

21. See Nicholas J. Mackintosh, *The Psychology of Animal Learning* (New York: Academic Press, 1974), 223–27.

22. Between 1949 and 1955, forty-five Iowa Ph.D. theses were published in the *Journal of Experimental Psychology*, the *Journal of Comparative and Physiological Psychology*, the *Journal of Abnormal and Social Psychology*, the *Journal of Consulting Psychology*, *Psychological Monographs*, and the *Journal of Applied Psychology*. Iowa's next nearest rivals were Columbia and New York University, with thirty-three each, Yale with thirty-two, and Michigan with twenty-seven (information taken from Spence's departmental reports in the Archives of the History of American Psychology).

23. I took this information from Howard H. Kendler's necrology of Spence, published in *Psychological Review* 74 (1967): 335–41; reprinted in *Essays in Neobehaviorism: A Memorial Volume to Kenneth W. Spence*, ed. H. H. Kendler and J. Taylor Spence (New York: Appleton-Century-Crofts, 1971), 1–8; and from Spence's papers in the Archives of American Psychology. The document listing total numbers of psychological doctorates from Iowa is hard to interpret because from 1952 onward, Spence's students are not listed. Spence did, however, make up a list comprising only his students (including some entries in ink that are very hard to read). I arrived at a total of 147 Iowa doctorates for the period 1940–64 by adding Spence's Ph.D.'s for 1952 onward to the total, concluding that Spence graduated 48.98 percent of them. Spence also graduated two Ph.D.'s from Texas.

24. That exception was Wilse B. Webb (Ph.D., 1946), who specialized in sleep research.

25. The people whose careers I will not discuss in detail were (the dates of their Ph.D.'s are given in brackets) G. Robert Grice (1947); David Ehrenfreund (1947); M. Ray Denny (1945); Warren H. Teichner (1951); Milton A. Trapold (1961); and Roger W. Black (1961). Allan R. Wagner (1959) was one of the leaders of the "cognitive revolution" in animal learning; however, he continues to be deeply influenced by Hull.

26. Ernest R. Hilgard and Donald G. Marquis, *Conditioning and Learning* (New York: Appleton-Century, 1940). Gregory Kimble's version was *Hilgard and Marquis' Conditioning and Learning*, 2d ed. (New York: Appleton-Century-Crofts, 1961).

27. See Frank Logan, *Incentive: How the Conditions of Reinforcement Affect the Performance of Rats* (New Haven: Yale University Press, 1960); and idem, "A Micromolar Approach to Behavior Theory," *Psychological Review* 63 (1956): 63–73. For a review of Logan's position, see Hilgard and Bower, *Theories of Learning*, 4th ed., 198–201.

28. See Abram Amsel, "The Role of Frustrative Nonreward in Noncontinuous Reward Situations," *Psychological Bulletin* 55 (1958): 102–19.

29. For a critical review of Amsel's position, see Mackintosh, *The Psychology of Animal Learning*, chap. 7.

30. Abram Amsel, *Behaviorism, Neobehaviorism, and Cognitivism in Learning Theory: Historical and Contemporary Perspectives* (Hillsdale, NJ: Lawrence Erlbaum, 1989).

31. Howard H. Kendler, "Reflections and Confessions of a Reinforcement Theorist," *Psychological Review* 58 (1951): 368–74.

32. Kendler, "The Iowa Tradition," 1129. Kendler concluded the passage by arguing that psychology could never reach the same certainties as a physical science like genetics because the gene was a physical entity with definite causal properties, whereas in psychology "the intervening variables of the past are still floating in imaginary space" (1129).

33. See Bernard J. Baars, *The Cognitive Revolution in Psychology* (New York: Guilford, 1986); and Thomas B. Leahey, *A History of Modern Psychology*, 2d ed. (Englewood Cliffs, NJ: Prentice Hall, 1994), 303 ff.

34. See Thomas S. Kuhn, "Logic of Discovery or Psychology of Research," in *Criticism and the Growth of Knowledge*, ed. Imre Lakatos and Alan Musgrave (Cambridge: Cambridge University Press, 1970), 1–23.

35. Even among animal scientists who have become cognitivists one sees remnants of Hullian thinking. I am thinking of Robert Rescorla (probably the most prominent living animal scientist) and Allan Wagner. See Barry Schwartz and Steven J. Robbins, *Psychology of Learning and Behavior*, 4th ed. (New York: Norton, 1995), 114–20 for a review of Rescorla and Wagner's theory of motivation.

36. See Leahey, *A History of Modern Psychology*, chaps. 12 and 13.

37. E.g., Cleanth Brooks and Robert Penn Warren, *Understanding Poetry*, 4th ed. (New York: Holt, Rinehart, and Winston, 1976); and Ivor A. Richards, *Practical Criticism: A Study of Literary Judgment* (New York: Harcourt, Brace and World, 1929). Both taught students to use a standard set of formal principles and apply these to any poetry whatsoever. Also note that in modernist visual art there were no theorists, only critics, that is, no discussion of fundamental principles was required; what was required was to train artists' and, even more important, critics' visual intuition. Once again, form overrode substance.

38. Comment in J. F. Hans van Rappard, "Meta Matters: A Comment on Agatti's Proposal on the Identity of Theoretical Psychology," *Theory and Psychology* 6 (1996): 296.

39. Patrick Rabbitt (lectures on cognitive psychology, Oxford University, 1976) commented that in the groundbreaking articles in cognitive psychology, the method and results sections were relatively short, whereas the discussion sections were exceedingly long. One saw the complete reverse in articles in the experimental literature published in the 1940s and 1950s. Cognitivists had to assert

their rights over a certain intellectual territory (and, to do them credit, were probably excited by the novelty of what they were doing). Neobehaviorists were simply not prepared to discuss fundamental questions; to do so would be to imply that the foundations of their enterprise were dubious.

40. For example, note a comment by Clement Greenberg about the New York abstract expressionist painter Jackson Pollack. Greenberg said that the abstract expressionists practiced "avant-gardism": they wanted to be noticed and were indifferent about the means. *Painters Painting: The New York Art Scene, 1940–1970* (New York: Mystic Fire Video, 1972).

Index

Adams, Donald K., 221
Aggression, Berkowitz on, 182
Allport, Floyd, views on political science, 31–32
Altruism, Blau on, 182
American Social Science Association, 23
Amsel, Abram, 188
Analysis of variance in psychology, 100–102; experimental designs implicitly using, 100–101
Anthroponomy, coined by Walter Hunter, 50, 51
Ausubel, David, 181
Ayllon, Teodoro, 166–68, 170–71
Azrin, N. H., 166

Baars, Bernard J., 237
Baerends, G. P., 197
Baldwin, James Mark, 5; compared with Watson, 57
Bawden, W. Heath, 200
Baxtrom v. Herold, 233
Beach, Frank A., 196
Behavioral science, 4, 24, 83; Skinner and, 123
Behaviorism: and animal psychology, 15–16, 25, 55; and civil rights, 21–22; and experimental method, 7–8; and mental health, 21–22; and philosophy, 32–38; and positivism, 5, 24; and pragmatism, 5; and psychology, 1–2; and social control, 6; and social science, 1–2; and values, 8; APA report of 1918, not listed in, 68–69; early forms of, in psychology, 38–40; features of, 4–18; in economics, 30–31; in political science, 31–32; in social sciences, 26–32; in sociology, 26–30; logical, 3; methodological, 3; philosophical, 2–3; radical, 2–3

Behaviorism (Watson), 75, 195
Behavior modification: William Burnham, role in, 162; civil rights and, 174; Fairweather, version of, 173–74; history of, 152–66; Hull's role in, 163; humanism and, 153–54; Kantor and, 165, 166; Mowrer's role in, 162–64; Progressivism and, 152, 154, 158–59; psychoanalysis and, 153–54, 162–64; Skinner and, 153; token economies in, 165–71; Watson and, 152–55, 157–59, 162
Behavior of Organisms, The (Skinner), 143
Bekhterev, Vladimir, 73, 154
Bellamy, Edward, 143
Bentham, Jeremy, 8
Bergmann, Gustav, influences Spence, 185
Berkowitz, Leonard, 182
Berman, Louis, 222
Bernard, Luther Lee, 28
Birnbrauer, 168
Bjork, Robert, 126
Blau, social exchange theory of, 182
Boakes, Robert, 56
Bode, B. H., 200
Boring, Edwin G., and operationism, role in creating, 87, 89–94, 179; on Skinner, 129
Boyer, David L., 131
Bregman, Elsie O., 210
Bridgman, Percy, 87, 93, 94
Brown, Judson S., 185
Brown, Roger, 62
Bruner, Jerome, 181
Buckley, Kerry, 206, 210
Bulmer, Martin, 28, 29
Burgess, Ernest, 28
Burnham, John C., 4; on origins of Watson's behaviorism, 58–59, 66, 67; on Progressivism, 198

Burnham, William H., 21, 154–55, 157–58, 162
Buxton, Claude E., 219

Calkins, Mary, 59, 69; Boring writes to, 92
Campbell, Donald T., 220
Carini, Louis, 222
Carmichael, Leonard, 92
Carnap, Rudolf, 93, 94
Carr, Harvey, and Watson, 57, 75
Cattell, James McKeen, 38–39
Cause, psychological analysis of, 9–18, 84, 86–87
Chicago school of sociology, 28–30
Chomsky, Noam, 132
Churchland, Paul M., 195
Cofer, Charles N., 184
Cognitive revolution, 190–91
Cohen, David, 210
Cohen, Jacob, 197
Coleman, Steven, 128, 210
Conditioning; Guthrie's views on, 80–81; instrumental, 56; operant, 16; Pavlovian, 11; Watson's research in, 73–74
Control, 4, 18; behaviorism, a defining feature of, 6–10; Skinner, theme in, 148–50
Conrad, Herbert S., 184
Coon, Deborah J., 209
Cowles, Michael, 214
Crespi, L. P., 215, 220
Crozier, W. J., 127

Danziger, Kurt, 192; and neo-Galtonianism, 13
Darwinism, 19
Dashiell, John F., 184
Davison, Gerald, 170–72
Day, Willard D., 195
de Laguna, Grace, 24; theory of mind, 36–38
Deficit theories of motivation, 180–83
Delayed reaction, Hunter's work on, 50
Dennett, Daniel, 124, 132, 140
Dewsbury, Donald A., 206
Dollard, John, 162
Dorcus, Roy M., 184
Drive theory, 14–15; Skinner's version of, 128–29
Dummer, Ethel Sturgess, 154
Dunlap, Knight, 68

Ebbinghaus, Hermann, 40, 88, 179
Economics, American, history of, 24, 30–31
Elms, Alan, 144–45
Empiricism, 21
English, H. B., 210
Ennis, Bruce, 174
Esper, Erwin, 19, 40, 41
Estes, W. K., 184
Experimentation in psychology, 8–18; Underwood's text on, 183

Fairweather, George, 173–74
Farber, Isadore E., 185
Faris, Robert Ellsworth L., 29
Fechner, Gustav Theodor, 88, 179
Fernberger, S. W., 184
Fisher, Sir Ronald, analysis of variance, 100
Flavell, John H., 181
Frank, Lawrence K., 154, 157
Freud, Sigmund, 180, 181; influences Skinner, 147; influences Watson, 71–72; Mowrer's reformulation of concepts of, 162–64
Fuller, Paul R., 230
Fundamental Laws of Human Behavior, The (Meyer), 40

Gantt, W. Horsley, 221
Geiger, Lazarus, 40
Gesell, Arnold, 181
Gestalt theory, 5; influence on Hull, 111–13, 119–20, 219
Giddings, Franklin Henry, 26–27
Gillette, King Camp, 144
Goldman, Eric F., 198
Gosnell, Harold F., 32
Goss, Albert E., 66
Gottlieb, Gilbert, 205
Gould, Lewis, 198
Grant, David A., 184
Grindley, C. C., 221
Guthrie, Edwin Ray, 1, 24, 187; conditioning, views on, 80–81; influence of Hull on, 116–17; influence of Pavlov on, 77; influence of Progressivism, 79; intervening variables, dismissal of, 78; learning theory, role in formulation of, 78; materialist, 6; as methodological behaviorist 3; operationism, version of, 79; role in behaviorist movement, 55–56; stimuli and

responses, treatment of, 80; theory of behaviorism, 76–81

Habit: Hull's analysis of, 114–17; Hunter on, 51; in learning theory, 84–86; Meyer's analysis of, 40–41; Watson's analysis of, 56, 57, 65, 69, 71, 72, 75–76
Hall, G. Stanley, 5
Harlow, Harry F., 184
Harrell, Willard, and Ross Harrison, history and review of behaviorism, 81–82
Harris, Benjamin, 210
Haskell, Thomas H., 198
Hayes, Edward Cary, 27–28
Hays, Ruth, 215
Hays, Samuel P., 198
Heidbreder, Edna, 205
Henderson, Charles Richmond, 29
Herman, Ellen, 228
Herrnstein, Richard J., 223
Hilgard, Ernest R., 196, 210, 216, 222
Hinde, Robert A., 196, 197
Hofstadter, Richard, 198
Holt, Edwin Bissell, 3, 19; theory of mind, 32–34; and Tolman, influence on, 94, 95–96
Horton, G. P., 211
Hovland, Carl, 116
Hull, Clark Leonard, 2, 4, 7, 20, 76, 184, 186, 187, 189, 190, 191; behavior modification, role in, 163; and biologism, 117–19, 122; Boring writes to, 93; compared to other learning theorists, 103; and deficit theories of motivation, 180; and gradient of reinforcement, 106–10; influence of Gestalt theory on, 111–13, 119–20; influence of Guthrie on, 116–17; Koffka and, 112, 120; Kohler and, 112; as materialist, 6; as mechanist, 106; influence of Pavlov on, 111; influence of Thorndike on, 107–8; influence of Washburn on, 107–8; as positivist, 105; *Principles of Behavior*, 103–4; and quantification, 106, 113–16; relationship with Spence, 103–4, 110, 112, 113, 114–19; as theorist, 106, 116–17; and version of logical positivism, 6, 105
Hunter, Walter Samuel, 20, 24, 68; compared to Watson, 51–52; Skinner and, 127; theory of behaviorism, 50–52

Institute of Human Relations, Yale, 104; and behavior modification movement, 162–63; influence of psychoanalysis on members, 228–30
Institutionalist school of economics, 30
Interbehavioral psychology, 45–50
Iowa, University of, site of Spence's graduate program, 184–85
Irwin, Francis W., 184
Israel, Harry F. and Goldstein, B., 14

James William, 5; influence on New Realists, 32–33
Jennings, Herbert Spencer, reviewed by Watson, 58
Johnson, Charles, 28
Jones, Mary Cover, 21, 227; works with Watson, 74
Journal of Philosophy, Psychology, and Scientific Methods, 24, 33

Kantor, Jacob Robert, 19, 24, 76; and behavior modification, 165, 166; compared to Skinner, 46, 47, 49; evaluation of, 49–50; and functionalism, 46; and learning, 46; and operationism, 46; theory, 45–50; and Watson, 46
Kazdin Alan E., 165, 231
Kendler, Howard H., 189, 190, 191; comments on Iowa program, 184
Kendler, Tracy S., 189
Kimble, Gregory, 107, 184; rewrites Hilgard and Marquis's *Conditioning and Learning*, 187–88, 210
Kincade, Kathleen, 149–50
Koch, Sigmund, 191, 216
Koffka, Kurt, and Hull, 112, 120
Kohler, Wolfgang, 112, 219
Krasner, Leonard, 21, 158, 159–60
Krasnogorski, N. I., 154, 158
Kumar, Krishan, 148
Kuo, Zing-Yang, 24; theory of behaviorism, 52–54

Lake v. Cameron, 233
Lamarckism, 7, 19
Langfeld, Herbert, 94, 183
Language; Meyer on, 41; Skinner's theory of, 131–34; Watson's theory of, 43–44, 73; Weiss on, 44

Lashley, Karl Spencer, association with Watson, 56, 73
Laski, Harold, 29
Lasswell, Harold D., 32
Laura Spelman Rockefeller Memorial, 29; and mental hygiene movement, 154–55
Learning, behaviorism and, 7–8; defined, 83–86; Guthrie on, 76–81; learning theory, 24, 83, 86; Watson's influence on research in, 74–76, 84
Levin, Harry, 181
Levine, Murray, 233
Lewin, Kurt, 112, 184, 189
Leys, Ruth, 71
Lindsley, Ogden R. and Solomon, H. C., 165
Little Albert, Watson's attempt to condition, 74
Loeb, Jacques, reviewed by Watson, 58; influences Skinner, 127
Logan, Frank, 188
Logical positivism, 6, 18, 42; operationism and, 87, 185; Spence's version of, 185
Logue, A. W., 208
Lorenz, Konrad, and innate releasing mechanisms, 12
Lovejoy, Arthur O., 209
Lovie, A. D., 208, 215

Maccoby, Eleanor E., 181
MacCorquodale, Kenneth and Meehl, Paul E., 214
Mackenzie, Brian D., 195
Mackintosh, Nicholas J., 220
Maltzman, Irving E., 190
Marquis, Donald, 187, 210
Marr, David, 197
Marvin, Walter Taylor, 32, 68
Maslow, Abraham, 180
Mateer, Florence, 154, 158–59
May, Mark, 106
McDougall, William, 39
McFarland, David J. and Sibly, R., 197
McGeoch, John A., 113
McGregor, Douglas, 94
Melton, Arthur W., 184
Menninger, William C., 160–62
Mental hygiene movement, 154–55
Mental testing, 18

Merriam, Charles C., 31
Meyer Adolf, influence on Watson, 70–71
Meyer, Max Frederick, 19, 24, 76; on language, 41; theory of behaviorism, 40–41
Miller, Neal, 164, 189
Mills, John A., 195, 196, 204, 212, 216, 217, 220, 222, 224
Mitchell, Wesley Clair, 30
Montague, William Pepperell, 32–33
Moore, R. Laurence, 198
Mowrer, O. Hobart, 180; interpretation of psychoanalytic concepts, 162–64
Mueller, Conrad G., and Schoenfeld, William N., 211
Munn, Norman L., 184
Murray, David A., 205

National Institute of Mental Health, 161
National Mental Health Act, 161
Neobehaviorism, 2–4, 20, 22, 55, 83; dominates psychology, 179–193; institutional dominance of, 183–84; Spence's version of, 185–87
Neo-Galtonianism, 13, 18
Newcomb, Theodore M., 184
New Realism, 19, 32–34, 94; New Realists, 24, 32–34
No-particular-behavior argument, 66, 131

Objectivism, 3, 38–41, 59
O'Donnell, John M., 195
Operationism, 3, 7, 10, 13–14, 16, 17, 18, 20, 24, 46, 49, 76, 79, 83, 191; Boring and, 87; 89–94; historical account of its rise in psychology, 86–100; learning theory and, 87; Skinner and, 10, 14, 87, 101–2, 128–29

Park, Robert, 28–29
Parke, Ross D., 182
Pavlov, Ivan Petrovich; and behavior modification, 154, 158, 159; and Guthrie, 77; and Hull, 111; and Skinner, 126–27; and Watson, 73
Peak, Helen, 91
Perry, Ralph Barton, 19, 24, 32–34; Tolman, influence on, 94, 95–96
Peters, Richard S. and Tajfel, Henri, 195
Piaget, Jean, 181

Piliavin, Irving M., 182
Pillsbury, Walter Bowers, 39–40, 68
Pinter, Rudolf, 66
Pitkin, Walter Boughton, 32
Political science, American; and behaviorism, 24, 31–32
Positivism, in American social science, 23–26; in behaviorism, 5, 6; in psychology, 16, 24, 26, 192; Skinner's version of, 129
Postman, Leo, 188
Pragmatism, in behaviorism 5; in American social science, 21, 23–24, 32
Pratt, Caroll C., 183
Principles of Behavior (Hull), 103–4, 111
Progressivism, 19, 21, 23–24, 26, 28, 29, 30, 32; and behavior modification, 152, 154, 158–59; influence on Guthrie, 79
Psychoanalysis, in American psychiatry, 162; in implicit American social theories, 177; influences behavior modification movement, 153–54; influences thinking of Yale group, 163–64, 228–230
"Psychology as the Behaviorist Views It" (Watson), analysis of, 62–66
Psychology from the Standpoint of a Behaviorist (Watson), 74
Psychology of the Other One, The (Meyer), 40
Purposive Behavior in Rats and Men (Tolman), 101

Quantification, 9; in Hull's theory, 106, 113–16

Rayner, Rosalie, 210
Razran, Gregory, 209
Realism, critical, 19
Reinforcement, 11; Hull's views on, 114–17; Kantor's views on, 49; Skinner's views on, 134–43
Rescorla, Robert, 237
Research Memoranda (Hull), 104
Response, 9, 47–48; and setting factors, 47
Roback, A. A., critique of behaviorism, 81
Rogers, Tim B., 13, 89, 90
Ross, Dorothy, 198
Rozeboom, William W., 222
Rucci, Antony J. and Tweney, Ryan D., 215

Ruckmich, Christian, 68
Ruml, Beardsley, 29, 154, 157

Samelson, Franz, 4; and history of behaviorism, 220; views on Watson, 61, 63, 64, 65–68, 225
Savage-Rumbaugh, Sue, 135–37
Schlosberg, Harold, 84
Schwartz, Barry and Robbins, Steven J., 197, 237
Science and Human Behavior (Skinner), 215
Scientism, 21, 38
Scott, Walter Dill, 88
Sears, Robert R., 181
Segal, Howard, 144
Shea, Christine M., 226
Sheffield, Fred D., 117, 210
Singer, Edgar Arthur, Jr., 19, 24; influence on Smith and Guthrie, 35, 76; theory of mind, 35–36
Skinner, Burrhus Frederick, 1, 4, 7, 8, 20–21, 76, 179; analytic behaviorism and, 130–32; animal behavior, theory of, 134–38; and behavior modification, 153; Boring comments on, 129; Coleman's analysis of work of, 128; control as theme in the work of, 148–50; Crozier and, 127; drive theory of, 128–29; Freud, influence of, 147; Hunter and, 127; influence of H. G. Wells on, 126; influence of Loeb on, 127; influence of Pavlov on, 126–27; language, theory of, 131–34; and logical positivism, 6; as materialist, 6; and moral theory, 8; as methodological behaviorist, 3; operationism, 10, 14, 87, 101–2, 128–29; philosophy of science of, 130; on subjectivity, 129; themes in creative life of, 123–25; theory, critique of, 139–43; theory, origins of, 125–29; *Walden Two*, 20–21, 143–51; Watson and, 126, 129–30
Smedslund, Jan, 17
Smith, Laurence D., 6, 105, 118
Smith, Stevenson, 6, 35
Social science, American, history of 24–32; pragmatism in, 23–24
Sociology, American, 24; history of, 26–30
Solomon, Richard L., 184
Somit, Albert, and Tanenhaus, Joseph, 199

Spaulding, Edward Gleason, 32
Spence, Kenneth W., 20, 183, 191; in behaviorist movement, 22, 184–90; as graduate supervisor, 187; relationship with Hull, 103–4, 110, 112, 114–19; theory and research of, 184–87
Spence, Janet Taylor, 190
Spiker, Charles, 185
Staddon, John E. R., and Simmelhag, Virginia L., 197
Stam, Henderikus J., 196
Stevens, S. S., 10, 179; operationism, 87, 93–94
Stone, Calvin P., 184
Stout, Dale A., 212
Stumpf, Carl, 40

Taylor, James G., 36
Theoretical Basis of Human Behavior, A (Weiss), 45, 203
Thorndike, Edward Lee, 5, 24, 31, 39, 56, 159; individual differences, 84–89, 94; influence on Hull, 107–8; learning, 84
Tinbergen, Nikko, 196
Titchener, Edward Bradford, 39; criticizes Watson, 67
Token economies, 165–78; Ayllon and, 166–68, 170–71; critique of, 170–77; early forms of, 165–68; Fairweather's version of, 173–74; Wexler on, 175–76; Winkler on, 168–70
Tolman, Edward Chace, 2, 4, 5, 7, 24, 76, 179, 187, 189, 190; experimental design, 100–101; and logical positivism, 6; as methodological behaviorist, 3; creates neobehaviorism, 4, 94–100; operationism, 94–100; influence of Perry and Holt on, 33, 94, 95–96
Tyler, Elizabeth, 143

Ullmann, Leonard P., 158
Underwood, Benton J., experimental psychology text, 183, 212; verbal learning, 188–89
Utilitarianism, 8

Valentine, C. W., 210
Variables, dependent, 9; independent, 9; intervening, 10, 14, 85–86; Tolman's treatment of, 97–99

Verplanck, William S., 48
Veterans Administration, 161

Wagner, Allan, 237
Walden Two, 20–21, 143–151
Wallis, Wilson D., critique of behaviorism, 82
Walters, Richard H., 182
Washburn, Margaret Floy, 36–37; influences Hull, 107–8
Watson, John Broadus, 1, 4, 5, 6, 20; association with Harvey Carr, 57, 75; "behavior" as a synonym for comparative psychology, 60–61; and behavior modification, 152–55, 157–59, 162; behaviorism, theory of, 55–76; and Columbia lectures, 63–64, 66; as comparative psychologist, 56, 60–61; compared to Baldwin, 57; conditioned emotional reaction, attempt to produce, 73–74; conditioning, research on, 73–74; on consciousness, 42–43, 64–65; Darwinism and, 57, 64; on emotion, 66–67; evaluation of, 74–76; as first acknowledged behaviorist, 55; functionalism and, 57; and habit, theory of, 57, 75–76; in Harper's, 61–62, 69–70; and Harriet Lane Home for Invalid Children, 73; and human research, 57, 73–74; images, treatment of, 66; influence of Freud on, 71–72; influence Skinner of on, 126, 129–30; Johns Hopkins, resignation from, 74; as laboratory scientist, 57; on language, 43–44, 73; and learning, 84; Little Albert, conditioning of, 74; makes psychology's first film, 74; "manifesto," and response, 67–68; as materialist, 6; methodological behaviorism of, 3; objectivism in his thought, 59; at Phipps clinic, 71; on prediction, 9, 74; "Psychology as a Behaviorist Views It," analysis of, 64–66; "Psychology as a Behaviorist Views It," publication of, 62–64; relationship with Yerkes, 58–63; on thinking, 65–66
Weiss, Albert Paul, 19, 24, 68; contrasted with Watson, 42; evaluation of, 45; on language, 44; as materialist, 43; on mental testing, 45; on social relations, 44–45; theory of behaviorism, 41–45
Wells, Frederic L., 156–57

Wexler, David, 175–76
Weyburn, Saskatchewan, 166–67, 171
Winkler, R. C., 168–70
Winston, Andrew, 10
Wolfe, Harry Kirk, 201
Woodbridge, Frederick James Eugene, 24; theory of mind, 34–35
Woodworth, Robert Sessions, treatment of experimentation, 10, 84

Wright, Quincy, 32
Wyatt vs. Stickney, 175

Yerkes, Robert Mearns, 5, 6; corresponds with Watson, 58–63
Yoshioka J. G., 217

Zeaman, D., 220
Zuriff, G. E., 130, 136

About the Author

John A. Mills started his working life as a geologist and then became a psychologist. He did his doctoral work at the University of Cape Town. After teaching at Cape Town for a year he took up a post at the University of Saskatchewan, Canada. His early research was in verbal learning, psycholinguistics, comparative psychology, and animal psychology. For the past twenty years his research has been in historical psychology, concentrating on eighteenth-century Scottish philosophy and on behaviorism. He is a member of the Cheiron Society, was a founding member of the International Society for Theoretical Psychology, and serves on the editorial board of the journal *Theory and Psychology*. He now lives on Hornby Island, British Columbia, Canada.